Decentering Advocacy in English
Language Teaching

Decentering Advocacy in English Language Teaching

Global Perspectives and Local Practices

Edited by

**Kate Mastruserio Reynolds,
Grazzia Maria Mendoza Chirinos,
Debra Suarez, Okon Effiong, and
Georgios Kormpas**

University of Michigan Press
Ann Arbor

Copyright © 2024 by the University of Michigan
All rights reserved

Published in the United States of America by the
University of Michigan Press
Printed and bound by CPI Group (UK) Ltd, Croydon, CR0 4YY

ISBN 978-0-472-03981-4 (print)
ISBN 978-0-472-22204-9 (e-book)

First published December 2024

No part of this publication may be reproduced, stored in a retrieval system, or transmitted in any form or by any means, electronic, mechanical, or otherwise, without the written permission of the publisher.

DEDICATION

Kate: I am so grateful to the authors who contributed their stories on top of their tireless advocacy work that is so valuable to students and communities all over the world. My thanks and gratitude to my fellow editors for all their hard work and keen insights that have driven this volume, particularly to Grazzia, who was reliable and steady throughout. Debra, thank you for your detailed eye. Okon, I am grateful for your social justice stance. George, I appreciate your energies. Thank you to my husband, Steve Close, who never ceases to amaze me about how much he will support me in my work. Hey, Alex, I hope this volume sheds a bit of light into the darkness. Of course, I must include a shout out to Maddy Reynolds, who wishes to change the world, too. Let these examples light your way. Don't let any obstacle stop you. You've got this!

Grazzia: I am truly grateful to Kate for spearheading this effort and bringing us all together to collaborate and make this volume a dream come true. Thanks to all the authors who stepped up and said "yes" to contributing and sharing their stories, lessons learned, and best practices; they are inspirational and represent the realities of our world, now at the service of hundreds of student teachers who, yes, will change their communities and their worlds! Thanks to my family, my husband and sons, who are always cheering for me whenever I embark on a new collaborative adventure. A huge thanks to my parents in heaven who taught me the value of collaboration, hard work, and perseverance; all my achievements are dedicated to you!

Debra: This work represents a labor of love—love, dedication, and commitment to the field of English language teaching (ELT) and to the students and teachers we serve around the world. I would like to express my appreciation to my fellow co-editors, Kate, Grazzia, Okon, and George, for joining together around our shared goal to advance the global ELT profession. Special thanks to Kate, our lead editor, for creating our international editorial group and for your intellectual leadership throughout this process. Kate, you are a generous and inspiring leader! Thank you to all the authors in this volume: your stories of your advocacy projects from around the world are powerful and exemplary. And, as always, thank you to my husband, Michael Cummins, for your enduring partnership and for sharing my work and my life.

Okon: My appreciation goes to the authors in this volume for overcoming the challenges in their different contexts and sharing their struggles and achievements in this volume with a wider global readership. Your efforts will serve as inspiration to others, and I cannot thank you enough. Keep up the good deed.

George: This book has been a realization of a dream to speak about advocacy around the world. My sincere thanks go to the chapter authors, who have come out of their comfort zones and have talked about situations that they are proud of and have worked hard on but that also may have been discomforting at times. My gratitude to the four co-editors, Kate, Grazzia, Debra, and Okon. I genuinely appreciate your work, ethics, and patience. You were all there when we all needed each other. Lastly, I would like to dedicate this publication to my beloved mother, who is currently struggling with her health, and I know she will be a winner as she always has been. This is what she taught me ever since my father went to heaven when I was three years old. It has been a great journey of perseverance and valor. I thank you all.

CONTENTS

List of Illustrations and Tables   ix

INTRODUCTION   1
Kate Mastruserio Reynolds, Grazzia Maria Mendoza Chirinos,
Debra Suarez, Okon Effiong, and Georgios Kormpas

**CHAPTER 1: IGNITING THE PASSION: ELT RENAISSANCE
AT ITOLU COMMUNITY HIGH SCHOOL, ILARO, NIGERIA**   18
Oluyemisi Oladejo

**CHAPTER 2: ADVOCATING FOR FEMALE ENGLISH
LANGUAGE TEACHING PROFESSIONALS IN CAMEROON**   32
Abigail Ekangouo Awanga

**CHAPTER 3: ADVOCACY AND EDUCATION AS A VEHICLE
FOR ECONOMIC DEVELOPMENT AND EMPOWERMENT
OF THE GARIFUNA IN BELIZE**   47
Enita Elecia Barrett

**CHAPTER 4: DE-COLONIZING ADVOCACY: ADVOCACY
EFFORTS FOR ENGLISH LANGUAGE TEACHING
AND LEARNING IN BELIZE**   65
Ethnelda Paulino

**CHAPTER 5: ENGLISH FOR A BETTER FUTURE: AN
INITIATIVE TO PROVIDE QUALITY EDUCATION
TO EL SALVADOR'S YOUTH**   86
Miguel Ángel Carranza Campos

CHAPTER 6: TESOL TRANSFORMATIVE ADVOCACY IN TERTIARY EDUCATION IN VIETNAM 95
Son Nguyen, Huong Lam, and Hong-Anh Nguyen

CHAPTER 7: USING ENGLISH LANGUAGE TEACHING AS A PLATFORM FOR DEVELOPING SELF-ADVOCACY: ENGLISH IS OUR FUTURE 116
Briana Rogers

CHAPTER 8: SUPPORTING YOUNG LEARNERS' ENGLISH IN PUBLIC SCHOOLS IN TÜRKIYE: SPOKEN CAFES PROJECT 134
Sumru Akcan

CHAPTER 9: EFL CLASSROOMS AS SPACES FOR ADVOCACY ACTS IN AREAS OF INTRACTABLE CONFLICT 147
Julia Schlam Salman and Brigitta R. Schvarcz

CHAPTER 10: THREE DECADES OF SUPPORTING ENGLISH TEACHERS IN PARAGUAY: PARATESOL'S NEW ADVOCACY RESPONSE 166
Valentina Canese, Susan Spezzini, and Rocío Mazzoleni

CHAPTER 11: METAGOGY AS ADVOCACY IN INITIAL TEACHER EDUCATION 178
Gabriel Díaz Maggioli

CHAPTER 12: GLOBAL EFFORTS IN ADVOCACY FOR ENGLISH LANGUAGE TEACHING AND LEARNING: CONCLUSIONS AND FUTURES 196
Okon Effiong, Kate Mastruserio Reynolds, Debra Suarez, Georgios Kormpas, and Grazzia Maria Mendoza Chirinos

Contributor Biographies 213
Index 221

LIST OF ILLUSTRATIONS AND TABLES

ILLUSTRATIONS

Figure 2.1: The Ladder of Three Collectives	35
Figure 7.1: Lone Buffalo Students. Photo courtesy of Lone Buffalo Organization	118
Figure 9.1: Identity Pie: Exploring Groups We Belong To	156

TABLES

Table 2.1: Weekly Schedule of Professional Development Presentations	38
Table 4.1: Enrollment and Number of Graduates by Academic Year	77
Table 10.1: PARATESOL Annual Conference and Workshop Five-Year Summary	173
Table 11.1: Policy Map for the Disadvantages of a Structural Approach to Language Teaching	190

Introduction

Kate Mastruserio Reynolds, Grazzia Maria Mendoza Chirinos, Debra Suarez, Okon Effiong, and Georgios Kormpas

> *In the case of advocacy in my context, freedom is to some extent, more theoretical than practical, because others may call advocates disrupters and silent revolutionaries.*
> —Abigail Ekangouo Awanga, "Advocating for Female English Language Teaching Professionals in Cameroon," this volume

The editors are honored to present *Decentering Advocacy in English Language Teaching: Global Perspectives and Local Practices*. The volume you now hold in your hands is a collection of narratives of diverse advocacy projects from around the world, written by the English language teaching (ELT) educators who spearheaded them, in their own words, in their own way, and reverberating with the resonance of their own voices. The ELT educators speaking to you in the pages of this book are champions of ELT advocacy within their individual educational context. The advocate authors defined a school-based need, borne from the challenges, hopes, and purposes that are unique to each specific context. They diagnosed the need, pinpointed the complexities, puzzled through options, determined a strategy, implemented the plan, delivered on outcomes, and now, they reflect on their experiences. Each singular project described is unique. Each and every one is luminescent and burning bright with the passionate voice of the ELT advocate. Our hope is that you find inspiration through the experiences in these pages.

Each chapter describes a narrative as a stand-alone testament to the power of ELT educators being agents of change within their school settings, and we celebrate each one. However, as a volume, these individual advocacy narratives create a collective that carries the power of a million voices.

This volume brings forth an expansive reflection of this collective voice, amplifying the essence of shared experiences, unveiling the multiplicity of the very nature and notion of "advocacy," and, in some cases, uncloaking the residual legacy of colonialism in education. This movement, from the personal to the political, is a transformative process that recognizes the interconnectedness of personal struggles with systemic injustices, such as poverty, racism, sexism, and colonialism (Freire, 2017), and with this recognition, we are invited and challenged to conceive the practice of education as a "project for freedom" (Giroux, 2010, p. 717) as we work toward mutual understanding and collective change.

While we celebrate the achievements embodied in these advocacy narratives, and while we amplify the nuances and complexities that they collectively reveal, we are mindful of the grim historical, sociocultural, and political realities that make a volume such as this of utmost necessity. Our motivation for undertaking this project was to gather diverse voices of ELT advocates representing diverse continents and countries and highlight global efforts in advocacy related to English language teaching and learning and how they come in different forms and shapes responding to the contextual realities in which they are implemented.

We hoped to learn what is possible in ELT advocacy worldwide in order to inform the development of principles and practices that work in more constrained contexts. Constrained contexts to us are those global contexts where educational innovation might be impeded (Murray, Liddicoat, Zhen, & Mosavian, 2023); where the efforts of teachers and other educators as agents of change might be restricted (Yazan, 2018); where the national focus might be more on governmental, top-down educational policies (Adams & Newton, 2009); where teachers' negotiation of their professional autonomy and legitimacy may not be welcomed (Chinpakdee, 2022); and where teachers' professional agency, impact, and publicly voiced dissent is conflated with complex contextual variables (Li, 2023) related to social, cultural, political, economic, historical, or religious concerns in education. The editors felt that individual ELT professionals working in markedly different contexts worldwide would be the most knowledgeable about and sensitive to the realities of their educational contexts, as is evident in the quote from Abigail Ekangouo Awanga at the beginning of this chapter. Of course, not all global contexts will be constrained by these factors; in the process of bringing together these narratives of global advocacy projects in local contexts, we began to see a clearer picture of the continuum from openness to constrained settings. This continuum relates to the political rights of individuals, for example, if they have the right to speak out to educational and political leaders. It also relates to whether these leaders will listen to the concerns expressed or if they will be dismissed. Top-down educational leadership systems tend to view educators' voices as non-essential since the leaders' voices are the only important authorities. In these sorts of settings, educators might not only waste time and energy but could also be perceived as loose cannons or as nuisances. When considering the influences of religious, economic, and sociocultural impact on the continuum, some individuals are entitled to more of a voice than others, *and* the groups of people they advocate for need to be perceived as valuable in the religious, economic, and sociocultural arenas in order to receive attention. The emic perspective (i.e., insider's perspective) of educators in these settings helps guide them in terms of how, why, and when they choose to advocate, and at what risk.

Understanding the contexts of advocacy actions then becomes an important part of the discussion of preparing teachers to advocate, which is part of the TESOL International Association's Teacher Education Standard 5, "Candidates demonstrate professionalism and leadership by collaborating with other educators, knowing policies and legislation and the rights of ELLs, advocating for ELLs and their families, engaging in self-assessment and reflection, pursuing continuous professional development, and honing their teaching practice through supervised teaching" (2019, p. 16). As we advance in our professional knowledge, we need to further understand the relationship between the variables mentioned above and educators' abilities and choices of when, how, and why to advocate in ELT contexts all over the world.

Roots of Advocacy Movements

Advocacy in terms of contemporary social movements/protests has its roots in Henry David Thoreau's philosophy, outlined in his book *Civil Disobedience*; Thoreau's work inspired global social and economic protests, starting with the U.S. abolitionist movement (notably Frederick Douglass) to secure the human rights of African Americans. This early advocacy was followed by the British and American suffrage movements, Gandhi's efforts to free India from British rule, the Zoot Suit Protest of the 1940s in California, the 1950/60's Civil Rights movement of African Americans, Cesar Chavez and the United Farm Workers 1960s protests for living wages; the feminist movement of the 1960s/1970s in the west, Ukraine's Orange Revolution of 2004, the U.S.-based Black Lives Matter protests, the #MeToo movement, and the Arab Spring from 2010–2019. Each movement learned from the next, building advocacy toolkits and protest tactics along the way. These worldwide social movements involved individuals standing up, voicing their opinions, and striving for change.

Advocacy efforts in education, drawing from the social movements above, began with equity for learners with special needs/disabilities and multilingual learners of English in the 1960s. Many of these advocacy efforts, including those efforts related to professional development in ELT with a focus on English speaking, began in the U.S. context, a Western context where individuals have rights to freely express their opinions and share their concerns with those in power without fear of direct reprisal.

The term "advocacy" and the practice of "advocacy actions" in English language teaching are understood and practiced in many ways by ELT educators. Advocacy can encompass promoting language learning, supporting language educators, empowering parents, influencing educational policies, and engaging with communities and stakeholders to advance language education and literacy. Furthermore, context plays an important, mitigating variable in our understanding of advocacy and our enactment of advocacy practices.

"Contextualized advocacy" recognizes the centrality of the professional context regarding how ELT teachers understand and enact advocacy practices (Linville & Vinogradova, 2021). At times, ELT advocacy professional development has appeared myopic, disconnected, and/or at worst imperialistic by promoting advocacy strategies that are simply not workable in some contexts. Since the majority of published advocacy work has appeared in the West, this volume is an effort to recognize the existence of advocacy efforts in additional contexts. We endeavored in this volume to *decenter* ELT advocacy initiatives. We seek to decenter by not sending implicit or explicit messages to our global colleagues that what works in Western countries will work in theirs. We aimed to add to the understanding of ELT advocacy professional development by identifying what advocacy looks like in various contexts worldwide. We wanted to *learn* about the ongoing advocacy work ELT educators already have underway that needs to be recognized in Western advocacy literature. Our aim is to *decenter advocacy* from a solely Western perspective and instead to *recognize the nuances of advocacy* by presenting real life examples, including its complexities, to highlight what advocacy looks like globally.

Myriad Approaches to Advocacy in ELT

Advocacy as it pertains to ELT work can occur within the classroom, in the school, in the district or region, or at the national or international levels. Staehr-Fenner (2014) noted the importance of advocacy in various settings:

Introduction 5

Advocacy in the classroom or in the building is just as important as advocacy within the district. Advocacy at the state level is just as important as advocacy at the national level. Where it's done, advocacy by TESOL educators is vital, so much so that advocacy is included in TESOL International Association's P-12 Professional Teaching Standards. (p. xi)

Within the classroom, advocacy has been recognized by Dubetz & de Jong (2011) to include "teaching as advocacy" (p. 251). Linville (2019) furthers this definition, indicating "Advocacy as noticing ways ELs' [English learners'] educational success is challenged and then taking action with the goal of improving their educational experiences and outcomes and life chances" (chapter 1, p. 2, para. 4). Classroom-based advocacy can include advocating for equity among students, social justice (e.g., diversity, equity, inclusion, and belonging initiatives), individual students (e.g., anti-bullying), or instructional choices that provide equal access to information and materials, for instance. Linville & Vinogradova (2021) describe classroom-based advocacy as, "such actions as choosing representative curriculum and allowing use of the L1 to support all students' linguistic and cultural identities" (para 2). It can also include teaching students to be self-advocates to get what they need in their learning process (Brulles, 2021; Salazar, 2020; Day, Prado, & Edmonds, 2022).

At the school, district, or regional levels, ELT professionals' advocacy may include advocating for learners' needs in terms of class time, program model, adherence to laws, policy or standards of instruction for multilingual learners of English (MLEs), materials or supports. According to Linville & Vinogradova (2021), "What TESOL professionals refer to as 'advocacy' can range from classroom and school actions to improve educational access and outcomes for English learners (ELs) or our own working conditions" (para. 2). Teacher advocates may also seek for themselves improved schedules, improved workload, lower numbers of students per class, fewer number of classes, better pay, better professional development opportunities, or a better work/life balance. An example is how one colleague recently worked with a student organization, Bilingual English Language Learning Association (BELLA), to advocate for increased educational preparation for all general educators/content teachers to work with multilingual learners of English (MLEs) (#ELL4ALL) by writing postcards to state legislators.

On a national and international level, ELT advocates can work on enhanced professional standards or efforts to elevate the professional recognition of TESOL professionals as comparable to other educational professionals. Social issues are areas ripe for advocacy social movements (Linville & Whiting, 2020);

they include immigration, peace, social justice for multilingual ELT educators, and support for communities such as immigrants; black, indigenous, and people of color (BIPOC); and individuals in the LGBTQ+ community. Haneda & Alexander refer to this type of advocacy as *transformative advocacy,* or advocacy seeking to change a socially inequitable or unjust situation (2015). ELT professionals can advocate for change in educational policy to enhance language standards, materials, and/or teacher quality/preparation to work with MLEs. "What TESOL professionals refer to as 'advocacy' can range…to political activism undertaken to change policies and improve the life experiences of ELs and their teachers" (Linville & Vinogradova, 2021, p. 2).

Decolonizing ELT Pedagogies: Decentering ELT Advocacy

The editors of this volume acknowledge the embedded colonialism within English language teaching and learning itself, given the world's history and legacy of English as a colonizing language. As we embarked on the journey of creating this volume, we realized that our work in decentering advocacy could be embedded within, and relevant to, larger academic conversations of colonizing pedagogies and the concomitant conversations of decolonizing those pedagogies. Colonizing pedagogies may be seen in many aspects of ELT, such as in the perpetuation of standard English as the idealized form, in the continued veneration of the native English-speaking teacher, and in the pervasiveness of pedagogy that ignores the social, cultural, and political context of language teaching and learning (Rice, 2021), to name a few. Broadly, the term "decolonization" can be defined as the undoing of colonialism (Tignor, 2005). More specifically related to ELT, a recent special issue of *ELT Journal* dives both broadly and deeply into what it means to decolonize the teaching of a language that has roots in imperialism (Canagarajah, 2023a, 2023b). Very much like the term "advocacy," the term "decolonization" is multifaceted, and thus, the decolonization of ELT requires a multiple-pronged approach. As the special issue delineates, "decolonizing" ELT involves decolonizing curriculum, methods, materials, classroom discourse, and teacher professional development (Canagarajah, 2023a). Yet even in this special issue, the decolonization of ELT advocacy receives tangential discussion. It became clear to us that our work in decentering advocacy could be a first step in exploring and contributing to larger conversations of what it means to decolonize ELT.

In coming to an understanding of *decentering* ELT advocacy, aligning with the purpose and intent of this book, we perceive the decentering of ELT advocacy from the perspective of the authors themselves, where they share the journey of their efforts to break the long-standing status quo, not only shifting paradigms in their own contexts but also creating new pathways to enact policy and bridge opportunities for future ELT educators. In decentering advocacy, the contextual nuances and complexities, the challenges to be mitigated, and the long-term sustainability of the changes brought about by advocacy actions converge into a new paradigm of what it means to contextualize realities and act accordingly.

Throughout our work in collecting, compiling, and editing the work of our contributors, we were mindful to practice decentering in our own editorial efforts. One key concern was to retain the words, voice, and tone of the ELT educators themselves. A haunting quote reminded us not to rewrite our contributing authors: as quoted in the opening of Bonnonno's (2006) translation of Memmi's *Decolonization and the Decolonized*, "I feared that my arguments would go unheard or be distorted, or might compound problems faced by still fragile societies in need of our support" (p. ix). Within this realization of decentering within academic discourse, we also heeded the words of bell hooks (1990), who writes, as she assumes the voice of the academic colonizer:

> No need to hear your voice when I can talk about you better than you can speak about yourself. No need to hear your voice. Only tell me about your pain. I want to know your story. And then I will tell it back to you in a new way. Tell it back to you in such a new way that it has become mine, my own. Rewriting you, I write myself anew. I am still the author, authority. I am still the colonizer, the speaking subject, and you are now at the center of my talk. (p. 152)

We did not rewrite our contributing authors. The narrative belongs to them.

Another concern in editing this volume was connecting the advocacy projects to the research literature of advocacy within ELT, since so much of the research is published with more Western viewpoints. Within this volume, in order to "decenter advocacy" and to minimize viewing global advocacy efforts from a solely Western perspective, we centralized our contributors' teachers' definitions of advocacy and encouraged the authors to align their working definitions with reference to the literature, when possible, but to also retain their own perspectives. These are just a few examples of editorial "decentering" efforts embedded in this volume.

The advocacy projects and experiences presented here are contextualized locally in each region represented, but, as said earlier, these narratives carry a collective voice. ELT advocacy is yet to be fully explored in the academic conversation of decentering ELT advocacy. We hope that as you read the advocacy projects highlighted in this volume, representing different global perspectives, that you also begin to make connections with these projects and the work that remains to be done in decentering advocacy and, ultimately, in decolonizing advocacy, as both a concept and a practice within ELT pedagogies.

The Purpose of This Volume

The chapters in this volume situate advocacy projects in real contexts that make the text valuable for the readers' awareness and knowledge. In each chapter, an ELT advocate describes the need for their project, the steps they took, the challenges they faced in their particular context (some of which were implicitly alluded to), what were the constraints/parameters they needed to work within, and how they worked within these constraints to achieve their goals. In some cases, advocacy efforts fail. Understanding why some advocacy projects do not achieve their goals, or struggle to, has value for other ELT professionals who engage in advocacy work.

The audience for this volume is educational professionals and students learning about advocacy in the field of English language teaching. It could be employed in initial and on-going teacher education programs to illustrate practical advocacy case studies. We imagine educators in far-reaching locations finding these advocacy efforts applicable to identify solutions to challenges they face.

ELT readers will learn about strategies and projects employed throughout the world. Readers will be able to relate to the contextual constraints and parameters and acquire new perspectives on how they may advocate within their context. They will be able to envision a new advocacy project that allows them to campaign in a personally and professionally safe manner for the needs of their multilingual learners of English and ELT colleagues that expands the repertoire of strategies and tactics currently employed in ELT advocacy work. The end goal of the text is to derive certain principles and practices that can be employed realistically worldwide in contexts that range from open and tolerant to constrained.

Editorial Leadership of This Volume

This volume has five editors whose work in ELT advocacy encompasses the globe. Three of the editors live and work in Honduras, Qatar, and Saudi Arabia and have worked, and served educators, globally; the remaining two editors have lived and worked in several different regions including the Caribbean, Central America, Eastern Europe, Mexico, South America, Southeast Asia, the Middle East, and West Africa. We have each engaged in advocacy on the levels described earlier and taught teachers to engage in advocacy to empower them in their work. We have also promoted the important role of advocacy in the field through our various leadership positions in national, regional, and international organizations.

We decided upon this collaborative effort because of our shared concern that advocacy as it is envisioned and defined in Western research literature may not reflect the realities of English-language educators in all contexts (as noted previously). Finding educators of ELT in global contexts who were engaged in advocacy efforts proved challenging when we first disseminated the call for proposals because many ELT educators had different perceptions about the term "advocacy." Not that they were not conducting advocacy initiatives, they were; rather, they just did not realize the definition described their efforts. As we have moved forward in our work on advocacy in global contexts, we realize the need for conversations about the concept of advocacy at regional ELT professional organizations worldwide in articles, following examples such as those described by Pentón Herrera's article in the *English Teaching Forum* (2022), and presentations, such as that from Reynolds, Schvarcz, & Liopoire, (2023), where they teach about the concept, connecting it explicitly to the unique contextual variables while discussing tactics for organizing teams and commencing advocacy initiatives.

Limitations of This Volume

We must make note of some limitations of this volume. First, while all of these advocacy projects are from non-Western environments, the global scope of this volume is limited by those who answered our call for submissions. Sometimes non-Western academics are hindered from participation in academic publications due to lack of belonging to an academic community, thereby limiting the invitations they receive to write, collaborate, and publish. Therefore, in order to improve our global reach and to include new and emerging ELT authors, we broadly disseminated our call for proposals and selected our contributing authors from that pool. Another potential limitation of this volume is that the chapters typically have few references to the extant literature. As already discussed above, it was an editorial decision to encourage the authors to reference the literature when possible, but to remain focused on telling their experience in their own words and letting their narrative and project efforts stand on their own. We believe this is a strength of the volume, but at the same time, it is a potential limitation for readers who might seek to read school-based activities embedded tightly within the extant literature. Therefore, we encourage readers to approach these narratives as we did—as an act of decentering—and to seek instead how the authors' experiences invite us to venture into newer ground and to explore new possibilities for understanding and enacting decentering. The acknowledged limitations of this volume notwithstanding, the voices of ELT advocates around the world add to the academic discourse of moving toward an understanding of decentering, and potentially decolonizing, advocacy in the sphere of ELT.

Overview of the Chapters in This Volume

Oluyemisi Oladejo writes in chapter 1, "Igniting the Passion: ELT Renaissance at Itolu Community High School, Ilaro, Nigeria," about her effort in a local Nigerian school where she was able to apply technology to her teaching in a disadvantaged rural setting. At the time of her assumption of duty, the school was experiencing shortages of human and material resources; however, Oladejo's classroom-based advocacy effort commenced with the development of an adjunct English class where she engaged students in listening games on her laptop computer at break and after school hours. The goal was to gauge the effect of computer-assisted language learning on learners' listening comprehension. Another step she took in her advocacy was to obtain funding for laptops, which she did when she won a grant from the Education Testing Service, a U.S.-based organization that provided laptops to facilitate the project with the aim of enhancing communicative competence of the learners in the four language skills. Despite the absence of supporting staff and epileptic supply of electricity, the advocacy project was concluded with students taking the TOEFL Junior Standard test. On average, students performed better in the post-study test than they did in the pre-study test, and she found that activity-based learning put the learners at the center of their own learning.

In chapter 2, "Advocating for Female English Language Teaching Professionals in Cameroon," Abigail Ekangouo Awanga's advocacy efforts focused on overcoming challenges, such as masculine dominance, societal stigma, and family constraints, that female ELT educators face. She set up a special interest group (SIG): the ELT Women of Cameroon within the

Introduction 11

Cameroon English Language and Literature Association (CAMELTA) was a female-only professional space with the intention to mentor at least 20 females every academic year to overcome the challenges females face and advance their understanding of teaching methodology. The goal was to raise the female English teachers' self-esteem and create an opportunity for female English language teachers to meet in order to network, share information, and support each other to achieve their full potential. The mentors were senior female colleagues in the SIG who volunteered to share their experiences and help younger female colleagues face professional setbacks. The SIG organized regular informative sessions online and in person to inform the women of available scholarships, training, and workshops. The major advancement was a weekly schedule that members followed to organize webinars, which ultimately changed the mindset in the group of women, which to Awanga was significant and encouraging.

In chapter 3, "Advocacy and Education as a Vehicle for Economic Development and Empowerment of the Garifuna in Belize," Enita Elecia Barrett described an ongoing advocacy initiative that she had individually undertaken to support the teens of the Garifuna community of Seine Bight Village in their academics and English language learning, so they would have marketable skills upon graduation from high school. Barrett described the Garifuna or Garinagu as indigenous people whose populations primarily reside in Belize, Guatemala, Honduras, Nicaragua, and urban centers in the United States (chapter 4 this volume). Her advocacy goals were to reduce the criminalization of the Garifuna teens, to disrupt the school-to-prison pipeline, to lessen the marginalization of the Garifuna in Belize, and to assist the community in the preservation of their culture. Her chapter discussed her efforts to "invest time and other resources in creating a safety net" that she called the Indigenous Youth Progress Nest. This multi-pronged initiative included a "homework hub" for teacher-assisted studying and researching; mentorship by a school success coach; discussion sessions; collaboration between the home, community, and school; workshops on life and soft skills; and a progress monitoring system.

Ethnelda Paulino described in chapter 4, "De-Colonizing Advocacy: Advocacy Efforts for English Language Teaching and Learning in Belize," her efforts to assist incarcerated youths to acquire English language and academic skills to access higher education opportunities. Many individuals of all ages in Belize, the Caribbean, and the world are denied entry into tertiary-level institutions due to lack of completion of secondary education. Incarcerated youths who have this problem face great difficulties when released from prison. Paulino's innovative and ground-breaking advocacy project supported at-risk youth through an online, accelerated, alternative high school program that allowed them to complete their secondary education and be ready for job opportunities or to further pursue post-secondary studies. Through this online high school program, youths who had dropped out of school for multiple reasons, including high-violence or high-crime contexts, as well as harsh economic situations, obtained high school diplomas and increased their potential access to better opportunities, including education, potential entrepreneurship, and access to the job market. Paulino discussed not only the social, political, and economic context of Belize but also how the multiple languages used in the country influence how learners learn the official language, English.

In chapter 5, "English for a Better Future: An Initiative to Provide Quality Education to El Salvador's Youth," Miguel Ángel Carranza Campos discussed a collaborative project reaching 3,000 high school students, funded by several institutions. English for a Better Future sought to support youth in El Salvador with a focus on learning the language as well as the development of life skills and competencies that would support them in becoming workforce ready. Through the project the learners developed their language skills in English as well as public speaking in both Spanish and English, the project included computer literacy skills and basic interpersonal skills that would lead to access to better jobs and study opportunities. This project aimed to increase youth abilities, skills, and competencies to support employment in the private sector, support growth in family economies, and allow access to better opportunities in the country.

In chapter 6, "TESOL Transformative Advocacy in Tertiary Education in Vietnam," Son Nguyen, Huong Lam, and Hong-Anh Nguyen delved into advocacy by emphasizing the need for equitable education for English learners. They underscored transformative advocacy, targeting systemic issues that marginalized English learners, and explored various forms of advocacy, including instructional, political, and transitive advocacy (i.e., collaborations among schools, stakeholders, and communities to support educational goals [Harrison & McIlwain, 2020]). The focus of the chapter was on the impact of advocacy on language education policies, especially within a majority monolingual society like Vietnam. Cultural factors, such as collectivism and Confucianism, posed challenges to advocacy efforts, limiting the power of teachers to advocate for their students. The chapter outlined challenges faced by English language teachers and learners in Vietnam, including unequal learning conditions and limited resources.

Introduction

Briana Rogers, in Chapter 7, "Using English Language Teaching as a Platform for Developing Self-Advocacy: English Is Our Future," wrote about a program in one small educational center in a rural area of Laos called Lone Buffalo, a grassroots organization named after a Lao man named Manophet that helps the children learn English to access a brighter future. The overall goal of Lone Buffalo is to help the local youth develop the life skills needed to become successful, educated adults. While English is still the main program in the center, volunteers also provide business and entrepreneurial training, videography, professional development for females, and leadership training. As a voice for Lone Buffalo and its students, Rogers shared her enthusiasm for its vision and expounded on Lone Buffalo's fantastic work. The center developed workshops, which resulted in students' participation in governmental study abroad programs.

Sumru Akcan detailed in Chapter 8, "Supporting Young Learners' English in Public Schools in Türkiye: Spoken Cafes Project," an advocacy project called Spoken Cafes she enacted in conjunction with Boğaziçi University and the Turkish Ministry of Education. The goals of this project were twofold: to advocate for interactive, communicative oral language development for young learners in Türkiye by demonstrating communicative and learner-centered methodologies, and to provide opportunities for pre-service educators to engage with young learners in authentic K-12 classroom environments. This chapter is an example of teacher educator advocacy, in which the teacher educator, in this case Akcan, recognized that the highly theoretical teacher preparation pre-service educators received in this context lacked experiential learning in authentic contexts, but also that the learning environments in Türkiye relied too heavily on more traditional forms of language instruction, which caused young learners to miss out on opportunities to engage meaningfully with English. Her advocacy project yielded changes in the ways the pre-service educators envisioned how they could teach language to young learners as well as how to co-plan, co-teach, and develop engaging materials. For the young learners, they developed more motivated and positive attitudes toward English.

Chapter 9, "EFL Classrooms as Spaces for Advocacy Acts in Areas of Intractable Conflict," Julia Schlam Salman and Brigitta R. Schvarcz reflected on the challenges and practices of their advocacy project implemented in the Israeli and Palestinian Territories, considered a complex context in terms of the sociopolitical realities as well as the historical aspects that influence language learning and teaching. The chapter gave special emphasis on decolonizing English as a foreign language teaching as well as orienting pedagogy toward negotiating recognition and respect for the multiple identities of learners in their contexts. They advanced three practices with the goals of mitigating conflict and promoting social and linguistic justice: (1) emphasizing appropriateness alongside correctness; (2) deconstructing binary thinking; (3) acknowledging societal inequities while maintaining high academic standards and promoting the use of learners' multilingual repertoires. Their advocacy project addressed and increased knowledge of traditions while promoting respect for multiple and varied worldviews present in the local context and communities.

In chapter 10, "Three Decades of Supporting English Teachers in Paraguay: PARATESOL's New Advocacy Response," Valentina Canese, Susan Spezzini, and Rocío Mazzoleni described actions implemented by PARATESOL to support teacher's professional development in Paraguay during the COVID-19 pandemic. They highlighted how going online due to COVID-19's impact became an opportunity even in the challenging circumstances. They gave a chronological account on how the association was able to make a comeback after a period of being dormant and how this helped them achieve their advocacy mission and vision to support ongoing professional development—offering free online seminars and an international conference. They further discussed their advocacy for the profession by creating partnerships with other organizations in the region.

Gabriel Díaz Maggioli's chapter 11, entitled "Metagogy as Advocacy in Initial Teacher Education," described his efforts to support educators' concerns and to address learning inequalities of a new Ministry of Education–developed curriculum, an outgrowth of neoliberal education reforms, in Uruguay. Employing the Metagogy theorem of adult education, his advocacy effort sought to raise educators' awareness of the dangers of structuralist curriculum through a mixed-methods project. The in-service educators investigated their learners' language learning while identifying strategies to improve their own professional understandings. The results of their investigation were shared with the educational community at large to highlight the issues surrounding the new curriculum.

The conclusion, chapter 12, "Global Efforts in Advocacy for English Language Teaching and Learning: Conclusions and Futures," by Okon Effiong, Kate Mastruserio Reynolds, Debra Suarez, Georgios Kormpas, and Grazzia Maria Mendoza Chirinos, identified patterns of advocacy in these global contexts in this volume's chapters. Patterns included the relationship between success, sustainability, and access to resources; the language learning goals and needs of multilingual learners of English, which served as an impetus for many of the advocacy projects; the types of catalysts for advocacy efforts stemming from intrinsic and extrinsic sources; the variety of approaches educators had to practicing advocacy; and the context of advocacy efforts, which often provided parameters for what efforts were undertaken. The chapter described lessons learned from the advocacy narratives, a reconceptualization of global advocacy, principles for advocacy within constrained contexts, and future directions.

Finally the intended purpose of this volume is to demonstrate advocacy work in global contexts. The chapters illuminate the advocacy efforts of educators, who understand the nuances and complexities of their contexts (what they are able to do and not able to do); other educators can explore how they can engage in advocacy efforts in different contexts and how they serve as agents of change in the face of challenges. The authors' advocacy chapters convinced us that our goals for this volume have been actualized. The resulting compilation of narratives kicked off additional questions and ideas for us. We hope readers find these advocacy narratives:

- familiar (readers can see alignments among the narratives, themselves, and their work),
- informative (readers can identify novel ideas to spur advocacy initiatives of their own),
- stimulating (readers become energized and excited by the advocacy projects and ideas),
- compelling (readers become motivated to become agents of change through advocacy),
- inspiring (readers identify themes, draft what they see as a "collective narrative," and explore future research and theoretical discussions), and
- worth replicating (potential advocates build on what resonates and create their own projects and experiences to create their own advocacy change)!

References

Adams, R, & Newton, J. (2009). TBLT in Asia: Constraints and opportunities. *Open Access Te Herenga Waka-Victoria University of Wellington.* https://doi.org/10.26686/wgtn.12720848.v1

Brulles, D. (2021). Leading gifted Hispanic learners toward self-advocacy. In J. Lawson Davis, and D. Douglas (Eds.), *Empowering underrepresented gifted students: Perspectives from the field* (pp. 43–57). Free Spirit Publishing.

Canagarajah, S. (2023a). Special issue: Decolonizing English language teaching. *ELT Journal, 77*(3).

Canagarajah, S. (2023b). Decolonization as pedagogy: A praxis of "becoming" in ELT. *ELT Journal, 77*(3), 283–293. https://doi.org/10.1093/elt/ccad017

Chinpakdee, M. (2022). Understanding teacher autonomy through EFL teachers' online teaching experiences. *rEFLections, 29*(3), 586–602. DOI:10.61508/refl.v29i3.262102

Day, E. J., Prado, J., & Edmonds, L. (2022). Initiating the third wave for English learners: Teaching self-advocacy. *GATESOL Journal, 32*(2), 3–13. DOI: https://doi.org/10.52242/gatesol.168

Dubetz, N. E., & de Jong, E. J. (2011). Teacher advocacy in bilingual programs. *Bilingual Research Journal, 34*, 248–262. https://doi.org/10.1080/15235882.2011.623603

Freire, P. (2017). *Pedagogy of the oppressed*. Penguin Classics.

Giroux, H. A. (2010). Rethinking education as the practice of freedom: Paulo Freire and the promise of critical pedagogy. *Policy Futures in Education, 8*(6), 715–721. https://doi.org/10.2304/pfie.2010.8.6.715

Haneda, M., & Alexander, M. (2015). ESL teacher advocacy beyond the classroom. *Teaching and Teacher Education, 49*, 149–158. https://doi.org/10.1016/j.tate.2015.03.009

hooks, b. (1990). *Yearning: race, gender, and cultural politics*. Boston: South End Press.

Li, X. (2023). A theoretical review on the interplay among EFL teachers' professional identity, agency, and positioning. *Heliyon, 9*(4), e15510. https://doi.org/10.1016/j.heliyon.2023.e15510

Linville, H. A. (2019). Advocacy skills for teachers: "A real careful little dance." In H. A. Linville & J. Whiting (Eds.), *Advocacy in English Language Teaching and Learning* (pp. 3–17). Routledge. https://doi.org/10.4324/9781351036665

Linville, H. A., & Vinogradova, P. (2021). Voices, perspectives, and actions of advocacy in diverse ELT contexts. In C. E. Poteau and C. A. Winkle (Eds.), *Advocacy for social and linguistic justice in TESOL: Nurturing inclusivity, equity, and social responsibility in English language teaching* (p. 152–165). Routledge. DOI: 10.4324/9781003202356-13

Linville, H. A. & Whiting, J. (2020). Social justice through TESOL advocacy. *TESOL Journal 11*(4), e553. https://doi.org/10.1002/tesj.553

Memmi, A., & Bononno, R. (2006). Introduction. *Decolonization and the Decolonized* (pp. ix–xiv). University of Minnesota Press. http://www.jstor.org/stable/10.5749/j.ctt5vkbnt.4

Murray, N., Liddicoat, A. J., Zhen, G., & Mosavian, P. (2023). Constraints on innovation in English language teaching in hinterland regions of China. *Language Teaching Research, 27*(5), 1246–1267. https://doi.org/10.1177/1362168820979855

Pentón Herrera, L. J. (2022). Advocacy for language teacher associations. *English Teaching Forum, 60*(4), 21–29.

Reynolds, K. M., Schvarcz, B., & Lopriore, L. (1 December, 2023). *"Get what you need": Creating an educators' advocacy toolkit.* Presentation for the 48th annual TESOL Italy conference, online.

Rice, P. (2021). Decolonising English language teaching pedagogy. *Journal of Useful Investigations in Creative Education.* Retrieved from https://juice-journal.com/2021/11/23/decolonising-english-language-teaching-pedagogy/

Salazar, M. (2020). Promoting self-advocacy by encouraging students' IEP participation (Doctoral dissertation, California State University, Northridge).

Staehr-Fenner, D. (2014). *Advocating for English learners: A guide for educators.* Corwin.

TESOL International Association (TESOL). (2019). *Standards for initial TESOL Pre-K-12 teacher preparation programs.* TESOL International Association.

Tignor, R. (2005). *Preface to colonialism: A theoretical overview.* Markus Weiner.

Yazan, B. (2018). Contexts of English language teaching as glocal spaces. In A. Selvi, and N. Rudolph (Eds.), *Conceptual shifts and contextualized practices in education for global interaction* (pp. 219–233). Intercultural Communication and Language Education. Springer. https://doi.org/10.1007/978-981-10-6421-0_11

Chapter 1

Igniting the Passion: ELT Renaissance at Itolu Community High School, Ilaro, Nigeria

Oluyemisi Oladejo

Overview

The Context of the Project

TOEFL Project CALL commenced at Itolu Community High School in Ilaro, Ogun State, in Nigeria on March 2, 2022, with 80 students in junior secondary class 2. This was with the sponsorship of Education Testing Service (ETS), a U.S.-based organization that provided the digital gadgets to facilitate the project. With the support of the school principal, the Ogun State Ministry of Education, Science & Technology, the government agency responsible for educational affairs in Ogun State, Nigeria, granted approval. The host school is a public school located in a low-income community in Ogun State, Southwest Nigeria, and I, the facilitator, teach English language in the school.

TOEFL Project CALL is a computer-assisted language learning (CALL) program designed to enhance the communicative competence of the learners in the four language skills—listening, speaking, reading, and writing—which made up the four modules of the program. Participation criteria included expression of interest via a poll and parental consent.

Participants were asked to complete a research form of the TOEFL Junior Standard test, which was antecedent to the study, while the completion of the study was marked by another research form of the TOEFL Junior Standard test. The goal was to gauge the impact of the computer and the digital environment on the teaching of the English language to learners of English as a second language (ESL).

Beatty (2010) defines CALL as any process in which a learner uses a computer and, as a result, improves his or her language skills. This project was a pilot study and took place mostly during breaks, after school hours, and during holidays.

What Is Advocacy?

Advocacy can be delineated as a chain of intentional activities piloted by an individual or a group of individuals and geared toward causing a positive shift in status quo. O'Neil and Tamaru (2017) have submitted that advocacy is a planned, deliberate, and sustained effort to advance an agenda for systemic change. Since advocacy is driven by intentionality, actions and activities that accidentally achieve positive results do not qualify as advocacy. A successful advocacy program is, therefore, one requiring resilience, tact, collaboration, sensitivity, communication, and strategy on the part of the advocate(s). Consequently, it requires planning and strategizing. Tufail and Lyon (2007) observe that planning helps advocates to get everything in order and take actionable steps toward the realization of set goals.

In most cases, either the advocates live with the realities of the beneficiaries of the advocacy initiative, or the advocates simply demonstrate empathy toward the circumstances faced by the intended beneficiaries of the advocacy program. Quite often, the desire for change is fueled by this reality or empathy. In some cases, the success of an advocacy program hinges on the cooperation and the support of the beneficiaries, who may be ignorant of the need for advocacy. This necessitates the creation of awareness by the advocate to educate the beneficiaries and gain their support. Casey (2014) believes that advocacy activities may be aimed directly at the decision makers; the advocacy may seek to influence indirectly through shaping public opinion and voter intentions or by disseminating alternative models of policy and practices. Effectively, advocacy only happens in a situation that is displeasing to an individual or a group of individuals who then decide to induce rather than wait for change. Advocacy may result in a common good for the beneficiaries.

As with all advocacy programs, the advocate's social or intellectual capital is leveraged for the good of the beneficiaries. Staehr-Fenner (2014) sees advocacy in English language teaching/learning as taking appropriate actions on English learners' (ELs) behalf, providing them and their families with a voice and having a deep understanding about the ELs' backgrounds in order to know which action to take. For learners who are speakers of other languages, English language advocacy is a series of activities embarked on by teachers, schools, government and/or other stakeholders in English language teaching to enhance the acquisition of the language. English language advocacy is germane then to effective teaching and learning in a multilingual country where English is the medium of instruction for all school subjects. Language learners need a voice if we are to change the predominant ideologies of multilingualism as a deficit (Ridley, King,Yoon, & Yi, 2019). Teachers of English to speakers of other languages should therefore prioritize English language advocacy in their classrooms by networking with other English language teaching (ELT) advocates while deploying strategies designed for the specific needs of their students.

The need for English language advocacy in Nigerian classrooms is made greater by the ever-changing Nigerian government's language policies, which often prioritize some Nigerian languages over others but never deny English language the prime place it steadily occupies. "From the fourth year [of school], English shall progressively be used as a medium of instruction and the language of immediate environment. For junior secondary school and senior secondary school, the stipulation for English is that of a core subject" (Federal Republic of Nigeria, National Policy on Education, 2004, para. 4 & 5).

The Goal and the Need for TOEFL Project CALL

I assumed duty as the teacher of English language at Itolu Community High School, Ilaro, in February 2021, to meet a multitude of students who had not taken English as a school subject for several months, because of the transfer and non-replacement of the former English language teacher five months prior. These learners, who are mostly children of illiterate parents, hardly have any contact with English language outside the school premises. This situation was quite disturbing when I considered the place of pride that English occupies in the Nigerian system. Ibrahim and Hamisu (2019) observe that English language is a language of instruction and a subject of study in Nigeria. It therefore serves as a catalyst for academic achievement and professional success.

English language is the medium of instruction for all school subjects; consequently, students' mastery of any subject depends on their English proficiency. Next, a minimum of credit score in English language at the Basic Education Certificate Examination, an academic assessment administered by the National Examination Council (Basic Education Certificate Examination, n.d.), is required for them to transition from junior secondary school to senior secondary school. Notably, English is the official language in their multilingual nation (Nigeria), which has at least 250 indigenous languages.

Olagbaju (2014) notes that Nigeria is a linguistic heterogeneous nation, qualifying as a multilingual nation with the problems of language choice, planning, and implementation.

The situation I found at this school was despicable, similar to other public secondary schools in Nigeria, which is evident in students' communicative incompetence and poor performance in English examinations. Some of the factors responsible for this include poor funding of the educational system, short staffing of schools, inaccessibility of teaching resources, and incompetence of teachers of the language. Yaro, Arshad, and Salleh (2016) observe how the funding of Nigerian schools fails to meet the demands of teachers and learners. This observation arose from the unavailability of teaching resources, dilapidated classrooms, and poor remuneration of teachers, among others.

When I commenced duty at Itolu Community High School (ICHS), it was experiencing the worst form of ELT inadequacy, yet the situation was/is not peculiar to ICHS. In my 13 years of teaching English across public schools in Ogun State, Nigeria, in my estimation, the teacher-student ratio was roughly 1:800 at its best and 0:3,000 at its worst. The situation of ICHS pre-February 2021 is a case in point. This was typical for schools in rural areas across the state. Holguin (2016) opined that isolation, cultural adaptation, misconceptions that rural families have about education, motivation, infrastructure, and violence are some of the shortcomings that inhibit English teachers from working in rural areas. This unfavorable situation is exacerbated by insufficient funding of schools (Akpoghome & Nwano, 2020), especially in the rural areas of Nigeria.

When I began my task as the only English teacher in the school, teaching about 3,000 students from secondary/high school junior class 1 to class 3, and juggling my 90 periods per week, each of which spanned 40 minutes, I realized that I could never be effective. Insufficient and overcrowded classrooms were my major limitations, as there were only 17 classrooms for about 3,000 students. My colleagues also decried the poor performance of the students in other subjects. From conversations and interviews with students, which were carried out in the students' mother tongue (Yoruba), my colleagues and I realized that English language incompetence might be a prime contributor to students' poor performance in the other subjects. According to Ibrahim and Hamisu (2019), communicative competence in English language where English is the medium of instruction serves as a pivot for academic and professional success for students. An unstructured informal experiment revealed that our students wouldn't answer questions correctly when taught in English and were permitted to express themselves in Yoruba.

Since it is a productive skill, writing is one of the most important components of communication; nonetheless, English as a Foreign Language (EFL) learners have difficulty composing texts that are both communicatively and linguistically competent (Chamba, Reinoso, & Rengifo, 2019). The school is the only place where these students have access to practice English, as many of them have illiterate parents from low-income communities and speak only their mother tongue, Yoruba, at home. Holguin (2016, p. 214) further states: "Rural students can also lack motivation." The importance of English as a global language remains abstract to students who hardly travel outside their county and are mostly in their local community with the occasional visit to a neighboring town, so they have little interaction with English. I projected that we could improve their performance in other school subjects if we found a mechanism to improve their English listening and writing skills. If English is the medium of instruction for all subjects, then students' English listening skills need to be whetted as well as their writing skills, since answers in tests and examinations are expected to be written in English.

Despite my individual efforts, and feeling inadequate for the task, no assistance was forthcoming. I was also statutorily bound to teach the specified content in the syllabus, disregarding the irreconcilable level of complexity with students' proficiency. I then set up an adjunct English class where I engaged students in listening games on my laptop computer during breaks and after school hours.

Combining that with my statutory duties was a daunting task; I could only work with five to eight students at once with my computer, which hindered my progress. In contexts with few resources, financial constraints, and a lack of infrastructure, the delivery of language programs and materials promoted as "solutions" by major international publishing companies can be problematic (Mahboob & Tilakaratna, 2012). I began to seek reinforcement because I could do more if the school had more computers and other instructional gadgets. Nevertheless, in line with the government policy, education is free; however, the necessary resources were not available to support teaching. I, therefore, began to look for external funding and sponsorship.

Luckily, I discovered the TOEFL English Researcher/Practitioner's Grant Award of Education Testing Service (see program website). I submitted my entry and was successful. The outcome is TOEFL Project CALL at Itolu Community High School, a project sponsored by ETS that spanned the six months from March 2022–September 2022. ETS provided licenses to the English Learning Center for a web-based, fun platform for learning English. The corporate goal of this project was to see how technology could enhance

English language learning, which was the reason for the pre- and post-study assessments. However, my personal goal with this project was for my students to attain communicative competence and confidence in English to improve their academic performance in other school subjects and to navigate the linguistic complexity of the world.

The Freedom and Constraints of English Advocacy at ICHS

A history of English advocacy, albeit on a personal level and a smaller scale, served as a springboard for my project at ICHS, Ilaro. A year before my transfer to the school, I had published a 531-page textbook of English grammar that was birthed by my disquiet years of inaccessibility of resources to grammar lessons and my subsequent resolve to write one based on need. The successful completion of my grammar book project shortly before my transfer to the school boosted my confidence about revamping the state of English language teaching and learning in the school.

Apparently, what fueled my zeal for this advocacy was my familiarity with the context. If I had been a new teacher of English language beginning my teaching career at ICHS, it might not have occurred to me to advocate. However, having 12 previous years' experience in similar circumstances and my consistent professional development undertakings made me feel ready to advocate at ICHS. Moreover, I had the approval and support of the appropriate authority, including the parents of the learners. The students themselves were not only welcoming of the idea but also excited about it. The licenses to the English Learning Center provided by ETS also made the work easier, because I did not have to design the learning resources.

The early progress, however, did not spare me the challenges that came with the execution of a project of this magnitude in the school. The first major challenge I encountered was the novelty of the digital environment to my students. Prior to this project, many of them had never come close to a computer, not even used one, yet they had to take the pre-study test, which was a computer-based test (CBT). It got messy and cumbersome as I tried to get all 80 students to take the CBT without prior knowledge of the use of the computer. Thankfully, participating in this project not only improved their English communicative competence but also offered technical skill development. As a result, many of them have basic knowledge on how to use a computer.

The biggest of the challenges was the absence of supporting staff. As the only English teacher in the junior section of ICHS, when I was about to officially initiate TOEFL Project CALL, I liaised with the teacher of English in the senior secondary section of the school who offered to assist me in the project. Unfortunately, due to unforeseen circumstances, she was unable to assist. It was at this point I realized the enormity of my task, and I braced myself to facilitate computer-assisted language learning to 80 students in the space of six months alongside my statutory duties. I saw Mahboob and Tilakaratna's (2012, p. 7) observation play out in my case. They explained "Often the ELT programs' need to enable enhanced English proficiency and to improve delivery of language programs in local contexts conflicts with other competing agendas by both the government and aid agencies." My extensive statutory obligations occasionally left me drained and unmotivated for this pilot study; nonetheless, I persevered in my commitment to fulfill my mandate. Additionally, other school-related activities in which the students and I were involved left limited time for this study. Despite these obstacles, through sheer determination and purposeful effort, we got to the finishing line.

Another major constraint was storage space for the equipment used for the project. At the time of this project, ICHS could not boast sufficient and conducive classrooms. Many of the classrooms where mainstream teaching and learning took place were in shambles, and there were no empty classrooms.

After a lot of clearing and rearranging, we were able to utilize a classroom-turned-storage where outdated and discarded computers were kept. Without security measures and because of previous cases of theft in the school environment, the participants of the project and I took on the extra task of retrieving the equipment from the principal's office in the morning for use in our makeshift TOEFL Project CALL room and returning it after use. This room was renovated to an extent after we commenced this project, but there were no security measures and gadgets were kept in the principal's office.

Time was another constraint because TOEFL Project CALL was an extra-curricular activity, and being the only English teacher in school, I was not relieved of my statutory duties. Despite my unrealistic workload of 90 periods per week, I continued to facilitate the TOEFL Project CALL. Due to my demanding schedule, we frequently crammed our work into a 30-minute break from 11:30 to 12 noon. Due to these time constraints, we were compelled to complete set tasks after school hours.

Moreover, we faced technical difficulties with an unstable internet connection. The server was often down, and we were unable to access the English Learning Centre or perform our tasks without hiccups. We wasted precious time trying to work with a poor server, which heightened the challenge posed by time. In addition, powering the computers and other gadgets was yet another challenge. As supply of electricity has been a major setback in every sector of Nigeria for a long time, and we heavily relied on a power generating set, which ran on premium motor spirit. The incessant hike in the price of premium motor spirit made us exceed our budget and threatened to stall this project at a point, but somehow, we were able to overcome this financial difficulty and reach the finishing line.

Advocacy Project

TOEFL Project CALL at Itolu Community High School

TOEFL Project CALL was the amplification of my previously unstructured and spontaneous ELT advocacy at ICHS. Sponsored by Education Testing Service, it involved the facilitation of English language learning to 80 students with the use of computer and digital learning resources. The goal was to gauge the effect of computer-assisted language learning on English language teaching to speakers of other languages. Participants took the TOEFL Junior Standard test to appraise their proficiency level before the commencement of this project.

The 80 students were placed in four groups of 20 each. Each group came for Project CALL at break on a particular day from Monday to Thursday, every week. Every learner also had a username and a password to access the English Learning Centre (ELC), a web-based English classroom provided by Education Testing Service. Moreover, there was the teacher's management portal in the English Learning Centre, which allowed me to monitor the activities and progress of each student in ELC, grade their assignments, and give feedback.

We adopted a simplified, learner-centered, fun-based approach to teaching English, vis-a-vis grammar, vocabulary, and the four language skills. For each English lesson, we used some of the following methods:

- Storytelling
- Role play
- Activities
- Speaking prompt
- Writing prompt
- Collaboration
- Games

- Project (activities based)
- Text analysis
- Visuals

The learning experience at Project CALL was so profound and engaging for the students since such learning designs were neither typical nor available in their overcrowded classrooms. Learners were excited about learning English in the ELC, as it took into account their individuality yet allowed them to work as a team. Learning was flexible and, to an extent, allowed students to learn at their own pace.

An activity-based learning design excited my students about learning English in Project CALL, just as Nunan (2015, p. 13) argues:

> Task-based language teaching (TBLT) is the practical realization of this philosophical shift. Unlike audiolingualism, there is not one single set of procedures that can be labeled TBLT. Rather, it encompasses a family of approaches that are united by two principles: First, meaning is primary, and second, there is a relationship between what learners do in the classroom, and the kinds of things that they will need to do outside the classroom.

The student-participants of this study and I demonstrated Nunan's argument by integrating psychomotor activities that involved the use of hands to create tangible products in our English lessons.

My students learned new words and gained some level of language competence while working on tasks that required them to work as a team. For example, in the week we learnt about Art Craft Fair in the ELC, not only did students play vocabulary games and respond to speaking and writing prompts, but they also consolidated their learning as I guided them to replicate certain crafts. We read about mosaics, among other crafts, and subsequently embarked on a mosaic-making project. We settled for making seed mosaics. This project required that they work as a team and communicate to get things done. In the process, they communicated more and improved their communicative competence in the English language. This validated the assertion that experiential learning refers to the organization of the learning process based on the pedagogical principle of "learning-by-doing" (Fragoulis & Tsiplakides, 2009, p. 113), which means that learners acquire knowledge after having experienced or done something new. It also corroborates Fedicheva (2011) that mastering English is only possible if the student is an active participant in the process of learning.

I found that activity-based learning put them at the center of their own learning. Working as a team helped them to communicate using their newly acquired vocabulary words relating to craft. Beatty (2010, p. 124) notes: "There are many benefits to collaboration including the above-mentioned socialization of learners. However, a concern of CALL is how collaboration promotes language learning through exposure to new language and opportunities to use it through negotiation of meaning with peers." Collaboration enhances and eases Second Language Acquisition (SLA) as they interact because they learn and use new words in the process of performing assigned tasks.

Fragoulis and Tsiplakides (2009) highlight other benefits of project-based language learning, including boost of confidence, increased self-esteem, collaboration, motivation, and engagements. We saw all of these play out in TOEFL Project CALL as students were given opportunities to collaborate and work together on various tasks. This collaboration enabled them to share ideas, knowledge, and experiences and fostered a sense of community and mutual support. As a result, the students became more motivated and engaged in their learning, which boosted their confidence and self-esteem. The project-based approach also allowed the students to take ownership of their learning and to develop their problem-solving skills. They were required to think critically and to apply their language skills in real-life situations, which helped them to become more confident and capable language learners.

As we wrapped up our TOEFL Project CALL, I also led the students into another major task that required collaboration to demonstrate their improved writing skills through this project. This writing project was the creation of a book. Students wrote short stories from the writing prompts I gave them. I assessed the stories and gave feedback. Then, I chose the best eight, proofread them, and compiled them as a collection of short stories, which we published with the approval and support of the school principal. It will be available to new intakes of the school every year as part of our efforts to promote a culture of reading in our school.

Outcomes of TOEFL Project CALL

This advocacy project was conducted along with a pre- and post-test using the TOEFL Junior Standard test. A comparative analysis of the pre-study and post-study test results identified an improvement in students' listening and reading skills. On average, students performed better in the post-study test than they did in the pre-study test, as shown in the statistics analysis.

This project, though carried out with the support and approval of stakeholders, was a personal project that did not involve any form of collaboration with another advocate, as I was the only teacher of English in the school as of the time of the study. However, there were student participants who assisted me in getting some tasks done. Students also demonstrated a significant improvement in academic performance. A comparison of first-term scores and third-term scores of some participants of the study randomly selected showed remarkable improvement in five other school subjects, notably basic science and technology, prevocational studies, national values, religious studies, and business studies. Moreover, three of the participants of the study participated in the online round of the Owlypia Intellectuals' Challenge, a science-based academic enrichment test, for which the preparation resources required the use of students' reading and listening skills. Their scores were 59, 48, and 48 out of 100 marks.

Reflections and Future Directions

A major discovery I made with this project is that students learn language better when they take responsibility for their own learning and the teacher only serves as a guide. The TOEFL Project CALL put students at the center of their own learning with an array of activities that required minimal input from the teacher. These activities allowed students to speak, listen, write, read, interact, communicate, solve, play, analyze, create, and collaborate. In all of these activities, students acquired language skills, grammar, and vocabulary while having fun all the way. The students were so zealous about the project that they gladly showed up in school when CALL classes extended to a holiday period. This activity-based student-centered approach used in TOEFL Project CALL is what Yafaei and Attamimi (2019, p. 2) refer to as Moodle when they say: "The implementation of Moodle encourages a student-centered approach in which both teachers and students take part in the classroom, and the focus of instruction is shifted from the teachers to the students."

This project also helped me to realize that ELT advocacy may not produce the desired result without the right resources in place. ELT advocacy not only requires sufficient funding but also an advocate who can strive for minimal achievements independently. It is best when educators, who are busy already, have collaborators on advocacy projects, so they can achieve more with minimal stress. I could not have achieved sustainable or remarkable progress if I had continued using my personal laptop. I am unsure whether there would have been a significant result, either. The reinforcement I got in the form of mentorship and supply of resources from ETS in no small measure fueled my desire, and I did more than I could have done unaided. Together, we can do more!

Though the TOEFL Project CALL officially ended with the post-study test in October, I do not plan to end my advocacy at ICHS. Thankfully, the resources procured are ours to keep. As our licenses to the ELC expire with the project, my plan is to model the lesson designs from the ELC to create local, customized, fun-based, and student-centered lessons targeted at improving students' four language skills, grammar, and vocabulary. At the time of this report, I only have a rough draft of the customized lessons I am designing and have no clear picture of the type of help I might require for implementation. I do wish to co-opt one or two other teachers of English as I unofficially continue with this project, but that does not seem feasible now. I am also currently writing a paper about the findings of this study where I compare data from the pre-study and post-study test, and the findings will be published in the ETS journal, *The Journal of Linguistics and English Teaching Studies*.

As an apologist for collaboration, I would suggest that all advocates of ELT in low-income communities of Ogun State, Nigeria, jettison individual efforts and join forces. While the lone effort of an individual teacher in a particular school may not yield much, collective efforts can do more. Going forward, we could form a movement. This way we can strategize, train more existing educators to become teachers of English, write grant proposals, and seek sponsorship for the procurement of computers, since computer-assisted language learning has proven to be an effective approach to the teaching of English to speakers of other languages. This in essence indicates that the goals of education are achievable when stakeholders join hands and share responsibilities (Yaro, Arshad, & Salleh, 2016). A unified approach can become a larger movement extending to other states in Nigeria, becoming a national movement. Obiegbu (2016) has identified the challenges facing the teaching of English language in Nigeria to include foundational problems, decline in reading culture, lack of textbooks, and lack of basic teaching needs. As a movement, we can collectively address these challenges, achieving more than we can individually.

References

Akpoghome, T., & Nwano, T. (2020). State funding of public institutions in Nigeria: Control mechanisms and legal challenges (schools and hospitals). *KAS African Law Study Library, 6*(4), 541–562. https://doi-10.5771/2363-6262-2019-4-541

Beatty, K. (2010). *Teaching and researching computer-assisted language learning.* Pearson Education Limited.

Casey, J. (2014). *Understanding advocacy: A primer on the policy making role of nonprofit organizations.* School of Public Affairs, Baruch College, City College.

Chamba, M., Reinoso, M., & Rengifo, E. (2019). Authentic materials to foster writing skills in college EFL learners. *English language teaching.* Canadian Center of Science and Education, *12*(6), 112–127. https://doi-10.5539/elt.v12n6p112

Federal Republic of Nigeria. (2004). *National Policy on Education.* 4th Ed. NERDC

Fedicheva, N. (2011). *Teaching English as a foreign language: Educational guidance for students, would-be teachers of English.* Lugansk SE Taras Shevchenko LNU

Fragoulis, I., & Tsiplakides, I. (2009). Project-based learning in the teaching of English as a foreign language in Greek primary schools: from theory to practice. *English Language Teaching, 2*(3), 113–119. https://eric.ed.gov/?id=EJ1083088

Holguin, B. (2016). *English language teaching in rural areas: a new challenge for English language teachers in Colombia.* Cuadernos de Lingüística Hispánica.

Ibrahim, A., & Hamisu, M. (2019). Appraising second language acquisition theory and English language teaching and learning in Nigeria. *Journal of Science Technology and Education, 7*(3), 258–262. https://www.atbuftejoste.net/index.php/joste/article/view/838

Mahboob, A., & Tilakaratna, N. (2012). *A Principles-based approach for English language teaching policies and practice.* TESOL International Association.

Nunan, D. (2015). *Teaching English to speakers of other languages: An introduction.* Routledge/Taylor & Francis.

Obiegbu, I. (2016). The challenges of teaching English language in Nigeria. *Journal of Modern European Languages and Literature, 5,* 53–60. https://journals.unizik.edu.ng/index.php/jmel/article/view/214

Olagbaju, O. (2014). Multilingual education in Nigeria: policy, practice, challenges and solutions. *Journal of Education and Practice*, 5(6), 66–73. https://api.semanticscholar.org/CorpusID:54677328

O'Neil, C., & Tamaru, N. (2017) *Introduction to advocacy*. Inclusive Security.

Ridley, J., King, N., Yoon, E., & Yi, Y. (2019). Exploring advocacy in an elementary ESL after school program in the United States empirically, What's there?. In H. Linville, & J. Whiting (Eds.), *Advocacy in English language learning* (pp 87–97). Routledge.

Staehr-Fenner, D. (2014). *Advocating for English learners: A guide for educators*. Sage.

Tufail, J., & Lyon, K. (2007). *Advocacy in action: A plain text guide to advocacy*. Jessica Kingsley Publishers.

Yaro, I., Arshad, R., & Salleh, D. (2016). Education stakeholder's constraints in policy decisions for effective policy implementation in Nigeria. *British Journal of Education, Society & Behavioural Science*. 14(1), 2–12.

Chapter 2
Advocating for Female English Language Teaching Professionals in Cameroon

Abigail Ekangouo Awanga

Overview

The English Language Teaching (ELT) Women of Cameroon is a special interest group within the Cameroon English Language and Literature Association (CAMELTA). It is a professional group for female teachers of English language and literature who feel the urge to grow professionally through volunteering in continuous professional development. As the Indeed Career Guide (2022) puts it, volunteering builds interpersonal skills, helps to establish new contacts, leads to career development, provides challenges, and keeps us healthy and happy. Moreover, English et al. (2021) noted the importance of volunteering for long-term professional growth. The English Language Teaching Women Cameroon Special Interest Group (ELTW-SIG) was founded two years ago (2021). This was after a group of women noticed that, despite the fact that women formed the greater majority in the profession in general and our teacher association in particular, few of the women were fully involved in continuous professional development activities in the teacher association. Sun (2010) clearly pointed out that "Institutions need to make a commitment to provide support for instructors to participate in ongoing professional development" (p. 149). The same faces actively participated in the continuous professional development and were always seen at the forefront of most, if not all, activities. This reminds me of the cartoon world, where the faces of Princess Anna and Elsa in *Frozen*, a Disney animated movie, are the same when you take a close look at both of them. They simply differ from each other in their eyes and hair color. Seeing the same females in positions and activities made me ask myself this question: How could I get more female professionals involved in professional activities and thus benefit from available professional opportunities? One needs to rise to the challenges they encounter, so

ELT Women of Cameroon was created. Through this special interest group (SIG), we aimed at raising the female English teachers' self-esteem, creating an opportunity for female English language teachers to meet in a place of their own to network, share information, and support English language female teachers to achieve their full potential. In addition, ELT Women of Cameroon facilitated their active involvement in teaching, learning, and community life, and provided female English teachers in Cameroon with access to professional information, scholarships, trainings, and mentoring.

The above objectives may sound like déjà vu (i.e., the same old objectives), but they have had a profound impact on the lives of many female ELTs in our SIG, especially the objective of raising self-esteem. So many of our members have realized their real values and have overcome low self-esteem thanks to their involvement in the SIG. Most skilled ELT females are wasted in our teachers' association simply because they were not noticed, and they felt like they did not have the required credentials to succeed.

As a SIG, it was important for ELT Women of Cameroon to collaborate with the mother group amicably. It was not easy establishing a collegial working atmosphere between us because many colleagues from the mother association did not share our ideology. The creation of a separate group sounded to most members, especially the men, like a willful act to destabilize the mother association. It was blurry and difficult to understand that the creation of a SIG of ELT women was an inoffensive attempt to put those women who found it difficult to express themselves among men at the forefront of their professional development. It was important to sensitize members to accept us as part of the mother association because we wished for nothing but the good of the association and its members. What sustained the relationship was the fact that a few of the leading members of our SIG also held leadership roles in the mother association. This was a strategic choice to avoid conflicts. However, depending on where you are in the world, definitions of advocacy may differ. For instance, in my context, there is an implicit meaning to advocacy. It is often interpreted as an excessive display of social justice. Advocates are often viewed in my context as what the French call "trouble fête," that is, someone who disrupts the norms to create nuisance. The audacity linked to advocacy in Cameroon stems from our cultural background. It was, and in some parts of the country it is still, a taboo to say "no" to an elder. Saying "no" is a gross sign of disrespect and may insinuate that one lacks proper upbringing. Advocacy is a form of saying "no" to a situation the advocate finds unjust. Supporting people in a way that considers their cultural needs is crucial to good advocacy.

I have a broader view of advocacy. I think it is or should allow for a peaceful transition of ideologies, stereotypes, and injustices from what they have always been to what they ought to be in a context of social justice. My vision of advocacy is more of an action that speaks louder than words, where those who feel unhappy about the initiative may gain admiration and want to join the cause. In Africa, we have been nurtured not to accept advocacy easily, or to view it as abusive freedom. We should thus expect some resistance and rejection. This explains why my view of advocacy is persistently a "communicative approach" (Cho et al., 2023), whereby those whom I advocate for understand their condition and voluntarily undertake steps to change. This group/project stemmed from a simple fact that although women constitute the majority in ELT personnel in our teacher association, many did not participate fully or proportionately to their numbers in professional development activities. I found it unsatisfactory that other women decided to stay comfortable in the background and clap for their fellow women. It is for this reason I decided to build a ladder of the three collectives; collective awareness, collective development, and collective efficacy (see Figure 2.1). First, the strategy was to create awareness through sensitization of the inter-gender gap arising from family constraints and or other issues, understanding women's situations and suggesting ways of tackling professional development collectively. Next was working from the standpoint that every challenge should be an opportunity, per Potts (2019) in her review talks about the use of design thinking to turn challenges into opportunities. Even though designers make significant use of creativity, she argues that creativity is not a specially endowed skill for designers only because everyone has it in them and can use it. Using design thinking in the face of adversity is a skill we need to cultivate if we do not want to remain professionally stagnant. This worked and still works for a minority of the women in the group. Lastly, the women in the association needed to pool their resources together to achieve collectively because it is through collective action that we can influence each other's outcomes and increase our achievements. Concisely, ELT Women of Cameroon was created because of the need to influence female professionals and further raise awareness of women's professional dormancy when they are not included in leadership or engaged in professional development. "To pursue opportunities and overcome global challenges, individuals must equip themselves with competitive skills and knowledge" (Sari, 2018, p. 112) was the motivation behind our advocacy.

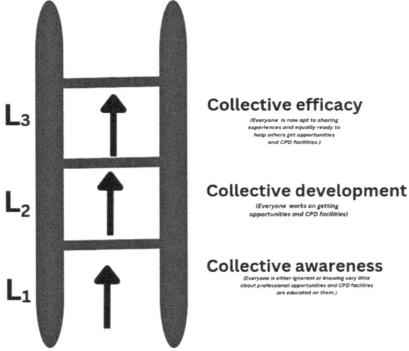

Figure 2.1 The Ladder of Three Collectives

Freedom and Constraints

Freedom without constraints is disorder; in the same light, constraints without freedom create a tense atmosphere. There cannot be one without the other. Government laws are legislated to ensure a balance and to create a conducive place for us to live. In the case of advocacy in my context, freedom is to some extent more theoretical than practical, because others may call advocates disrupters and silent revolutionaries. Constraints are necessary to develop respect for views and beliefs. Without constraints, it might not be possible to control violence and settle disputes because stronger groups will impose their ideology on the weaker ones. However, establishing a difference between constraint and freedom of speech and ideology is a pertinent issue in advocacy.

According to Arno (2014), there are three types of freedom. The first kind of freedom is freedom from, or freedom from the constraints of society. The second is freedom to, or the freedom to do what we want to do. Thirdly, there is freedom to be, freedom not just to do what we want but also to be whom we were meant to be. Advocacy, as I conceptualize it, is a concentration of the three types of freedoms mentioned above. This explains why, in my context, advocates are not usually appreciated, because being an advocate in itself is getting to appreciate things from your own perspective, being what and who you want to be, without taking on societal constraints. My perception of advocacy is therefore a peaceful negotiation between the constraints of nature, tradition, and society to fit our various freedoms. I think "advocacy can be a powerful, multidimensional way to put social justice aims in action in English language teaching and learning" (Linville & Whiting, 2020, p. 4) because when things go the wrong way, "effective social justice advocacy-fused practices are something all TESOL professionals need to be well versed in" (Linville & Whiting, 2020, p. 4).

Advocacy Project

The daring project we carried out was to create a forum of women ELT professionals. A space where a same-gender group could meet and greet, and share experiences about their professional and social lives. This was not the first professional group that existed; however, the marked difference between previous undertakings and this project was the fact that it was a female-only professional space. We hoped to get more females involved in professional development by raising their awareness, developing them, and making them effective professionals. Notably, most of our female colleagues were not novices to professional groups. The difference was in their degree of active participation in the group projects. Empowering and inspiring myself from the interesting story of Princesses Elsa and Anna in the film *Frozen*, I took a bold step ahead to unfreeze the gender apathy toward professional development and engagement. The main lesson in Disney's *Frozen* is to be bold and courageous. Elsa fleeing her home to live on her own was bold; Anna following her to stop the freezing of their kingdom was bold, too! This boldness, which is uncommon in our culture, something we are struggling to rectify, led to the birth of a vibrant group of women interested in changing their career history through cooperation and commitment.

The ELT Women of Cameroon (ELTWC) is barely two years old and is still in its infancy. We have many objectives to attain over time. However, we do not relent on any effort to bring professional development courses to our women. Our advocacy work is continuous and relentless. Teachers need to be up to date with knowledge, so they never stop learning. Advocating for ELT females' greater participation in professional development is a job we do not intend to relent from.

Advocacy Activities

Our project is an ongoing one. We have general and specific objectives. Specifically, we hope to mentor at least 20 females every academic year to ameliorate their struggles with teaching methodology. Mentors are senior female colleagues in the SIG who volunteer to share their experiences and help younger female colleagues face professional setbacks. We also focus on activities and world days that have a direct impact on teaching and our wellbeing. For instance, last year we celebrated Literacy Day with international colleagues from Kenya and the United Kingdom (UK) during a symposium that we organized to that effect. We equally celebrated World Mental Health Day in almost all the regional chapters. We started by organizing a sports walk, encouraging the women to do physical warm-ups regularly to keep the brain fresh and avoid stress, which can lead to mental breakdowns. All our female members in each town participated on the same day and time. After that, we organized a Zoom session on last year's topic, inviting mental health specialists who gave the women a series of detailed presentations on the effects of poor mental health and how to avoid mental health problems.

Our audience was international because we feel that mental health is a global issue. We also collaboratively produced a short film on the importance of checking on each other in our teaching careers. The short film showed the frustration English female teachers suffer, which can lead to mental breakdown if unsupported. According to the UK Mental Health Foundation, "Today, women are three times more likely than men to experience common mental health problems. In 1993, they were twice as likely. Rates of self-harm among young women have tripled since 1993. Women are more than three times as likely to experience eating disorders as men" (2022, n.p.). Despite the fact that female teachers are a working group, they are not exempted from the struggles unemployed females face, such as single parenting, domestic violence, and oppression by superiors in the office, by the other gender, by learners, by tradition, and by stigma. We found it proper to sensitize the female members of our SIG on the dangers of not taking care of themselves in moments of mental imbalance. Last year's celebration was a tremendous success, and we are looking forward to next year. Many of the female members of our SIG participated in the event and gave presentations, some for the first time, and the results were satisfying. In addition, our SIG has representation nationwide, so we hold at least one seminar per term to update the women on the latest teaching improvements.

Collaboration and Strategies

Given that our SIG is comprised of female members who are also members of our main teacher association, our SIG often collaborates with the mother association first. Notwithstanding, we have minor projects with other teacher associations in other countries, such as Mali English Teachers, and non-governmental organizations (NGOs), for example, African Women in Tech-Start-Up (AFWITS), with whom we are gradually building liaisons. English language is taught in all sectors of education in Cameroon, and we chose to

Table 2.1 Weekly Schedule of Professional Development Presentations

Day	Activity
Mondays	ESL teachers' professional development presentations
Tuesdays	Technical education sector professional development presentations
Wednesdays	Primary education sector professional development presentations
Thursdays	English as a Foreign Language (EFL) professional development presentations
Fridays	English for Specific Purposes (ESP) professional development presentations
Saturdays	Question and answer sessions
Sundays	Business orientation and advertisement professional development

Advocating for Female English Language Teaching Professionals 39

employ a variety of teaching strategies for our own professional development. The best collaborative strategy we put in place was to have an inclusive association of female teachers from the various sectors and draft an inclusive schedule with and for all of them, so we would know when professional development programs were available (see Table 2.1).
Our work schedule and programs aim at encouraging members to find their niche in the SIG based on their affiliations, such as those shown below.

- Technical language teachers
- General language teachers (ESL/EFL)
- Primary language teachers
- Secondary language teachers
- University lecturers
- Literature about English teachers

On Sundays, we encourage our women with other skills in business to advertise their work in the forum. This acts as an additional motivation for them and is a way of mixing business with pleasure. ELTWC engages its female professionals in many personal and professional development activities. We have weekly presentations by the special interest section where inspired teachers discuss pertinent and challenging topics in their English language teaching sector. Furthermore, we introduced a nine-month mentoring program, which consists of senior female professionals guiding the younger ones throughout the academic year. At the end of the academic year, the mentee authors a report on how they benefited from the mentorship. Other opportunities come from exchange programs we have negotiated with other female English language interest groups in Tanzania, Ghana, Argentina, and Mali. We also organize regular informative sessions online or in person to inform the women of available scholarships, trainings, and workshops.

Amidst all these professional development activities, we wish to inculcate a fighting spirit in our women. The strong message we put forth is to encourage them to learn not to accept and not to be comfortable with the least as far as their career and social lives are concerned. We also advance the idea of turning challenges into opportunities and using those opportunities as life changers for them, their learners, and their communities at large. Our group is dynamic, and everybody plays a significant role in its success. One hand cannot tie a bundle of wood, as they say in my country, and as such, our continuous efforts cannot and should not be attributed to one person because we work collaboratively. One challenge, though, that we have is finding sponsors and funding. Many proposed programs are still pending because we do not have, or rather are still in search of, sponsors who can help us reach our goals.

Achievements

When we started the group, it was a vague virtual idea. We had nothing concrete to share apart from the urge to bring female English language professionals together in a forum to create an impact by having a sense of purpose. The forum remained dormant for quite some time while we explored ideas to make the women want to stay. Nothing more boring than joining a group that has no activity—most people would leave at some point. As humans, whenever we find ourselves in an inactive space, we get bored and feel like filling the vacuum or leaving the space.

We used WhatsApp as our virtual space because it has lately become one of the most common and easiest spaces to gather and communicate with a large number of people within a relatively short period. Talking about concrete advances, we have a weekly schedule that we follow, we organize webinars, and we have changed the mindset in our group of women, which to me is significant and encouraging. The forum is a mixture of young and old, experienced and inexperienced teachers who share their challenges and find common solutions to them. In addition, we encourage the women to register for webinars, conferences, and scholarships on a regular basis, and show them the numerous benefits they will have by taking courses, attending online conferences, and getting scholarships. The Africa English Language Teaching Association's (ELTA) Female Mentoring Program's latest report indicates that five women from our group participated in the mentoring program after the information was shared in the group and a session was held to help the women in their application process. We equally have one female teacher who secured funding to attend a conference in Senegal due to the opportunities and constant encouragement she had in the forum.

Testimonials

The testimonials below (names have been changed) show that our SIG is working wonders for female ELT professionals, and we have many testimonials

Advocating for Female English Language Teaching Professionals

that illustrate how our SIG is changing women's professional lives. Some examples of the testimonials include:

> I have benefited a lot from ELT Women Forum. I am currently undergoing my OPEN program thanks to the ELT women group. I also benefit a lot from the teaching resources shared in the chat forum on a daily basis.
> —Rita

> ELT Women gave me the opportunity to connect with other ELT professionals in other countries. After having served as the moderator for a panel discussion in September 2022, l received a lot of appreciative feedback and grew the connections friendly and professionally. In addition, a presentation by the founder of ELT Women SIG on the importance of membership in an international teachers' association enabled me to become a member of TESOL international. So far, l enjoy the membership. ELT Women and CAMELTA are my windows to the world.
> —Gina

> I have been a professionally blind teacher for many years until I was added to the ELT Women forum. It helped me discover the most interesting part of my career (professional development). Ever since, I work towards achieving greater things. I am currently attending an online course thanks to ELT Women, and I can't wait to share what I am learning by the end of the training.
> —Clara

> Significant advances have also been made in the domain of enhancing leadership skills. Our group is represented in all 10 regions of our country, each having a regional branch. We equally have a subgroup of regional leaders and their assistants where we brainstorm and harmonize decisions that will affect the regions. There, we do mini trainings on leadership skills to encourage our leaders to withstand the challenges.
> —Cynthia

What can be observed from these testimonials is that these female educators desired a professional network that would allow them to have interpersonal support, access to resources, and professional development in areas of their interest and need. They valued the access to weekly online connections and local communities of practice.

Setbacks

Setbacks are part of professional journeys that will happen to almost everyone at some point and can be devastating. Wherever human beings interact, and as in every situation or project in life, there are certain setbacks. For our SIG, the first challenge we encountered was dormancy in the regional groups. Despite the fact that we work to have all ten regional chapters as active as the main group, it is exceedingly difficult to invigorate all regional leaders with the same enthusiasm and energy as the main group. Regarding regional dormancy, we have a regional leader's group where we exchange ideas about activities that can boost the groups. We encourage regional leaders to think creatively and bring up ideas that could be helpful. This has brought some major positive results, since some leaders are already organizing training and workshops for the women in their regional chapters. In biology, seed dormancy is a "resting state of a viable seed that must be broken either by time or by deliberate conditions before the seed germinates at temperature and moisture levels suitable for required growth" (Abubakar & Attanda, 2022 p. 96). The leaders at the main chapter help the regional leaders decide when to stop resting, just like the seed, and germinate ideas in their chapters. This remains a critical situation to deal with as a whole.

A weak online presence is another setback we experienced. Despite all the advantages, we have been trying to show the members about the importance of online presence for professional growth. It is not easy to have a handful of women ELT professionals show up at the professional development sessions, trainings, and workshops. There are many reasons for this. For example, women have a complex routine as teachers, wives, and other roles. As far as we understand, it causes considerable conflicts in our schedule, resulting in poor attendance. Poor internet connectivity and prohibitive cost are other challenges. It is not news that in developing countries, the internet is a luxury. The poor network coverage that we experience in most areas discourages us from participating in online activities. Similarly, the cost of the internet does not make the situation easy. Quite paradoxically, it takes a very conscious and selfless professional to endure the frustrations caused by poor connectivity. While hoping that those in authority will handle the problem, we keep encouraging females to subscribe to cheaper internet rates to maintain online presence.

Another setback is the women's reluctance to financially underwrite their own trainings and workshops. They know how important these professional development sessions are, but for some reason, they are not willing to pay for training because, most of the time, these trainings could be expensive. Most of them prefer free trainings. Paying for training is quite a challenging experience for teachers in general, not just females. Teachers feel more comfortable with free offers and, sometimes, remunerated ones. There is still a long way to go to help the women come to terms with paying for professional development. When we offer workshop sessions at even a small cost, the numbers of attendees are ridiculously small. We encourage the women to understand that free trainings are sponsored. If there is no sponsor, then the training cost will be high, and we need participants to understand and support it.

Above are some considerable setbacks that we encounter. The ELTWC is just a year old. Similar to any newly founded SIG, we hope that, with time, most of these challenges will be overcome. I am the fail-forward type of professional, and I hope my female colleagues will learn the value of failing forward. Failures can be upsetting, but a mature and determined mind should look beyond them. Despite the numerous setbacks we have encountered, and continue to encounter, the way forward is our focus. We need to learn the lessons in the setbacks and grow from them. It is not an easy task, though, especially because some setbacks encountered are beyond our control.

However, we are determined not to fall prey to the law of abandonment. In law, "abandonment is the act of surrendering a claim to, or interest in a particular asset" (Chen, 2022, para. 1). The ELTWC is in an infancy that we are nurturing, and surrendering to setbacks is therefore equivalent to abandonment. With respect to online presence, we have undertaken a six-month-long online open therapy session with all women in our group. In these sessions, we discuss ways in which we can find and use opportunities for the collective benefit of our members and others. The sessions take place once per month, at the end of which a task is assigned to each woman to carry out through the following month. They need to complete the task and bring feedback at the next therapy session. Here, everyone has a duty and responsibility. The sessions bring about 40% of the women online, and we hope this number will continue to grow with time.

Our project is a long-term one, and given that it is still in its infancy, outlining our achievements may be a bit too early. However, we are making some considerable advances as time passes. For example, we now have 15% of females applying for available scholarships because the ELTWC shares them in the main WhatsApp group on a daily basis. Three out of the 45 women who underwent the training in digital skills are now trainers. They in turn train their female members in their regions, and we hope this circle continues. Two female members have been preselected for two different scholarships and are awaiting the results. Many women also volunteer to lead topical sections of the main group and organize presentations for those with the same special interest.

Reflections

This journey is one of the most inspiring I have embarked on since I started teaching. I did not know where we were heading because our objective at the beginning was just a WhatsApp forum where female teachers of English could share experiences. The determination to accomplish something unique encouraged us to create a SIG, and with the help of co-leaders, advisers, and members, we continue to grow and adapt our mission and objectives. I believe there is a direct link among an individual's personality, grit, and professional competence. Personality can be measured through five indicators: extraversion, agreeableness, conscientiousness, openness, and neuroticism. Extraversion refers to the tendency to seek stimulation and to enjoy the company of other people. Agreeableness is a tendency to be compassionate toward others. Conscientiousness reflects a tendency to show self-discipline and strive for competence and achievement, whereas openness refers to enjoying new experiences and innovative ideas. Finally, neuroticism suggests experiencing unpleasant emotions (Windodo, 2021). I can identify with all of the above because I possess these qualities, and they spur me to engage and encourage other women to develop professionally. I have learned a lot about advocacy through these experiences. Firstly, I have learned that advocacy does not necessarily mean fighting stereotypes openly or directly. Professional manners obliged me to see advocacy as a polite and constantly convincing procedure or series of procedures with the aim of changing the opponents' thoughts without letting them hold grudges against you. I also learned that advocacy is an effort to not only change old, aching habits but also work toward reawakening our professional consciousness. Many women have been awakened, and that was our first goal and our best achievement.

Dealing with the complexity of human interactions was and is still a learning experience for me in this project. It has not been easy to interact. Sometimes my decisions were openly criticized, and this led to some misunderstandings. I did apologize to the group, because I believe humility is the key to a successful leadership. I have grown a step higher in that respect. I have also learned that we all do not have the same energy and motivation. Therefore, I deal with members in groups. From those who are highly motivated but lack experience, to those who are less motivated but have experience. Considering the impact our activities have had on the members of ELTWC in the past years, I think if I had to start all over, there is nothing significant that I would change.

Advice

The advice I would give to other ELT advocates is that they should address their problems with passion, patience, selflessness, and resilience. Laying the foundation for change is not an easy task, especially when ideologies have not been questioned for a long time. Playing the positive disruptor role should be a tactful exercise where the main objective is to stimulate positive change and gain more allies than enemies. We can thus conclude by saying that as TESOL teachers who wish for a change in mindset, advocacy is the key. "We need to understand what skills are involved, which personal characteristics are shared by effective advocates, and how to do advocacy at the various levels and within our spheres of influence" (Harrison & McIlwain, 2019, p. 15).

Discussion Questions

1. Which continuous professional development activities do you think could engage a group of female teachers more actively in a teaching community? And why?
2. In this chapter, we encourage personal development alongside professional development. Which ideas do you think are teacher oriented and could be recommended to female English language teachers as personal development projects?
3. How do you view this kind of advocacy? Will it work in your community? Why or why not?

References

Abubakar, M. S., & Attanda, M. L. (2022, September 20). Factors that cause seed dormancy. IntechOpen. Retrieved from https://www.intechopen.com/chapt 8 para(3)

Arno. (2014, July 27). Three types of freedom. The Warriors Way. Retrieved from https://warriorsway.com/three-types-of-freedom/

Chen, J. (10 April 2022). Abandonment: What is means, how it works. Investopedia. Retrieved from https://www.investopedia.com/terms/a/abandonment.asp#:~:text=Abandonment%20is%20the%20act%20of,the%20purchase%20of%20deliverable%20securities.

Cho M., Xu S., & Boatwright B. (June 2023) A personal communicative approach to CEO advocacy & employee relations. *Science Direct*, 49(2) para. 4. http//doi.org/10.1016/j.Pubrev.2023.102295

English, P., de Villiers Scheepers, M.J., Fleischman, D., Burgess, J. & Crimmins, G. (2021). Developing professional networks: The missing link to graduate employability. *Education + Training*, 63(4), 647–661. https://doi.org/10.1108/ET-10-2020-0309 https://www.emerald.com/insight/content/doi/10.1108/ET-10-2020-0309/full/html

Harrison, J., & Mcllwain, M. J. (2019). ESOL teachers' experiences in their role as advocate: Making the case for transitive advocacy. *TESOL Journal*, 11(1) 1–18. https://doi. org/10.1002/tesj.464

Indeed. (2022). Why volunteering is important in a personal and professional capacity. *Indeed Career Guide*. Retrieved from https://www.indeed.com/career-advice/career-development/why-volunteering-is-important

Linville, H., & Whiting, J. (2020). Social justice through TESOL advocacy. *TESOL Journal*, 11(4), 1–5 https://doi.org/10.1002/tesj.553

Potts, E. (2019, March 11). Using design thinking to turn challenges into opportunities. CreativeLive Blog. Retrieved from https://www.creativelive.com/blog/how-use-design-thinking-challenges-opportunities/

Sun, Y. (2010). Standards, equity, and advocacy: Employment conditions of ESOL teachers in Adult Basic Education and literacy systems. *TESOL Journal*, 1(1), 142–158. https://doi.org/10.5054/tj.2010.215135

Sari A. P. (2018). More than teach: English teachers' advocacy in the online globalized era. *Lingua: Jurnal Bahasa Dan Sastra*, 18(2), 110–118.

Windodo, J. (2021). Enhancing teachers' professional competence through grit, personality, and creativity. Retrieved from https://www.researchgate.net/publication/348119505_Enhancing_teachers'_professional_competence_through_grit_personality_and_creativity

Chapter 3
Advocacy and Education as a Vehicle for Economic Development and Empowerment of the Garifuna in Belize

Enita Elecia Barrett

Overview

As a TESOL practitioner, I have witnessed the complex interplay of language and culture, shaped by a history of colonialism and marginalization. My role extends beyond language instruction. It involves ethically advocating for learners' rights while emphasizing the preservation of native languages alongside English proficiency and confronting linguistic imperialism while promoting ethical teaching practices. I have engaged in efforts like the Saint Alphonsus Roman Catholic School (SARC) teacher training program to alleviate the negative effects of unfair language policies and practices by implementing uplifting programs that address systemic disadvantages in vulnerable low-income contexts.

Teaching English to Speakers of Other Languages (TESOL), as the acronym suggests, is a field dedicated to instructing individuals from diverse linguistic backgrounds in the English language. However, within this endeavor lies a complex interplay of linguistic and cultural dynamics, often prompting questions regarding the perceived superiority of English over the native languages of learners. Depending on the context, many learners of English as a second language belong to social minority groups, many of whom have historically endured the impacts of colonialism and other oppressive systems that eroded their ethnic cultures and identities. Naturally, this intersects with advocacy; as TESOL educators we often find ourselves evolving into a multifaceted role that includes advocating for the rights, needs, and aspirations of their learners.

At its core, teaching English as a second language (TESL) is far more than just imparting language skills, but is a discipline that inherently involves complex sociocultural dynamics, power structures, and the promotion of linguistic diversity. As such, it facilitates access to global communication and empowerment for individuals from diverse linguistic backgrounds.

While many TESOL educators see their primary goal as empowering students by imparting the skills of speaking a foreign language in addition to their native tongues, they unavoidably face the legacies of colonialism and the linguistic hegemony established. Included is the notion of subtractive education, as elucidated by Skutnabb-Kangas (2017), which seeks to replace a child's indigenous culture with an alternative one. With this in mind, contemporary TESOL educators are now educated to advocate for learners' rights to maintain and celebrate their native languages while acquiring English proficiency.

TESOL practitioners play a critical role in promoting social justice and equity in education (Shohamy, 2022). This involves challenging language policies that may undermine linguistic diversity and advocating for bilingual or multilingual education models. They work to level the playing field for learners who face systemic disadvantages due to their backgrounds. This includes addressing issues like access to quality education, fair assessment practices, the incorporation of culturally relevant materials, the promotion of multiculturalism, and the fostering of an inclusive learning environment not only in the classroom but also at local, national, and international levels. They collaborate with educational institutions, policymakers, and non-governmental organizations (NGOs) to influence language policies, funding allocation, and teacher training programs. Within this, ethics play a central role. Educators must grapple with questions of linguistic imperialism, ethical language teaching practices, and the potential for linguistic and cultural exploitation. This ethical dimension often shapes their advocacy strategies and decisions.

Linville (2014) cited her observations of systemic inequities against minorities at an institution as a significant catalyst for her engagement in English language teaching (ELT) advocacy. Similarly, I too was motivated to act based on my observations of disparities in the village of Seine Bight, Belize. This village has undergone many changes, especially in recent times. While some are to the benefit of its residents, many are also to their detriment. My concern is that according to the Belize Crime Observatory (2021), there has been an increase in criminal activities in the community. What caught my attention the most is that, in reaction to this widespread issue, Seine Bight now has one of the highest numbers of police officers assigned to a single post in the region. While I applaud the attempt to respond to the rise in crime,

I am concerned about the lack of other resources that could influence changes in the youths' ways of thinking and steer them away from the cycle of crime and poverty.

Though the tourism boom has brought economic growth to the peninsula, unfortunately, its effects on the village and the Garifuna[1] villagers is minimal. Rapid demographic shifts are represented in an increase in the number of Chinese; Mayas; Hispanics; Creoles; Caucasian expats from the United States, Canada, and other countries; and others who are not shy about laying claim not only to traditional Garifuna lands but also to the economic hubs of the village. As such, they systematically exclude Garinagu from even menial jobs by giving preferences to those of other cultures. They are not shy to say that Garinagu are lazy, unreliable, and not trustworthy (Bonner, 2001; Koenig, 2015).

Sadly, our people's attitude seems to be one of acceptance, and we too often do participate in this self-fulfilling pattern. For example, there has been a decrease in the number of students from Garifuna villages who successfully complete high school or earn marketable skills. More concerning is the fact that there is no data on record regarding what may be some of the specific factors that primarily contribute to the decline in the completion rate. In addition, there is no data on where these students end up once they leave primary school. I realized that there was nothing in place that focused specifically on an individual student's path to success. Instead, I observed an increase in police presence in this small village. This caused me to wonder what can be put in place that can avert youth from leaving school, which leads straight to prison cells and a lifetime of prison records.

The absence of both individuals and systems dedicated to engaging students in meaningful conversations, listening to their perspectives, and offering resources aligned with their identified needs becomes apparent. This observation finds support in Palacio's (2013) work, which highlights how Garifuna students' underachievement in schools can be attributed, in part, to the "failure to identify what problems they are having in the school system arising from their status as an ethnic minority together with the failure in public policy to ameliorate these conditions" (Palacio, 2013, p. 133). These shortcomings can be traced back to a longstanding lack of communication, reflecting a traditional disregard for this minority group (Kroshus, 1998). Stenner (2005), approaching the issue from a social constructivist epistemological perspective, reinforces this point by emphasizing the importance of considering the perceptions, experiences, and viewpoints of individuals directly involved in social or educational contexts (Rebar, 2005). Consequently, to enhance our ability to develop relevant interventions aimed at addressing educational failure, retention challenges, and dropout rates, it is imperative to pay specific attention to this population, ensuring that interventions are tailored to maximize their potential benefits.

To get a better picture of the dynamics that have influenced the attitudes of the youth of Seine Bight Village, one would need to understand its geographical location and the history of prejudices between the Garifuna and the Creoles within the context of the booming tourism industry on the peninsula.

Seine Bight Village

Seine Bight Village is a Garifuna village located on the pristine coastline of the Placencia Peninsula. According to the recent census, there are around 1,100 residents in Seine Bight Village—90% are Garifuna. The Garifuna—also known as Garinagu, formerly referred to as the Black Caribs—are indigenous people whose populations primarily reside in Belize, Guatemala, Honduras, Nicaragua, and urban centers in the United States (Servio-Mariano, 2010). They are a hybrid group, being descendants of Carib-Arawak indigenous peoples who migrated from South America to the Antilles, where they embraced escaped slaves and incorporated them into their community. In 2001, UNESCO declared the Garifuna culture a Masterpiece of Oral and Intangible Heritage for Humanity (UNESCO, 2001). The Garifuna in Belize constitute 6.1% of the Belizean population (Central Intelligence Agency, 2016).

Geographical Location and Sociopolitical and Economic Realities

Three miles north of Seine Bight is Palencia Village, which is among the most popular tourist destinations in the country. Palencia is recognized as a Creole village but is inhabited by multiple ethnic groups, including expatriates from the United States, Europe, and other parts of the world. Creoles, who make up 25.2% of the Belize population (Statistical Institute of Belize, 2021), are descendants of European and African people (Boles et al., 2011) and are the only ethnic group that bears physical resemblance to the Garifuna. In fact, it is only the language and ethnic pride in their self-identity that differentiates these two groups. Yet, historically, there has always been animosity between the two groups, dating back to the arrival of Garinagu on the shores of Belize. Upon learning that the Garinagu were migrating to Belize, colonialists sowed

Advocacy and Education as a Vehicle for Economic Development   51

the seed of discord and warned the local population not to mix with the new group. That seed of marginalization took root and grew into the legacy that lives on today.

The current strain between the Garifuna and Creoles is also propagated by politics and the lack of equity in the distribution of economic and other opportunities yielded by the ever-changing political tide and the booming tourism trade (Koenig, 2015). Though manifested in much more subtle ways than in previous years, this history is the root of the prevailing attitude of other Belizeans toward Seine Bight Village and its people.

Key and Pillai (2006) report that recently, political leaders are succeeding in forging some level of reconciliation between the two groups, brought on by a level of co-dependence on the tourism industry. This may be true, as most hotels on the peninsula rely on performance groups from Seine Bight to provide cultural entertainment to their guests. On the other hand, in an interview conducted by Koenig (2015), a Seine Bight resident lamented the disparity between the economic opportunities afforded them compared to those being enjoyed by the Creoles and other ethnic groups on the peninsula. For example, Garifuna performers are paid a very small percentage of what hotels charge tourists. One performer complained, "They pay ten dollars to see the monkeys and refuse to pay me three dollars for my performance." In addition, when we consider how the village appears and feels, including its physical layout, buildings, and general atmosphere, it does not match the impressive look that other communities on the Peninsula have. This is because decisions made by people in charge, both socially and politically, have influenced things like the village's size, safety, the types of people who live there, land ownership, and the village's overall sense of identity.

With this in mind, I reflected on sociolinguistic theories, especially critical social theory (Leonardo, 2004), which looks at issues of race, class, ethnicity, language, and culture as embedded in relationships of power and provides the framework for conceptualizing the role of different stakeholders in the community and human capacity building. When thinking about the stakeholders, however, I realize that not many of the community stakeholders surrounding the village are committed to promoting the change I envision because the current conditions are convenient to the promotion of their personal agendas. People who are not armed with knowledge and experiences that can propel a desire for change are less empowered and more easily manipulated. Therefore, it is in the best interest of others to keep this population in a socially, economically, and academically oppressive state (Freire, 2000). This perspective aligns with the evident agenda of recent arrivals who are assertively claiming ownership of the valuable beachfront properties and other resources traditionally belonging to the village and its residents. Loperena (2022) observed that Garifuna territorial rights remain under threat due to the actions of land developers, who simultaneously espouse rhetoric that does not foster respect for the local community, its culture, or its prospects for progress.

As a stakeholder myself, providing relevant education programs to raise a generation of critical thinkers and leaders is one way the current cycle may be broken.

Advocacy Projects

In a discussion with the village primary school principal, she explained her frustration and embarrassment over the fact that the high school children who left the k–12 school she directs were not reading at high school level when attending higher education institutions. She said she had been doing her best but the reading levels in the entire school were below par. The students are native Garifuna and Spanish speakers but mostly speak an English-based Creole, which is the lingua franca of Belize. The language of instruction in Belize is English. As an ELT practitioner and being aware of the challenges such linguistic dynamics can pose to second- and in some cases third-language learners, I was moved to utilize my expertise to advocate for these children by focusing on the education of youth in the village of Seine Bight, in the Stann Creek District of the country of Belize. I believe that investing in their education and development can lead to a more skilled and productive workforce, which can ultimately drive economic growth and prosperity in the village. Youth are the potential future workforce and contributors to society. Therefore, I believe there is a need to rethink the quality of education provided so that it reflects the on-the-ground realities.

To achieve this vision, I have undertaken a multifaceted advocacy program through an NGO that includes: an indigenous youth progress nest, free teacher training; and a school reading program.

The Indigenous Youth Progress Nest

In 2022, I was invited to be the guest speaker at the graduations of two Garifuna community high schools in Belize. While addressing the students, I experienced overwhelming sadness as I looked into their faces, shining with pride. I was saddened by the thought that in the community where they live, all the odds are stacked up against these kids and that this graduation was expelling them from the safety net of perceived childhood and thrusting them into the world beyond the village. Yet, they did not possess the economic, social, or academic tools needed to successfully undertake the journey. It was then that I decided to invest time and other resources in creating a safety net around these 46 high school graduates. I would provide the resources that may mitigate the possibility of falling by the wayside during their journey, and I would monitor them for the next four years to see if the high school completion rate could be higher than usual. This gave birth to the Indigenous Youth Progress Nest (IYPN).

The aim of the IYPN is to account for every individual who completed eighth grade in 2022 from the villages of Seine Bight and Georgetown. Our objectives include:

1. To establish a comprehensive tracking system that will facilitate accounting for the academic, home, and other experiences of students who completed or dropped out of eighth grade in 2022. In line with the recommendations of Alam, Ashikullah, and Rahman (2018), who emphasize the significance of family in shaping children's development and educational outcomes, my approach includes a situation analysis that involves reviewing school records for all participating students and collecting biographical information and relevant data that will provide a better understanding of the students' family dynamics, economic circumstances, and social situations, all of which can significantly influence their academic experiences and outcomes.
2. To provide life and soft skills workshops in response to specific issues that are found to be needed by participants. Quite a few of our students have gotten into situations where they ended up escalating a situation and getting into more trouble than necessary due to their inability to think strategically. Therefore, life and soft skills are necessary to help students develop important personal qualities, including self-awareness, self-confidence, and resilience. According to O'Niel (1996), every child should be taught the essentials of handling anger, managing conflicts, developing empathy, and controlling impulses. These skills empower them to navigate challenges, set goals, and make informed decisions.

3. To provide a mentor for each student. Mentors are sourced from the local and international communities. Qualifications to be a mentor include being of sound character and moral fortitude, having achieved academic and professional success, or being known in the community as being of sound character and dedicated to community activism. Most importantly, the mentor must be willing to give of his or her time to attend self-development workshops with the students twice per year and to keep in touch with students enough to build personal relationships with them. By so doing, the students know they can go to that person if they have issues that may affect their ability to succeed in school. Most importantly, I know the mentors personally, because I am very careful not to expose the students to individuals who may cause them more harm than good. Currently all our mentors are educators, mostly from the Belize Ministry of Education.
4. To hold at least two whole-group meetings with all participants per year. A primary purpose of the whole-group biannual meetings is for students to spend a day with their mentors. Most of the communication between the students and their mentors is done via distance communication. The biannual meetings are the place where they get together in person and in a relaxed environment. The meetings also provide an opportunity for clear and direct communication when important information, updates, and announcements are shared with everyone simultaneously, ensuring that everyone is on the same page. These meetings also facilitate opportunities for collaboration and team building among participants. Students, mentors, and parents participate in activities where individuals come together, share ideas, discuss challenges, and work collectively toward common goals. They also review goals, milestones, and progress, and hold each other accountable for their commitments and responsibilities. In his book *The Five Dysfunctions of a Team*, Lencioni (2002) cites the absence of these characteristics as the main cause of a dysfunctional team. These meetings, therefore, foster a sense of belonging to a team with a shared purpose. Having to wear their IYPN t-shirts also gives students the opportunity to publicize their identity as Nesters who belong to something positive.
5. To invite community involvement in the project. I collaborate with the village school to send out notifications to parents via their WhatsApp group chat. I also walk around the village, give word of

Advocacy and Education as a Vehicle for Economic Development

mouth invitations, and post flyers in the village and on the villagers' Facebook pages.
6. To collect and maintain running data on each student. A teacher from each high school is responsible for keeping data on each student. This information is sent to me, where it is compiled and saved.
7. To find funding sources to alleviate the cost of providing needed resources for participating students and for funding the projects. Grant applications were made.

Start-Up Project Plan

The project started in August 2022 when I held a first meeting with all students and their parents. The purpose of the meeting was to follow up on a letter notification that was sent to parents and to meet them for the first time, face to face, to further explain the program and answer any questions they may have. Unfortunately, only five parents and their children attended. I continued the meeting with the five parents. They had many questions, most of which were related to financing and funding their children's education. It took a bit of explaining for the parents to understand that the focus of the Nest was beyond funding. I used social temptations, such as hanging out with friends and playing games, as examples to show them the need to minimize the possibility of their children falling into the more popular traps that have resulted in derailing other children's high school education. Once understood, the parents eagerly agreed and without hesitation signed commitments to the program, promising to explain it to other families and urge others to participate.

December 22, 2022: The First Indigenous Youth Progress Nest

The second meeting with the Nesters was at the Indigenous Youth Progress Nest First Bi-Annual Personal Development Workshop. I hosted this workshop at my residence, Barrett's Peraansah Beach. A bus was chartered to bring students and parents from Seine Bight and Georgetown villages. A total of 35 students and 8 parents and mentors attended. At the workshop, guest speaker Marshal Nunez, director of the Disabilities Desk in the Ministry of Families, who is blind, gave a well-received motivational talk on resilience. The students participated eagerly, and their responses indicated high levels of cognitive engagement. The second speaker was Pastor Agatha Lambey, psychologist and counselor at Agape International Ministries, who challenged the students to utilize effective conflict resolution strategies. I, along with Marsha Mejia, a Garifuna youth activist and president of the Dangriga branch of the National Garifuna Council, engaged the students on the topic of "Coping with Changes/Self-Identity." In this session, students were assigned to groups and each group was given a problem scenario. Group members were asked to role-play how they would deal with the scenario and explain or advise their peers on positive ways of dealing with such issues. It is gratifying to say that the presentations were intriguing.

For this event, a strict dress code was enforced. Boys wore shirts with buttons and jeans/pants, and girls wore modest-sleeved blouses and jeans/pants. No shorts were allowed. The rationale behind this is that we are teaching our students how to dress and groom themselves appropriately. A few students were turned back to change their attire. They came back dressed as required. In one case, however, one female lingered around when sent home. When I saw that, I asked her why, and she told me she did not have any "good" clothes to change into. I took her inside my home and gave her a pair of jeans. This is a very poignant point: often as advocates, if not careful, we can alienate the very people we want to help—by, for example, forgetting that the attire the student arrived in may have been the best they had. It is indeed a delicate line that we must carefully navigate. Similarly, I suggested we form a WhatsApp group to keep in touch. Though I pride myself on being realistic about the conditions, I was still very surprised that out of the 35 students who were present, only one had a cell phone. Again, as advocates, even with our best efforts, our realities are sometimes very removed from the realities of those for whom we are advocating. This can sometimes be dangerous, because it causes our perceptions to misalign with the on-the-ground realities. When this happens, the service we provide may be less relevant to the receiver than we think.

Providing Scholarships

Three students were awarded scholarships for tuition and fees to attend the Georgetown Technical High School. At present, all Nesters are doing very well. I have asked the principal to inform me if any students from the Nest default on fees. An agreement was made that no Nester will be contacted regarding non-payment of fees. From personal experience, it is an empowering relief to know one will never be sent home because of arrears on school fees. As a high schooler, I was one of those whose names often rang over the PA for owing fees, and was told not to come back until it was paid. This is something I wish I could protect all students from experiencing.

Providing Laptops and Tablets

Though we are no longer under COVID pandemic restrictions, teachers have found it impossible to return to the pre-COVID style of teaching. The use of electronic devices has become the norm in today's face-to-face classroom. Unfortunately, our students do not have laptops or smartphones. Many students do not have internet access to be able to research and do the necessary assignments. I am trying to get each of them a device. To date, I have vetted the quality and bought 13 refurbished laptops. I am hoping to buy 10 more in each of the next three months. I have also been asking for donations of good working condition used devices, but so far, I have not received any donations.

Indigenous Youth Progress Nest (IYPN) Tutoring and Home-Work Hub

In Seine Bight, the students do not always have internet access. I dedicated a property I own in the center of the village to house the Indigenous Youth Progress Nest Tutoring and Home-Work Hub. I solicited the cooperation of the local teachers and parents to volunteer to supervise the hub. For now, the hub opens from 5:00 to 8:00 p.m. daily. There are three laptops in place for students to do research, and at least one adult is always there to supervise the students and assist with tutoring.

Language and Culture Summer Camp

In summer of 2022, I planned and implemented the Garifuna Language and Culture Summer Camp in Seine Bight Village. The goal of the camp was to raise the awareness and consciousness of the youths regarding their own identity as Garifuna people. The objectives included learning the Garifuna language and cultural dances and songs, translating English to Garifuna words and short sentences, reflecting on the ways of our ancestors, learning virtues that promote good citizenship, and reflecting on their own practices that demonstrate good citizenship. For example, one of the issues that sets the village apart from the others on the peninsula is the fact that the culture of cleaning around the homes and streets is not always practiced. At this camp, the virtue of cleanliness is enforced, and children are taught how to rake the yard and keep the environment clean. Other virtues discussed are the primacy of God, respect for the spirit of our ancestors, respect for our elders, cleanliness, honesty, resilience, strategic thinking, self-reliance, and consensual governance.

The camp was held with the moral support of the Seine Bight Village Council and other villagers who donated food, money, and time. Other expenses include providing daily snacks and stationery. Local teachers and parents assisted in facilitating the various sessions. The camp was held at the Seine Bight Multipurpose Building on July 26 to August 5, 2022, and 50 children and young adults attended. Participants were required to do an end-of-camp assessment. An award ceremony was held on the last day, and each child received an award for areas in which he or she excelled. To facilitate the awards, I traveled to the neighboring village to purchase gifts, which included personal hygiene items, school supplies, and t-shirts for the students.

While the decision to offer the Garifuna Language and Culture Summer Camp may be notable in itself, what truly stands out is the underlying motivation behind my decision. This motivation arose from my observation of a significant presence of Caucasian and Hispanic evangelists organizing various summer camps throughout the village. Throngs of children attended daily. It dawned on me that while the missionaries were pushing their agendas, there were no plans in place for the children to learn about themselves, their village, their language, or their culture. I started to see the summer camps offered by others as part of the problem that contributes to the erosion of the identity of the villagers. Given the historical marginalization of the Garifuna (Bonner, 2001; Palacio, 2013; Ravindranath, 2001), particularly on the Placencia Peninsula, it is extremely necessary not to ignore these activities that are so lacking in cultural responsiveness. These are all part of a process; this process signals to Garifuna children a subtle need to assimilate to something other than their native identity. It is clearly contrary to decolonization theories, which expose the unequal power relationships that so often lead subordinated populations like the Garifuna to suppress their native linguistic and cultural practices and identities to be accepted (Matthei & Smith, 2008). As such, I felt that there was an urgent need to counter such an impact. By conducting the summer camp, I feel that I proactively provided an alternative and more relevant experience for our children. Based on feedback from children and parents, the Garifuna Language and Culture Summer Camp was a resounding success and will continue to be an annual event. Plans are already in place for Summer Camp 2023, which will be held on July 24 to August 4, 2023. I am planning to add basic reading and math.

In tandem, these programs represent a concerted effort at providing specific skills. Each part of these projects is needed to empower students and influence positive changes regarding how they see themselves and how they see future possibilities. Fortunately, the Seine Bight community has a very friendly and collaborative attitude toward advocacy, especially when community members are consulted and included in decision making from the planning stages of the project. Communicating on a regular basis and allowing them to take ownership of the project is key to keeping them engaged in the process. In this case, parents and teachers especially have particularly bought into these programs. There is still time in the project to determine the progress and meet expectations, but it is expected that our success rate will be high.

Saint Alphonsus Roman Catholic School (SARCS) Reading Program

The SARCS reading program also began in December 2022 after Principal Loris Moreira reported that the issues with poor reading skills among her students had reached worrisome proportions. After meeting with her to look at the documentation to have a better understanding of her concern, I decided to seek the services of a reading specialist who could then advise us on a way forward. Reading specialist Dr. Rose Bradley responded to my call for assistance, and I traveled to Belize City to meet with her to discuss a plan for SARCS. She also took me on a visit to a school where she had helped to develop a very robust reading program. After the visit, I agreed that a program like that was what was needed in Seine Bight. Dr. Bradley agreed to have a first workshop with the teachers to set some parameters.

The first workshop was held via Zoom on December 14, 2022. The main outcome of this workshop was that teachers were instructed to collect data on their students' word and letter recognition at all grades. A second meeting was held a week later, where teachers reported on their findings. From those reports, Dr. Bradley was able to arrive at a plan of action, which included visiting the school and having a face-to-face training session. This was done on January 12, 2022. Though the cost of travel to Seine Bight was expensive, Dr. Bradley explained the need for two more facilitators so that they could cover all the classes in a limited time. Both facilitators were flown in from Belize City to conduct the training.

On that visit, the facilitators observed the teachers as they taught. This was followed by a workshop where a three-month plan was outlined, which included the application of strategies and data collection to track improvements in students' reading skills. On the recommendation of the specialist, the reading program A to Z Plus was purchased so that the teachers could access contemporary material to support their teaching strategies. Printer and ink were also bought so that they could print documents instead of drawing them by hand for each student, as was the practice.

In addition, I provided a laptop so that the teachers could have a dedicated device from which they could print the handouts they wished to use. Furthermore, an electrical and computer engineer was hired to ensure that the principal's laptop and the one we donated were hooked up to the printer to ensure that they could print from both devices.

Currently, the teachers are implementing plans discussed and approved by Dr. Bradley and the principal at the last workshop and submitting updates to the principal.

Another workshop was scheduled for February 9, 2023, where the facilitator walked the teachers through the A to Z Plus program and taught them how to maximize the use of the resources. It is hoped that the goal of raising each student's reading level by at least one point was met by the end of the academic year, 2022–2023.

Free Teacher Training

Another step in the advocacy projects was to build relationships with the school, principal, and teachers. In conversations with them, I discovered that they were having problems accessing teacher training professional development (PD) workshops, which are pertinent to maintaining their teaching licenses. With the permission of the Belize Ministry of Education (MOE), I started offering free workshops to teachers in 2015. These PDs allowed them to earn the continuous professional development (CPD) credits needed for license renewal. This work let me gain first-hand knowledge about the realities that both teachers and students face in the school system. Through this relationship, I was able to assist in specific plans for progressing both students and teachers, following the timeline below.

    June 13, 2022—Reading Comprehension
    June 14, 2022—Assessment Strategies
    December 7, 2022—Read Aloud: A Focus on Prosody to Teach
        Punctuation

December 14, 2022—Planning a Reading Program
January 12, 2023—Reporting on Word and Sound Recognition Data
   (all grades)

Reflections: What Did I Learn?

By participating in these projects, I have learned that it is important to pay attention to the opinions of the people you are advocating for. We should not only listen to what they say, but also pay attention to what they do not say. Frequently, our intense passion for a cause can cloud our judgment and influence our decision making during project implementation. Additionally, in my experience, I have come to realize that effective communication and negotiation skills serve as the backbone of any advocacy project. They play a vital role in maintaining the stability and progress of your initiative. It is important to acknowledge that communities can be swayed and persuaded to turn against your intentions, even when they are genuinely positive. A successful advocate must be patient and willing to engage those with opposing opinions. Often, what may seem like opposition is sound reason, based on the person's firsthand knowledge of the community. Therefore, advocates can benefit a lot by respecting those opinions. I also learned that networking, especially with the community appointed leaders, is beneficial, as it facilitates breaking down barriers that may exist between you and the community.

What Would I Do the Same or Differently Next Time?

As I continue the projects, there are a few things that I plan to do differently. First, all my programs are currently self-funded. This is not sustainable. I will take courses in grant writing, and I will actively engage in finding funding sources for my projects. I will also create more opportunities for the beneficiaries of these programs to invest more capital in the programs. For example, I bought the A to Z Plus reading program. It requires an annual renewal of license. I also bought ink for printing handouts. I will now put a system in place for the recipients to demonstrate a plan on how they will ensure that they will have the funds to renew their reading program license as well as provide the supply of ink they will need. Building the mentality to do for oneself will help to break the dependence of handouts.

What I plan to continue doing is to maintain a close working relationship with the administrators and teachers at SARCS. I find that the principal does a very good job of keeping the pulse of the parents, so they tend to get on board quicker when project activities are rolled out via the school's social media and other communications systems. Also, since the projects often need manpower, teachers are always willing to volunteer, so they remain a crucial factor in the success of the programs.

What Advice Would I Give?

I perceive advocacy as a matter of the heart, demanding deep-rooted convictions. Without this, an advocate can easily give up on a projected plan. The undergirding framework for advocacy varies among individuals and groups. Therefore, one must be definitive about where one stands. For instance, my advocacy is informed by two underlying assumptions of Grassroots Development Theory, which promotes organizing efforts that reflect the wishes of people directly affected by the problem and requires building the capacity of those affected by the problem to address it (Stachowiak, 2007). Leaning on this framework keeps me focused on my stated goals and minimizes the possibility of wavering when conditions for advocacy become less favorable.

Summary

Overall, it will be interesting to see what will unfold over the next four years. With these programs fully engaged, it is hoped that we can start to see the impact on the lives of the 46 students who are in the Youth Progress Nest, the youths who are in the reading program, and the youths who participate in the summer camp. Many of these students are recurrent in all projects, so this too will result in a level of consistency in the messaging, which urges them to take ownership of the course of their lives. If these programs can awaken a hunger in these youths, then there will be no stopping them from charting their own path and being the source of economic and other motilities for themselves, their families, and the community.

Note

1. The Garifuna—also known as Garinagu—are indigenous people located in Central America. The terms Garifuna and Garinagu will be employed intermittently throughout this chapter to align with references' uses of the terms.

References

Alam, M. J., Ashikullah, M., & Rahman, M. M. (2018). The role of the family in English language. *International Journal of English Language Teaching*, 6(2), 36–46.

Belize Crime Observatory. (2021). https://bco.gov.bz/

Boles, E., Anderson, A. Cawich, R., Figueroa, V., Franco, J., Grijalva, D., Mai, D., Mendez, K., Peralta, A., Requena, L., Rodriguez, M., & Sánchez, E. (2011). *Rapid Assessment of Effects and Issues Related to Development in the Placencia Area, Dry Season*. NRMP 4552 Integrated Coastal Zone Management, Course Project. University of Belize.

Bonner, D. (2001). Garifuna children's language shame: Ethnic stereotypes, national affiliation, and transnational immigration as factors in language choice in southern Belize. *Language in Society*, 30(1), 81–96.

Central Intelligence Agency. (2016). Belize. In *The World Factbook*. Retrieved from https://www.cia.gov/library/publications/the-world-factbook/geos/bh.html

Freire, P. (2000). *Pedagogy of the Oppressed* (30th anniversary ed.). Continuum.

Key, C., & Pillai, V. K. (October 2006). Community participation and tourism attitudes in Belize. *Revista Interamericana de Ambiente y Tourismo*, 2(2), 8–15.

Koenig, R. (2015). Baiting sustainability: Collaborative coastal management, heritage tourism, and alternative fisheries in Placencia, Belize. [Unpublished master's thesis]. University of South Florida.

Kroshus, L. M. (1998). History, culture, and place-making: Native status and Maya identity in Belize. *Journal of Latin American Anthropology*, 4(1), 134–165.

Lencioni, P. (2002). The five dysfunctions of a team. Jossey-Bass.

Leonardo, Z. (2004). Critical social theory and transformative knowledge: The functions of criticism in quality education. *Educational Researcher, 33* (6), 11–18.

Linville, H. A. (2014). *A mixed methods investigation of ESOL teacher advocacy: "It's not going in and just teaching English."* (Publication No. 362431). University of Maryland, Baltimore County. Retrieved from: https://llc.umbc.edu/wp-content/uploads/sites/15/2013/02/diss2014_Linville.pdf

Loperena, C. (2022). *The Ends of Paradise: Race, Extraction, and the Struggle for Black Life in Honduras.* Stanford University Press.

Matthei, L. M., & Smith, D. A. (2008). Flexible ethnic identity, adaptation, survival, resistance: The Garifuna in the world-system. *Social Identities, 14*(2), 215–232.

Palacio, Joseph O. (Ed.) (2013). The Garifuna: A nation across borders. *Essays in Social Anthropology* (4th edition). Cubola Productions. Original work published 2005.

Ravindranath, S. (2001). *The Extent of Urban Bias in Belize.* Unpublished manuscript, Williams College, Williamstown, MA.

Rebar, B. M. (2005). *Children's Conceptions of Nature as Influenced by Residential Environmental Education Program.* [Unpublished master's thesis]. Oregon State University.

Servio-Mariano, B. M. (2010). Garifunaduáü: Cultural continuity, change and resistance in the Garifuna diaspora (Doctoral dissertation, University at Albany, State University of New York), ProQuest 3433375.

Shohamy, E. (2022). Critical language testing, multilingualism, and social justice. *TESOL Quarterly, 56*(4), 1445–1457.

Skutnabb-Kangas, T. (2017). Language rights and bilingual education. In O. Garciá, A.M.Y. Lin, & S. May (Eds.), *Bilingual and multilingual education,* 3rd edition (pp. 51-63). Springer.

Stachowiak, S. (2007). *A Guide to Measuring Policy and Advocacy.* Retrieved from https://www.orsimpact.com/DirectoryAttachments/132018_13248_359_Center_Pathways_FINAL.pdf

Statistical Institute of Belize. (2021). *Abstract of statistics 2021.* Retrieved from http://sib.org.bz/wp-content/uploads/2021_Abstract_of_Statistics.pdf

Stenner, K. (2005). *The Authoritarian Dynamic.* Cambridge University Press.

United Nations Educational, Scientific and Cultural Organization (UNESCO) (2001). UNESCO universal declaration on cultural diversity. Retrieved from http://portal.unesco.org/en/ ev.php-URL_ID=13179&URL_DO=DO_TOPIC&URL_SECTION=201.html

Chapter 4

De-Colonizing Advocacy: Advocacy Efforts for English Language Teaching and Learning in Belize

Ethnelda Paulino

In online schooling, the students are separated from the instructor because the students are taught online. Even in the year 2013, online schooling in Belize was a very new concept and was a cause for doubts and aspersions. As a high school teacher for more than 35 years, l had witnessed expulsions that were only justified because of rules that were based on the colonial system. Examples of offenses that caused expulsion were smoking cigarettes or marijuana, possession of either or both, speaking up justly or unjustly, getting pregnant, long hair and long nails, dreadlocks, being in a bar, getting arrested, attending school without proper uniform or shoes, and inability to pay school fees These practices still exist in Belize, today.

Ironically, individuals who did not receive a high school, college, and/or university education were not prevented from securing employment in the public service and in the private sector. In her research article entitled "Educational Policy Studies," Lewis (2002) noted that Mullens, Murnane, and Willett (1996) state,

> In an attempt to promote economic growth, the government places a high priority on providing its citizens with a sound foundation of basic education. In Belize, "Basic education" means attendance at primary school since only 50% of students continue their education past eighth grade. Thus, while primary school is a stepping-stone to further schooling or job training for half of the citizens of Belize, it has the full extent of formal education for the rest. (p. 146)

In the 1980s studies conducted by the government of Belize and outside observers revealed that up to one-third of primary school students dropped out before they turned 14. Dropout rates and absenteeism were notably higher in rural areas, where the seasonal demand for agricultural labor led many students to opt for work rather than school. The studies indicated that many poor parents did not regard education as a priority for their children, seeing few benefits from secondary or tertiary schooling. Only a small percentage of Belizeans received any kind of post-secondary education. This means that some Belizean men and women who were born in the 1980s and are now in their thirties and early forties may not have received a high school education. That probably explains why some of the students who are enrolled in Kaina Online High School are 35 to 45 years old.

Evening divisions or night schools are face-to-face classes that are held at night for adults who wish to earn a high school education. An evening division is a night school in which adults pursue a high school education. It is usually managed by the same authorities who are in charge of the traditional day school for youngsters. The school makes use of the same facilities that are used during the day, and, in many cases, they are taught by some of the same teachers. In Belize, adults are not allowed to attend classes during the day along with the youngsters. Night schools have existed in Belize for many years; but for many, attendance is too difficult for those who do not have enough support to consistently attend classes and earn a high school diploma. Traveling to the school and paying baby-sitting fees, tuition, and duties for shift workers, like nursing aids, security officers, and police officers, is too costly. The climate of Belize is unpredictable and not everyone has a vehicle. The increase in traffic has also rendered traveling at night to be uncomfortable and very dangerous, not only because of the weather and accidents but also because of the steady increase of crime. Four high schools in Belize City now offer free education. Unfortunately, increased gang activity, especially in Belize City, prevents many people from leaving home to attend a traditional school. In addition, our incarcerated youth also need to be in a place called "school." Hopefully, earning a high school diploma while in prison would mean that their return to society would be their final departure from prison.

Due to the inability of many employees to earn a high school diploma, some Belizeans were unable to access tertiary-level education, thereby preventing them from enjoying higher pay scales and, in some cases, becoming permanent, pensionable employees. Public officers and policemen who have not completed high school have less command of the English language, especially because of the language situation in Belize.

The current population stands at 441,471. Some of the languages that are spoken in Belize are English, Spanish, Belize Creole, Q'eqchi' Maya, Mopan Maya, German, and Garifuna (Statistical Institute of Belize, 2021). According to McKissey (1972), "Belizean Creole is the tongue used by Belizean Creoles and acquired by other segments of the society." English is the language of instruction and the official language of Belize. Belize's English-based Kriol is the main language of communication. This includes business discussions. Official news broadcasts are done in English but callers on talk shows use Kriol and some English. However, all Belizean official documents are written in English. All textbooks are written in English. In classrooms, one often hears lessons being delivered in Belize Kriol; but all examinations and answers must be written in English. This renders the language situation in Belize phenomenal.

Most do not realize that English and Belizean Kriol are not the same and expressions in the English language do not necessarily mean the same in Belizean Kriol. This places the public servants at a constant disadvantage. Misunderstandings are not unusual.

Historical and Geographical Background of Language in Belize

The historical and geographical background of Belize has contributed to its ethnic and language diversity, and therefore, they are worthwhile points of reference in any attempt to understand the culture and linguistic situation of the country. Belize is situated on the eastern coast of Central America. It is situated below the Yucatan Peninsula and above the eastern seaboard of Guatemala. It shares borders in the north and northeast with Mexico and in the west and south with Guatemala. Belize occupies 8,867 square miles, including 266 square miles of coastal islands. It extends approximately 174 miles and is 68 miles at its widest point. Belize is divided into six districts: Corozal, Orange Walk, Belize, Cayo, Stann Creek, and Toledo. Belize City in the Belize District was the former capital of Belize, but the capital is now Belmopan.

Belizean Ancestry

The Mestizos are immigrants and descendants of immigrants from the neighboring Central American territories. People of largely African and African European ancestry, who are called Kriol, predominate in the central coastal regions. The Maya and Ketchi, indigenous people of Central America, account for 10% of the population. Several thousand Garinagu, formerly called Black Caribs, also live in Belize. They are descendants of Caribs and Africans who were exiled from British colonies because they resisted European domination in the Eastern Caribbean (Lesser Antilles) in the eighteenth century. They mostly live in communities in the southern coast of Belize. People of European and East Indian ancestry are also present, as are smaller numbers of Chinese, Indians, Nigerians, and Arabs.

Ethnicity and Language in Belize

According to the Statistical Institute of Belize, the present composition of the country's population is as follows: Most Belizeans are of multiracial descent. About 52.9% of the population is of mixed indigenous (mostly Maya) and European descent (Mestizo), 24.9% are Kriols, about 10.6% are Maya, and about 6.1% are Afro-Amerindian (Garifuna). The remaining population includes European, East Indian, Chinese, Middle Eastern, and North American groups. Indeed, with such a diverse ethnic background, it is inevitable that the language situation in Belize would be a complex one. It is no wonder, then, that there exist in Belize numerous issues regarding the acquisition of English.

Enslavement of Africans may have contributed to the presence of various varieties of English in the Caribbean and the Americas. In the early seventeenth century, Africans were shipped to the Caribbean islands and the American coast, where they were exchanged for sugar, rum, and molasses. There are conflicting ideas about the origins of English-based Creoles. One theory is that the slave traders brought people of different language backgrounds together in the ships in order to prevent them from rebelling. This strategy may have resulted in the forging of pidgin forms of communication between the enslaved Africans and the sailors, many of whom spoke English. These circumstances would account for the presence of English and English-based Creoles in the English-speaking Caribbean islands, Guyana, and Belize.

The Contemporary Language Situation in Belize

Children who grow up in contemporary Belize are surrounded by a complex language situation. Belize, formerly British Honduras, is the only English-speaking nation in Central America. It is a multicultural, multi-ethnic, and multilingual nation with an English-based Kriol as its lingua franca and with English as its official language and language of instruction; therefore, it is necessary for Belizeans to have a thorough command of the English language if they wish to succeed in the education system. Craig (1963) suggested that "one result in daily life is the frustrating shortage of people available for employment in positions where an ability to write clearly and accurately is needed" (p. 1). The medium of education in English is different from Kriol, and it is different, for example, from languages like Spanish, Mopan Maya, Garifuna, Kekchi Maya, the languages of the Asian immigrants, and German (spoken by Mennonites). This means that children who speak these various languages may be found in any Belizean classroom, and, in that regard, they learn English as a second language.

Second Language Learning in Belize

Like their counterparts in different parts of the Caribbean region, Belizean students are expected to learn English as a second language. Currently in Belize, there is a new awareness and a healthier respect for Belizean Kriol than there was during colonial days. In Belize, members of all ethnic groups try to learn Kriol because it guarantees social acceptance. The nationalist movement and a healthier view of non-English languages created rapid change in how the various groups thought of themselves and their languages. Additionally, each group adopted Kriol as the best language for intergroup communication; however, the language of instruction is English, a language in which the students appear to be no longer interested but know that they need it for academic advancement. It is also the students' tool for communicating with the rest of the world.

The fact that certain procedures need to be employed in the teaching of English has long been recognized. Buhler and Hadle (1975) suggested that English should not be taught as a first language. They believed that this caused Belizean youngsters to appear to be unable to keep pace with their British and American counterparts in the development of reading and writing skills (p. 3).

State of the Nation

Belize became a nation on September 21, 1981. About the 2017 Independence Day Celebrations, the editor of *Amandala*, which is the leading newspaper of Belize, wrote the following:

> In the moment of Belize's so-called independence that it had commemorated on September 21, 2017, there is a burning anger that still engulfs the mind and the soul of its people as to whether the country has made any real progress since September 21, 1981.

Today, Belize still struggles with issues like the Belize Guatemala Claim, which is now in the hands of the International Court of Justice. Much to Guatemala's annoyance, the Honduran Claim to Belize, has also been submitted to the International Court of Justice.

Another source of discontent among some citizens of Belize is the presence of a governor general who represents the monarch of England. Popular opinion is that like the Central American and Caribbean nations, Belize should become a republic and that political reform is necessary for Belize to become a truly independent nation.

The above notwithstanding, Belize is a popular tourist destination. It boasts great visiting sites like San Pedro Ambergris Caye, Caye Caulker, Placencia, the Maya sites, Hopkins, and a kaleidoscope of people.

My Personal Definition/Understanding of Advocacy

There is a thin line between advocacy and service. Advocating for solid education requires that those who need to be educated must be served. Advocacy means improving the circumstances and lives of all persons and other creatures, especially the most unfortunate. We need to detach and develop a culture of advocacy that can be transmitted from generation to generation as a legacy that we can bestow upon our descendants and for those who will lead our countries in the future. The respect that our ancestors had for every creature, every plant, and all that mother nature has provided us needs to be revived. The culture of requesting permission to use only what is necessary to survive and to be comfortable, instead of abusing animals and plants, will go a long way. If we advocate this philosophy, we may still be able to save the people, animals, and plants of the world in which we live. In his article entitled "Elevators to Heaven: Advocacy Groups in Belize," Barrow (2021) posits that:

De-Colonizing Advocacy   71

One very salient strategy is for the country to have a critical mass of advocacy groups advocating for more specific targeted changes in the social fabric of the Belizean social changes in the fabric of the Belizean social ecosystem. These include groups that would focus their advocacy in such targeted areas as land reform, constitution reform, public service reform, constitution reform, public service reform, political reform, poverty alleviation and to push the envelope on gender and equity as well as education and finance sector reforms.

What is in it for me? This is the question I have been asked repeatedly. I refer especially to the Belize TESOL Association. The would-be members, especially teachers, are reluctant to participate because the benefits are learning, teaching, and professional development; not cash. There is always an excuse not to be an active participant, and the excuse is generally, "I am too busy." Support for movements like TESOL is not forthcoming because "Belize is an English-speaking nation." My experience is that the multilingual situation in Belize has never been considered. Whoever wants to advocate for language improvement must foot his or her own bills (expenses). The move to encourage advocacy and the "What is in it for me?" culture must be replaced with a more positive attitude toward advocacy.

Belize is a melting pot of cultures, each deserving equality, social justice, recognition, and empowerment. Belize must preserve and maintain the unique cultural diversity that is the foundation of its history. Finally, the Belizean people must unite in efforts to be strategic in crafting an educational and language policy that supports the development and preservation of language diversity, which would attract many culturally curious people from across the globe Guettler (2018).

The Project—2013

In the year 2013, I decided to fulfill the dream of advocating for women and men who needed to earn high school diplomas while going to work and taking care of their households, their children, and the elders in their families. This required a fully online high school that students could access 24 hours per day, seven days per week. To satisfy the Ministry of Education and obtain license to operate, I found ways to turn the "I" into "we," filled out forms, created and executed a survey, sought the attention and approval of the chief education officer and the board of directors, found a number of licensed volunteer instructors and efficient volunteer technicians to create a website, and pulled together virtual classrooms and a volunteer accountant, a volunteer lawyer, and financing.

Phase 1

The survey was sent to people of all ages. We especially targeted individuals who had not completed high school, their parents, and their siblings. Since the Young Women's Christian Association is intimately involved with people from all walks of life, the director distributed the survey among students who were enrolled in English and Spanish learning, sewing, food and nutrition, barbering, tailoring, and manicuring classes. I took it to the University of Belize because in many cases, the students came from families in which the students were the first in their families to attempt to acquire a university-level education.

The results of the survey were positive. The questionnaire was distributed at the office of the Young Women's Christian Association and in each district. A hundred percent of respondents thought that an online school would be a good idea, but with reservation, because most thought that the greatest challenge would be learning how to use the technology. Eighty-four percent said that they would dare to become online students.

The goals of the Kaina Online High School are therefore based on responses to the issues identified in the survey, responses during focus groups, the observation and experience of the founder, as well as research done by founders and others.

Research indicated that there has been a scarcity of male students in the Belizean classroom and that the number decreases in the upper division of elementary schools, high schools, and in tertiary-level institutions. According to members of the male population in Belize, they are not only absent from the classroom due to financial constraints but also because they feel restricted by the physical environment of the traditional classroom. Some of our respondents think that being in school is boring and not time effective. Members of our female population are more visible in the classroom, but this initiative will empower our stay-at-home mothers, single mothers, working women, and those women who did not attend high school due to our cultural traditions. For example, the practice that allowed females to marry at the age of 14 prevented our Belizean women from attending or completing high school, and in turn they were unable to access tertiary-level education. In fact, there was no high school in my district until 1960, and girls were not expected to attend high schools. Their role was to get married and take care of their families. When I graduated from high school, only two of us were females. Parents who allowed their daughters to attend high schools in those days were severely criticized by the public.

On October 9, 2020, UNICEF Belize announced that Belize had the second-highest level of child marriage and early unions in the Caribbean region. The National Committee for Families and Children (NCFC), in collaboration with UNICEF and the United Nations Population Fund (UNFPA) Belize, launched a five-year Road Map to End Child Marriage and Early Unions in Belize. The Road Map highlights worrying trends in child marriage, early unions, early sexual debuts, and teenage pregnancy across regional, urban/rural, and social divides—with girls being the worst affected.

"In Belize, one in five girls (20.8%) and one in ten boys (10.7%) aged 15 to 19 years are married or in a union" (UNICEF, 2020). This has tremendous repercussions on the physical, emotional, and educational health and livelihood opportunities of both girls and boys, with girls being the hardest hit. Girls who are married as children are more likely to be out of school, suffer domestic violence, contract HIV/AIDS, and have a higher risk of morbidity and mortality due to complications during pregnancy and childbirth.

Phase 2

Having received positive results from citizens about the possibility of opening an online school, the next task was to approach the Ministry of Education. My search for an application form for opening an online school was futile, but carefully prepared paperwork is a necessity in my country. I created a form and filled it in. A letter of explanation accompanied the form. The letter was addressed and delivered to the chief education officer. Some weeks later, I received a response. While I was waiting for a reply, the accountant and the lawyer (both volunteers) proceeded to form and register a company in the hopes that the chief education officer would send a positive response. The company consisted of four people and was named Kania Online High School Limited. The company consisted of a long-time friend, an accountant, a technician, and myself.

The first response from the Ministry of Education arrived in 2013. We were instructed to present the information to the board of directors in Santa Elena, one of the border towns west of Belize. We traveled to Santa

Elena in February 2013. Apparently, the presentation captured the interest of the panelists, perhaps because it was an idea that was hitherto unheard of in our country and perhaps because it did not seem to be something that could work. A few weeks later, I received a letter. We had the license to start an online high school. We were not allowed to encourage students to leave their present schools nor recruit actively from other schools, and we were not to expect any type of funding at any time from the government of Belize. We were not discouraged. Dr. Alberita Enriquez became co-founder of Kaina Online High School and I, the founder.

Surprisingly, we attracted some interest and some much needed help. The four founders were retirees, and we decided to use our money and our electronic equipment to pay the initial expenses. I used a Scotia Online Cheque to open a bank account. The volunteers I contacted were former teaching colleagues and licensed teachers whom I had taught in university or in high school. They were willing to serve. All we needed was some of their free time. A former co-worker offered to build the site, and my son offered to create the virtual classrooms, manage application forms, and perform a host of other internet related issues.

Having been granted license from the Ministry of Education to operate, the portals of the Kaina Online High School were opened on March 14, 2014, to some 45 students. They were students registered in first to fourth form of ages varying from 14 to 35 or older; they were employed, self-employed, and not-yet-employed, and from various parts of the country. The first and second semester were accelerated, and by September of that year, we were able to begin classes along with the other schools in Belize.

Who Does Kaina Cater For?

Who may apply?
The following is a description that I wrote for the website. It aptly describes our intentions:

Mission

The Kaina Online High School strives to make serious, diligent, independent youth and adults return to or remain in the school system by providing quality high school education for persons who need to complete high school and for persons in the workforce who wish to attend high school by using online technology.

Vision

The Kaina Online High School envisions an affordable, student friendly online high school environment dedicated to the inclusion of more persons into the Belizean school system, thus enabling them to transition into higher education, promote and increase economic sufficiency and accelerate efficiency in the Belizean workforce. The school envisions equitable education for members of all ethnic groups, including individuals in rural or disadvantaged urban areas and correctional facilities in Belize and elsewhere.

Kaina Online High School of Belize Limited aims to reduce crime; alleviate criminal tendencies among our youth; educate and prepare the incarcerated for a more seamless return to society; improve communication skills—master the language of instruction/official language to become experts at self-negotiation and comprehension. Understanding the target language and others promotes peace and reduces loss of temper, violent language, as well as aggressive and criminal behaviour.

Setbacks

In the beginning, things did not go smoothly. The volunteer technician did not ask for a salary; however, the requests for him to remedy constant technical difficulties became too numerous for him to continue in this role. In addition to technical difficulties, the name of a government-aided school began to appear on the screen. A young man who was enrolled in Kaina Online noticed our plight and reached out to us. He worked for a firm that had a server. He was a technician, the site was enhanced, and for a short few months, things went well. However, the complaints about technical difficulties and server and domain fees soon increased. In a nutshell, we had jumped from the proverbial frying pan into the fire.

The first few weeks were fine, but the bills for server and security increased so dramatically that I began to realize that we were being taken advantage of. Each week the system was disabled, and I found out that the technician kept charging us over a thousand dollars per month for using kaina.edu.bz when, in fact, it only costs $147 per year. He was deliberately disabling the system. When the co-founder offered to continue to pay him, I did not think that we should. I explained to her that eventually, no money would be left and the weekly glitches that were affecting the progress of the school would continue. Finally, we agreed that we should part ways with him. We would look for help elsewhere.

After four years of technical stress, we found an extremely reliable technician in August of 2018. He then turned the process over to a nephew of his and my son. The system has worked extremely well, and we have been able to offer the students access to Kaina Online night and day since September 2018. Sadly, and to our surprise, the young man who guided the process suddenly passed away a few months after the site was built.

The Pandemic

The advent of the coronavirus sparked some interest in Kaina Online High School. People became aware of the fact that a fully online high school was indeed present in Belize, and had been since 2014. Because our main objective was to produce as many useful high school graduates as possible, we reluctantly accepted young students, fresh from elementary school.

The Kaina Online High School of Belize Limited was not fazed by the onslaught of COVID-19. Even as we hope that Belize will continue to witness less COVID-19 cases, Kaina Online High School of Belize Limited marches along without interruption. Our academic year is in progress and consequent academic years will begin in August and January of each year.

Enrollment

Table 4.1 shows that Kaina Online High School opened its portals in the year 2014 with 45 students. We had students from first to fourth form. By the end of 2014 our form-four students were ready to move on. In September of that year, we joined the rest of the country by starting classes in September. We followed the traditional system until July of 2018. Thereafter, we instituted the accelerated 24/7 program, as indicated in the table below.

Since 2014, 1,536 people have applied to attend Kaina Online High School. They have done so for various reasons. In some cases, we hosted some students who, one could say, were on borrowed time. There is the case of Belizean parents and Belizean residents whose children were attending Belizean traditional schools but who were transferred to countries abroad for one or two years, but who wanted to take their children with them. Those children were

De-Colonizing Advocacy 77

Table 4.1 Enrollment and Number of Graduates by Academic Year

	Enrollment and number of graduates by academic year				
	Year	Enrollment	Graduates	Male	Female
Traditional	2014	45	4	3	1
Traditional	2015	61	7	3	4
Traditional	2016	84	10	3	7
Traditional	2017	84	10	1	9
Accelerated	Aug 2018	69	12	3	9
Accelerated	Jan 2019	123	14	4	10
Accelerated	Jul 2019	85	10	3	7
Accelerated	Jan 2020	74	15	5	10
Accelerated	Jul 2020	123	20	8	12
Accelerated	Jan 2021	74	18	8	10
Accelerated	Jul 2021	152	27	10	17
Accelerated	Jan 2022	133	18	6	12
Accelerated	Jul 2022	129	27	5	22
Accelerated	Jan 2022	150	16	8	8
Accelerated	Jul 2023, 2023	150			
	TOTAL	1536	208	70	138

enrolled in Kaina Online and were able to attend classes in a Belizean school. Fortunately, the students have been studious, so far. They worked from the confines of their parents' temporary homes while they were abroad, took examinations, and got promoted. When the parents returned to their substantive positions in Belize, the students were returned to their original schools, from which they graduated.

In 2018, a group of young cadets were enrolled in a special program called the Challengers. Because this was an intensive course, the Challengers were enrolled in Kaina Online High for one year and were then sent back to their schools to complete their respective high school programs. Incarcerated students also got enrolled. Those who remained in prison continued to complete their courses and graduate. Alas, those who left before they completed the program faced the harsh reality of not owning a gadget or having internet access. So far, 208 students have graduated from Kaina Online High School. Finally, there are applicants who take their leave immediately after they find out that to earn a diploma, schoolwork must be submitted. The others are committed. They apply themselves, they study, and they successfully complete the program. Their self-confidence gets a boost. They get promoted and/or pursue tertiary-level education.

As aforementioned, our instructors offered to be voluntary workers. We asked the first intake to pay a registration fee of $12.50 USD and a tuition fee of $150 USD per semester. This would help us to offer the instructors a token sum of $100 for each course. Some students paid $12.50; most did not. Bearing in mind that the goal is to educate and increase the number of high school graduates at home and abroad, we did not bill the students, and students began to graduate and proceeded to attend junior colleges.

Note that during the pandemic, from 2020 to June 2022, 118 students graduated. To date, the number of graduates has risen to 210. So far, nine students have graduated from Kolbe Foundation. The Kolbe Foundation houses young offenders at the Belize Central Prison, which is the correctional facility of Belize. Noteworthy is the fact that I did not envision how much Kaina was doing for Belize until we got applicants from soldiers, policemen, cancer patients, and others with various types of illnesses that make them unable to attend regular traditional schools. In some instances, students work from hospital beds, at home and abroad, complete their work, get promoted, and graduate from Kaina Online High School.

So far, the graduates from the prison who have been released have not returned to the prison. In the year 2019, the first pair of Kaina Online High School students from Kolbe Foundation, Belize Central Prison, had the pleasure of attending the Kaina Online High School graduation ceremony.

In their research on advocacy in English language teaching and learning, Linville and Whiting (2019) explain that throughout the iterative analytical process, the following themes related to tutors' conceptions and enactment of advocacy emerged across transcripts and were coded accordingly:

> Advocacy as welcoming, advocacy as voicing, and advocacy as promoting student learning. Advocacy as welcoming refers to tutors' desires

De-Colonizing Advocacy 79

and active attempts to create spaces where students feel welcomed, cared for, and accepted. Advocacy as voicing occurs when tutors act on behalf of their students. Finally, advocacy as promoting student learning encompasses tutor efforts to advocate for and take actions to promote the equitable and high-quality education of ELs [English learners] in formal and in informal contexts.

In July 2019, just before the coronavirus infected the world, we held our last face-to-face graduation ceremony. Getting our two inmates to attend the ceremony was an ordeal. Special permission had to be sought from the courts. They were allowed to wear civilian clothing under their graduation gowns. Thankfully, our request to allow security officers to be dressed in civilian clothing was granted. The ceremony was an event that may forever be etched in the memories of the people who were there. Normally, each student's private information is concealed. However, our guest speaker, Mr. Nuri Mohammed, an outstanding Belizean who has a long-standing relationship with the Belize Central Prison and the Kolbe Foundation, became emotional. He put his speech aside and spoke from his heart. The moment was profound. When the ceremony and the reception ended, the students were whisked into an armored vehicle and returned to their place of abode. The above gives credence to Linville's (2014) suggestion that advocating for English language learners (ELLs) includes:

> Speaking up, sharing information, or providing resources, for ELLs and/or their families, with other potential co-advocates at the classroom, school, community, state, or national level, in order to improve ELLs' treatment and access to educational resources with the larger goal of improving their life chances. (pp. 2-3)

Inmate One, High School Graduate

"When I began to focus on myself and change myself, I began to realize that there are a lot of people who love me and care for me and are there for me. I don't take that for granted. I take advantage of every situation which comes well into my hands. And I decided that I really don't want to give any trouble and focus more when I come out and what I will do afterward."

Hipolito Novelo: "Was it difficult?"

"It is difficult because you can't say it is just easier or so because there are times that difficulty happens. And you have subjects that get to your head.

When I graduated, I felt very proud of Mr. Dawson and my family. I was very happy that you know what I can be someone in life. It does not have to be here."

Regrettably, it has taken incarceration for him to value the importance of a sound education.

Inmate Two, Third-Place Student

"It was a bit challenging because of the incarceration, I was away from my family, but I built a close relationship with each and every one, so it was a bit easier to focus on what I was doing."

Isani Cayetano: "Now you've come in third which is a fairly high rank in terms of the number of persons enrolled in the program this time around. How do you feel?"

"Well, it's a very good feeling. I feel excited that I have made my family members proud, Mr. Dawson, Mr. Murillo, everyone."

Imprisonment does not mean an end to academic pursuit. In fact, it is mandated under the Nelson Mandela Rules.

Virgilio Murillo, CEO of Kaina Online High School

"Education of inmates is a must. When a person comes to prison it does not mean that they are deprived of education or the opportunity for an education."

Isani Cayetano reporting for News Five.

Inmate One is currently attending St. John's College Junior College. Inmate Two was offered a scholarship by a sponsor to attend Galen University, and he was doing well. During the coronavirus pandemic, his sponsor fell into hard times, and the scholarship was discontinued. He was discouraged. He started a delivery service during the pandemic, and he is doing well. He also has a wife and a son. He says that he will make sure that his son "does not get into the kind of trouble he got into."

The young men's testimonies give credence to Linville's (2014) suggestion:

> Advocating for ELLs includes: Speaking up, sharing information, or providing resources, for ELLs and/or their families, with other potential co-advocates at the classroom, school, community, state, or national level, in order to improve ELLs' treatment and access to educational resources with the larger goal of improving their life chances. (pp. 2–3)

Our students and graduates would benefit from some help. Although the fees appear to be affordable, some students do not have enough funds.

Consequently, some graduate but claim that they do not have the funds to pay for their fees and receive their diplomas on the date that is scheduled for graduation. Unlike all the other schools in Belize and elsewhere, we never withhold report cards, nor do we ever ask students to withdraw when they do not pay fees. They are not required to buy books or any other school equipment. The only fees they have ever been asked to pay have been school fees. This is done because our mission is to increase the number of graduates. Such students pay monthly or whenever or however they can afford it.

As aforementioned, the teachers in Belize have a "What is in it for me?" mentality when it comes to actively participating in TESOL, for example. It is possible that the children they teach are exposed to this attitude throughout their school days. We have observed that whenever students really need their diplomas, they pay what they owe.

Our fees are affordable. In other schools, adults pay $350 BZD for 11 months each year. Another school charges $300 per month for 10 months. These students receive their diplomas at the end of four calendar years. Our students pay $2,800 BZD to complete the entire program. Our Belizean population is small, and Facebook is also an information provider. We have a very good idea of who can afford to pay but do not wish to, and we know who would like to pay and cannot do so. So far, we have two friends from Kaina Online High School (Dr. Angela Joseph and Mrs. Delmarie Fuller) who send up to $300 for needy students each academic year. These funds help students who have arrears.

Accelerated Program

In September of 2018, a friend who meant well met with me and severely criticized me for subjecting adults to a four-calendar-year high school program. "They are adults. This thing can be accelerated," he said.

We used the 24/7 rationale and accelerated the program to a six-month academic year for those who could handle it. Some students take their time. Students who choose to apply themselves graduate in January and July of each calendar year.

Students who are willing and prepared to accept the challenge can be enrolled in a program in which they can earn a high school diploma in two calendar years. With the site reliably operating during the semesters, students can login to Kaina Online without fear, 24 hours per day, 7 days per week. Before the launch of Kaina Online High School, all instructors created the weekly lecture notes, videos, lessons, and assignments. When we decided that it was okay to offer an accelerated program, the instructors merged the four-year program into two academic years, and our technicians made sure that Kaina Online would be accessible to all students any day, hour, minute, or second from the start of the academic year until the last minute of the academic year. The final week of the academic year, which also marks the end of the second semester, the students take a final examination. The finals are one-attempt-only examinations, and the students are free to take their seven or eight examinations, depending on which class they are in, night or day during that week. Thereafter, the final year students graduate if they meet graduation requirements and are promoted.

Student enrolment has increased; therefore, the instructors now receive $150 USD for each subject that they teach. This means that someone who teaches two classes receives $300 USD every eight weeks, when students receive report cards. Each instructor is committed, and they have remained in this project since 2014. No one has left. The quality of their work has improved, they are open to professional development, and, above all, they remain enthusiastic.

The government has been relentless. In one instance, personnel from the Ministry of Education suggested that they give us 15,000 USD. They would then be in control of the entire project. We could not agree, as we are aware of why Kaina Online High School was established. The government remains relentless; we have received no assistance from them, but they do pay fees for some of their workers.

The Way Forward

A group of young men and women from the New Beginnings Youth Development Centre (formerly the Princess Royal Youth Hostel) from the Ministry of Human Development, Families & Indigenous People's Affairs have been allowed to attend Kaina Online High School.

According to Minister Dolores Balderamos Garcia, it is now described as a "residential care facility rather than a certified institution under the law and that means that it is no longer a place for punishment, but to provide short-term urgent care as needed and to turn over a new leaf" (Humes, 2023). However, there is more work to be done. To date, no female from Belize Central Prison has ever been allowed to attend classes. That problem needs to be taken care of.

In Belize there is much more work to be done. Incarcerated women are not allowed to attend high school. We need to advocate for our women.

Micro Classes

Some adults experience great difficulty with online learning. If there were more funds, we could have a micro tutoring service in various parts of the country. Kolbe Foundation has micro classes because the inmates are constantly supervised. Some students who are at-large need this type of discipline.

Autonomy

We need far more adults and young people who can develop the courage to dare to lead. Perhaps the culture of enslavement persists. If we are to become a truly independent nation, people will need to pick up the proverbial "mantle" instead of waiting for commands. This is my wish for our people and for our instructors, because our students can be better citizens if leadership skills are modeled for them.

Question to Reflect upon and to Take Action for Future Projects

Would a country like Haiti, perhaps through our TESOL associations, benefit from an online model, like Kaina Online High School for the teaching of English?

"In 2023, UNICEF estimates that more than 4 million children will need humanitarian assistance in Haiti. Affecting them are many difficult conditions: increased gang-related violence, internal displacement, civil unrest, political instability as the country still reels from the killing of the president and indefinitely postponed elections, a socioeconomic crisis, rising food insecurity and malnutrition, the resurgence of cholera, and the continued expulsion of Haitian migrants from several countries in the Americas, including the neighboring Dominican Republic" (Reliefweb, 2023). Would a program such as Kaina Online High School's English program provide support for the children of Haiti?

The above rules out an opportunity that could be given to Haitians, Haitian educators, and students. They would participate in a program that

I would call the Haitian/Belize TESOL Experience. This alternative would entail the use of an online platform, like what is done in the Kaina Online High School of Belize. Since students can be enrolled in Kaina Online High School from anywhere in the world, it would be possible to teach English—or any other subject—to Haitian learners from the Kaina Online Platform in Belize. In collaboration with Haitian educators, from TESOL for example, we could create a program using the Kaina platform in Belize to teach Haitian learners who live in Haiti. This program would educate Haitian students and eliminate immigration problems, because they would not have to travel from their country.

References

Barrow, D. (2021). Elevators to heaven: Advocacy groups in Belize. *Belize Breaking News*. Retrieved from https://www.breakingbelizenews.com/2021/05/24/point-and-counterpoint-elevators-to-heaven-advocacy-groups-in-belize/

Buhler, R., & Hadle, R. (1975). Why Juanito can't read (pp. 1-4). Belizean National Studies 3, 1-4.

Craig, D. (1963). A comparative study of the written English of some 14-year-old Jamaican and English children. Doctoral dissertation, University of London. WorldCat.

Guettler, R. (2018) *Belizean tongues: The socioeconomics of language and education in Belize*, EBSCO Publishing: eBook Collection (EBSCOhost).

Humes, A. (May 17, 2023). New beginnings formerly, princess royal youth hostel. *Breaking Belize News*. Retrieved from https://www.breakingbelizenews.com/2022/05/17/new-beginnings-for-former-princess-royal-youth-hostel/

Lewis, K. (2002) Educational policy studies. *AERA*. University of Illinois at Urbana Champaign. Retrieved February 12, 2023. https://education.stateuniversity.com/pages/159/Belize.html#ixzz7t5iAXQb7

Linville, H. A. (2014). A mixed methods investigation of ESOL teacher advocacy: "It's not going in and just teaching English." (Publication No. 362431). University of Maryland, Baltimore County. Retrieved from: https://llc.umbc.edu/wp-content/uploads/sites/15/2013/02/diss2014_Linville.pdf

McKissey, G. (1972*). The Belizean Lingo*. National Printers Limited, Belize.

Reliefweb. (2023). *Humanitarian action for children 2023—Haiti.* Retrieved from https://reliefweb.int/report/haiti/humanitarian-action-children-2023-haiti

Statistical Institute of Belize. (2021). *Abstract of statistics 2021.* Retrieved from http://sib.org.bz/wp-content/uploads/2021_Abstract_of_Statistics.pdf

UNICEF (2020). Belize launches road map to end child marriage and early unions. Retrieved from https://www.unicef.org/belize/press-releases/belize-launches-road-map-end-child-marriage-and-early-unions

Chapter 5

English for a Better Future: An Initiative to Provide Quality Education to El Salvador's Youth

Miguel Ángel Carranza Campos

Background

El Salvador is the smallest country in Central America with only just 21,000 square kilometers; yet it is home to 6.3 million people. The nation has endured wars, earthquakes, and other natural disasters. In 1992, an agreement was signed to end the bloody civil war between leftist rebels and government representatives. The war took the lives of over 75,000 Salvadorans. The post-war proved also to be damaging to the country's social fabric. Consequently, documented and undocumented migration (Orozco & Jewers, 2021) to other countries escalated, and the United States was the main place of destination. Due to migration, families were broken. Parents, in most cases, left their children to be raised by grandmothers. Youth delinquency increased in an uncontrollable manner, and it is still felt 30 years later. "The current "gang problem" in El Salvador is not a reflection of what is inherently wrong with Salvadorans but rather a reflection of the lack of care toward children in policies during war-torn and post-war El Salvador (Parada, 2022).

Approximately 2.3 million Salvadorans live in the United States. "Migration has deprived El Salvador of human capital, and insecurity has weakened the country's appeal to foreign direct investment" (Plewa, 2021). Also, a comprehensive survey conducted by Creative in 2021 revealed that economic insecurity coupled with crimes that further damage people's economic well-being were significant drivers of intention to migrate during 2019 (Orozco & Jewers, 2021).

To remedy the social issues, multiple efforts have been made by the Salvadoran and U.S. governments to improve the country's social, political, and educational conditions. The United States government, through the U.S. Department of State (USDoS) (BECA, 2023), has supported a variety of educational projects. One of the most successful ones is the English Access Microscholarship Program, "which provides a foundation of English language skills to bright, economically disadvantaged students, primarily between the ages of 13 and 20, in their home countries. Access programs provide participants with English skills that may lead to better jobs and educational prospects" (BECA, 2023).

Another interesting but less-known project is Empower, which was developed at Universidad de El Salvador, the state college, from 2014 to 2015, with the financial support of the USDoS in the country. The grant was worth $50,000. The university provided the labor (the work of the teachers who taught classes), valued at approximately $160,000. Empower had 400 students from 12 public educational high schools for two academic years. These 400 students were divided into 20 groups of classes; each group consisted of 20 students (Callejas and Quintanilla, 2016).

The private sector has a similar project called Supérate (Fundación Sagrera Palomo, 2022). It also aims to "provide high-quality training in English, computer science, and values. The idea is to focus on the students from local public schools with the best academic performance, high potential, and commitment for self-improvement." Both Access and Supérate have become flagship programs in the country, and entrance to both programs depends on students' GPA and a commitment to complete the program. Supérate started in El Salvador in 2004 and then expanded to Panama. It now has six academic centers in El Salvador. With both countries combined, Supérate has graduated a total of 4,308 students. All graduates from the different programs represent a small but invaluable influx of quality students for colleges and for the social and economic development of El Salvador.

Regarding employment opportunities, in the last 20 years, international call centers have opened offices in the country and provided job opportunities to many young people without job experience. "The industry has grown by 29% over the past six years, now employing 12,000 people in 45 different facilities around the country" (Voices, 2011). These jobs have provided a boost to the youths' families and to the economy of the country. However, one of the limitations to growth over the years has been the relatively small bilingual workforce. In 2006, PROESA, the Agency for Promotion of Exports and Investments, tried recruiting English-speaking Salvadorans in the United States, promising salaries as high as $1,500 a month to move to El Salvador and work in call centers. And according to Barrera (2021), executive director of the

American Chamber of Commerce of El Salvador (AmCham), "growth in call centers was expected to reach 12,000 new jobs by the end of 2021, although the need for coverage of new jobs is 55,000" (Barrera, 2021). It is clear then that the country needs to prepare the youth with quality education and with better job opportunities, allowing them to thrive in a sustainable manner that would support the country's much-needed growth.

Advocacy for Quality High School Education and Better Opportunities

According to the online Merriam-Webster dictionary, advocacy is the act or process of supporting a cause or proposal: the act or process of advocating. Haneda and Alexander defined advocacy as "acting proactively on behalf of students to ensure that they are treated equitably and have access to needed resources" (as defined in Norman & Eslami, 2022, para. 9). Likewise, it is equally pertinent to note Linville's (2019) definition of advocacy as noticing ways English learners' educational success is challenged and then taking action with the goal of improving their educational experiences and outcomes and life chances. In this particular case, advocacy will be understood as the act of supporting and involving several key role players in the process of contributing to an important goal: providing free online quality English classes to 3,000 high school students for two years. Along this line, the project pretends to answer sustainable goal four of the United Nations, "which aims to develop quality education for all. UN goal four also aims to provide equal access to affordable vocational training, to eliminate gender and wealth disparities, and to achieve universal access to a quality higher education" (United Nations, 2015).

Fernando Herrera, the cultural specialist at USDoS in EL Salvador, envisioned a new project with a much bigger impact than previous programs: teaching 3,000 high school students of El Salvador ten hours of English classes a week for two years, following an after-school format. The project involved a total of 300 college students from six universities of the country in conjunction with the Ministry of Education and the Office of Public Affairs at the USDoS in El Salvador. Additionally, the project included a component in Spanish where volunteers would be trained by Soul.com. The main purpose of this last component is to prepare high school graduates to be agents of change to lead to more satisfying and productive lives. The project was proposed to former alumni with degrees in education who were working in

English language teaching in the country. The innovative idea was accompanied by convincing statistics and arguments concerning the current economic and work situation of the country as well the experiences gained in the last years supporting and funding different initiatives aimed at improving the country's education.

The Ministry of Education of El Salvador had already provided public high school students with laptops for their classes in response to the COVID-19 pandemic context. These devices would prove to be highly useful for the success of the new project, given the fact that all classes would be virtual and synchronous. Students from all departments of the country would be able to join classes at the same time with a given instructor.

Additionally, the proposal also stipulated that laptops would be assigned by the Ministry of Education to college students (English and Spanish volunteers) for them to plan and teach their online classes. Many of the college volunteers would have their practicum courses and their community service requirements waived as a result of their participation in the program. High school principals have promoted the idea with their students, and their students have registered and are already receiving English classes online. High school students have already engaged in talks about self-esteem, stress, and college planning, among other topics. These discussions have been led by psychology and social work majors at the university, who have been in charge of conducting the sessions every two weeks. The English teaching volunteers and the life skills volunteers represent excellent role models for high school students to imitate.

Several key stakeholders are voluntarily participating in the project: the Ministry of Education; the USDoS in El Salvador via its cultural specialist; college professors in charge of preparing future educators of the country; college students majoring in English teaching or in psychology, social work, or related fields; high school principals; high school students; and alumni of different U.S. scholarship programs offered in El Salvador.

High school students of public institutions are using their laptops, which were provided during the coronavirus pandemic. Additionally, funding for continuous training, polo shirts and certificates for the volunteers, and other needed expenses is expected to be provided by the generosity of the USDoS in El Salvador. The first six months of the program did not require any economic expense, except for the cost of the 300 laptops (MINED, 2022) that the Ministry of Education provided to the volunteers. This project is financially responsible and viable; all the work done in the first five months has been free and done by volunteers at all levels. Committed Salvadorans helping in the success of other Salvadorans is another one of the project's lofty goals. This initiative mainly focuses on students from low-income families, particularly those from public institutions, who have not had opportunities to study English intensively. Just as Brooks and Adams (2015) noted, educational change should challenge marginalized students.

Origins of English for a Better Future

English for a Better Future is an ambitious project that aims at teaching 3,000 high school students in El Salvador ten hours of English classes in an after-school format, weekly for two years. The project, in conjunction with the Ministry of Education and the Office of Public Affairs at the American Embassy of El Salvador, utilizes 300 students of English teaching majors from six of the nation's universities.

The cultural specialist at the USDoS in EL Salvador, Fernando Herrera, invited educational leaders employed by different colleges all around the country and who are also alumni of the different scholarship programs the embassy offers. These professors and educational leaders in their universities would be in charge of identifying and recruiting students in their B.A. programs who could volunteer and serve as teachers of English and life mentors for high school students interested in participating in the project. There were several online meetings to discuss the project and brainstorm ideas to recruit high school students as well as the volunteers who would conduct the classes (some for English courses and others for life skills courses).

Some of these leaders had good relationships with local public high school principals. These connections were used to encourage the school principals to recruit high school students interested in committing to receiving ten hours of English classes a week. A program coordinator was also needed, and Danny Membreño, a professor at Universidad Tecnologica and Ugrad alum, was chosen for the job. He would oversee coordinating the work with six college representatives for the English classes and five coordinators of the Spanish component.

The Syllabus

The course syllabus does not need textbooks; it only requires free material already available on the internet. The course is composed of linguistic functions, vocabulary, and grammatical structures necessary for a learner using the communicative approach. The designed program includes several free interactive exercises, materials, and videos available on the internet from sources such as Kahoot, Nearpod, Wodwall, Quizizz, ESL games, Bamboozle, and others. This syllabus was proposed and designed by Professor Joel Peña at UNIVO University. Professor Peña, who holds an M.A. in TESOL, is also an alumnus of the U.S. programs in El Salvador. He has been in charge of sharing the contents, the corresponding materials, and links for the English classes via Google Drive weekly.

With the proposed program, young Salvadoran high school graduates are expected to reach a B1 English language competency according to Common European Framework of Reference for Languages (CEFR), which will allow some of them to find their first job as call center agents. If 60% of the students achieve the intermediate level, the program will be considered successful. The graduates would then get money to pay for their college education, get help at home, have better career opportunities, and thus thrive and contribute to the country's economy. If 80% of the participants register for college, the program will also be considered a success.

Likewise, the call center sector is highly interested in the results of the project, and they have even promised their support. There is a strong need for bilingual personnel in the country, and the current initiative will provide an influx of new employees for the sector. In the end, everyone would win. Young high school graduates would obtain their first job as call center agents, and these companies would fulfill their vacant posts.

The program counts on the invaluable support of 300 college students from different universities in the country who are the English teaching volunteers. Finally, the five private colleges involved in the project have envisioned new academic majors, and some have already been designed. These plans will be offered mainly in English. Preparing bilingual professionals is key for the future and having college graduates with an intermediate level of English will be an advantage for these universities and for the development of the country as well.

The First Months

After weeks and months of planning, classes finally started on May 2, 2021. Currently, students have received almost six months of online English classes. The group of teacher volunteers has, for the most part, persisted; a few have dropped out. Most of these volunteers will have their college community service requirement waived in exchange for this experience, and some others will get credit for their practicum courses. However, there has been a relatively high dropout rate (around 30%) for high school students who initially registered for the classes. Probably many did not know what the commitment involved, or they preferred to focus more on the last period activities of the 2022 school year.

Six consistent months of virtual and synchronous classes have been delivered. There are groups of classes served at different times of the day: from 9 to 11 a.m., from 4 to 6 p.m., and from 6 to 8 p.m., Mondays to Fridays. And there are a few groups of classes on Saturdays and Sundays. Looking toward the future, more students have been invited to participate and have already accepted. New groups of students will be created, and more volunteers will join the project. The initial number of 3,000 expected high school students could be higher by the end of the project in October 2023 (Joma, 2022).

A Program Worth Replicating

Working toward the goal of improving the nation's future is rewarding for everyone involved. All stakeholders work toward the major goal of helping prepare a better society for the country. Colleges have great human capital to be utilized, and university students are benefiting from this experience. They are gaining skills, networking, and providing useful and important community services. The student volunteers are being exposed to intensive practicum, where they are putting into practice what they are learning in their colleges. It will be important to continue boosting their professional development so their impact can be bigger, just like Ballantyne, Sanderman, and Levy (2008) stated: "Providing quality instruction to English language learners requires teachers who are skilled in a variety of curricular and instructional strategies."

There are questions on the horizon worth discussing: will virtual classes alone help high school students improve their language competencies? Is the designed syllabus appropriate and challenging enough to take students to higher levels of language competence? Will the volunteers commit to teaching their classes for two years without any monetary incentive? A work plan has been set up to address these challenges. Each college will meet and monitor volunteers' work frequently and closely to improve the quality of instruction and make corrections in the process. At the end of the classes in October of 2023, a standardized test will be administered to measure students' proficiency in the language and the impact of the program. It is expected that those who finish the program will have improved their English competencies and will have achieved an intermediate level, which will allow them to get their first jobs in a call center and at the same time apply for entrance to college, and some to the new bilingual college degree programs.

There have been similar projects in the country, but the economic cost of those has been higher, and the impact has only benefited fewer than a hundred students. This is a major visionary program, and it has been an enriching experience in many areas. It has not involved major economic investments up to now, except for the 300 laptops assigned to the teaching volunteers. However, funding will be needed to pay for face-to-face workshops, facilitators, transportation, and per diems, among other expenses. It is expected that either the Ministry of Education of El Salvador or the USDoS in EL Salvador will help with the necessary financing of key needs of the program.

Colleges are improving their image within the Salvadoran community by committing to the noble goals of the initiative. Together, everyone involved is doing their best to make this project a successful one, so that our nation may have a brighter future. Most likely, intercollegiate experiences like this will continue being replicated in the following years.

References

Ballantyne, K. G., Sanderman, A. R., & Levy, J. (2008). Educating English language learners: Building teacher capacity-roundtable report. National Clearinghouse for English language acquisition. Retrieved from https://eric.ed.gov/?id=ED521360

Barrera, J. A. (2021, June 30). Industria de "call centers" anuncia que generará 12,000 empleos en El Salvador en 2021. Diario El Mundo. Retrieved from https://diario.elmundo.sv/economia/industria-de-call-centers-anuncia-que-generara-12000-empleos-en-el-salvador-en-2021

BECA. (2023) English access microscholarship program. U.S. Department of State. Retrieved from https://exchanges.state.gov/non-us/program/english-access-microscholarship-program

Brooks, K., & Adams, S. (2015). Developing agency for advocacy: Collaborative inquiry-focused school-change projects as transformative learning for practicing teachers. *New Educator, 11*(4), 292–308. Retrieved from https://doi.org/10.1080/1547688X.2015.1087758

Callejas Quijano, D. V., Quintanilla Navidad, G. M., Navidad Morales, F., & Landaverde, M. A. (2016, May 6). *A partial evaluation of the economic benefits arising from the empower project in Instituto Nacional General*

*Francisco Men*éndez in the metropolitan area, San Salvador, El Salvador, year 2015. Ri.ues.edu.sv. Retrieved from https://ri.ues.edu.sv/id/eprint/12464/

Fundación Sagrera Palomo. (2022, December 1). ¡Supérate! Retrieved from https://superate.org.sv/nuestra-historia

Joma, S. (2022). La embajada de Estados Unidos impulsa la enseñanza del Inglés a 3,000 estudiantes. Noticias de El Salvador. Retrieved from https://www.elsalvador.com/noticias/nacional/embajada-estados-unidos-clases-ingles-estudiantes-mined/1003331/2022/

Linville A. H., & Whiting, J. (2019). Advocacy in English language, teaching and learning. *Advocacy in English Language, Teaching and Learning.* Routledge.

Ministerio de Educación. (2022, July 29). MINED entrega 300 computadoras a jóvenes tutores del programa Inglés para un Mejor Futuro. Retrieved from https://www.mined.gob.sv/2022/07/29/mined-entrega-300-computadoras-a-jovenes-tutores-del-programa-ingles-para-un-mejor-futuro

Norman, L. N. M., & Eslami, Z. R. (2022). English learner teacher advocates: A systematic literature review. *Teaching English as a Second or Foreign Language-TESL-EJ, 25*(4), n.p. Retrieved from https://doi.org/10.55593/ej.25100a8

Orozco, M., & Jewers, M. (2021). Economic insecurity & irregular migration from El Salvador Center for Migration and Economic Stabilization Creative Associates International. Retrieved from https://www.creativeassociatesinternational.com/wp-content/uploads/2021/12/Economic-Insecurity-and-Irregular-Migration-from-El-Salvador.pdf

Parada, D. (2022, April 20). Imprisoning children: How El Salvador's adults fail young people involved in gangs. Global Voices Online Blog. Retrieved from https://globalvoices.org/2022/04/20/imprisoning-children-how-el-salvadors-adults-fail-young-people-involved-in-gangs/

Plewa, P. (2021, April 14). Migration from El Salvador to the U.S.: A Background Brief, Duke University Center for International and Global Studies. Retrieved from https://igs.duke.edu/news/migration-el-salvador-us-background-brief

United Nations. (2015). Sustainable development goal 4: Quality education. *Unoosa.* Retrieved from https://www.unoosa.org/oosa/en/ourwork/space4sdgs/sdg4.html

Voices. (2011, November 23). Call center industry growing in El Salvador. Voices on the Border Blog. Retrieved from https://voiceselsalvador.wordpress.com/2011/11/23/call-center-industry-growing-in-el-salvador/

Chapter 6
TESOL Transformative Advocacy in Tertiary Education in Vietnam

Son Nguyen, Huong Lam, and Hong-Anh Nguyen

Overview

Advocacy is defined as "working for English learners' equitable and excellent education by taking appropriate actions on their behalf" (Staehr-Fenner, 2014, p. 8). In other words, it represents acting agentively on behalf of English learners (ELs) and/or their families to ensure they are treated equitably and have access to needed resources (Haneda & Sherman, 2018). Therefore, advocacy in the field of teaching English to speakers of other languages (TESOL) is becoming more and more critical, especially in the context of social inequalities among English learners.

This chapter focuses on transformative advocacy (see more in Haneda & Alexander, 2015; Norman & Eslami, 2022). Transformative advocacy takes place when policies and practices regarding English language teaching promote inequities for learners at the school level and/or beyond the classroom, and then EFL teachers challenge those policies and practices, such as colonial conceptions of language education or lack of teaching facilities and learning resources. Arguably, this advocacy needs special attention because EFL lecturers are the direct agents in implementing the policies, and they are especially responsible, on behalf of the students, to raise their voices for better qualities. In this case, EFL teachers would question such inequities so that their students could be more involved in the educational process and experience better language education.

Advocacy in the Field of TESOL

English learners' voices are sometimes not much heard due to their being allied to the lowest level under the management of higher education in a monolingual society. Therefore, they need staunch advocacy, generally identified as agentive actions on behalf of ELs to ensure they are treated equitably and have sufficient opportunities to access needed resources (Haneda & Sherman, 2018). Despite its undeniable importance, TESOL advocacy in tertiary education is still under-researched.

Definitions of advocacy may vary in the fields of TESOL and language education, but the commonality clearly seen in the literature is that of representation on behalf of ELs to achieve desired educational outcomes and positive societal changes for these students (Linville, 2015). We are proponents of Linville's definition because she is concerned about equality among ELs. Advocacy is considered as noticing challenges to students' educational success and then addressing the situation (Linville, 2016, 2019, 2020). As a critical component of social justice language teaching, teachers have a responsibility to stand up for students' rights and access to equitable and high-quality education so that students' voices can be heard in and beyond the environment of classrooms and schools (Linville, 2016).

Advocacy is not only mentioned in learning English but also as a critical term of professional engagement. It is reflected in the concept of teacher leaders. Teachers are not only instructors but also crucial professionals, committed to an education inside and outside their classrooms. They are always willing to take risks, time, and responsibility to encourage school reform efforts to ensure equitable treatment for their students (Christison & Lindahl, 2009).

Types of Advocacy and Transformative Advocacy

There are several types of advocacy, known as transformative advocacy, non-transformative advocacy, instructional advocacy, political advocacy, and transitive advocacy. These types of advocacy models are explored in light of the Multifaceted Nature of Language Learning and Teaching model by the Douglas Fir Group (2016). This model consists of micro, meso, and macro levels. The second/foreign language learning process begins at the micro level of social activity, where individuals interact with others in multilingual contexts. The engagement in these contexts uses semiotic resources, including prosodic, interactional, linguistic, nonverbal, graphic, pictorial, auditory, and artifactual resources. At the meso level, these contexts are shaped by sociocultural institutions and communities that involve social identities of language learners. The meso level is also related to learners' families, schools, neighborhoods, workplaces, places of worship, and social organizations. The macro level of ideological structures, which orientate toward language use and language learning, includes belief systems and cultural, political, religious, and economic values (Douglas Fir Group, 2016).

In educational policy at the state and national levels, English teachers typically enact instructional and political advocacy for more equitable treatment of their ELs. Another type of advocacy is termed "transitive" by Harrison and McIlwain (2019), and is mainly performed at a meso level. It is related to collaborating with teachers and other community members, including parents and administrators, to advocate for students. Transitive advocacy allows those working with ELs to share responsibility for the students' educational and life outcomes in classes, schools, and communities. It is a form of advocacy that aims to create an academic environment where ELs can develop and thrive. This type of advocacy is considered as a practical approach that Vietnamese schools adopt to push for greater English proficiency in their students. Stakeholders, including school leaders, teachers and parents, have a strong impact on language education. The literature (e.g., Dang, Le, & Ha, 2021) highlights the constructive role of parents in their children's development of positive attitude and desire to learn English. Moreover, teachers' and students' difficulties in teaching and learning will not be left behind thanks to the close collaboration between school and family. Therefore, the efforts and cooperation from administrators, teachers, and parents are able to enhance the quality of language teaching (Nguyen, Fehring, & Warren, 2015; Mai Ngoc & Iwashita, 2012).

Non-transformative advocacy occurs when inequities are not challenged at or beyond the school levels (Linville, 2020). Teachers can conduct this kind of support to ensure their students' access to curricular and linguistic resources. This form of advocacy may take place within the micro and meso levels.

The most crucial type, which will be discussed in detail because of its significant impact on language education, is transformative advocacy. Transformative actions occur where the educational structure, system, or policies marginalize ELs and their families. ELs' inequities are brought to the surface and challenged within and beyond the school levels. That is why alternatives need to be developed and potentially put into practice (Harrison & McIlwain, 2019; Linville & Whiting, 2019).

Transformative advocacy can take place at the meso level of sociocultural institutions and at the macro level of ideological structures. Firstly, at the meso level, teachers require a place at the table where decisions are made so that their learners will be more included in institutions' curriculum development and states' policies. The support from teachers at this level can ensure the students as beneficiaries in any activities and strategies of their schools and communities. Studies on English tertiary education in Vietnam reveal the challenges that students faced in relation to inappropriate teaching and learning materials, time constraints, lack of facilities, and testing-oriented systems (e.g., Trinh & Mai, 2019). Fortunately, English teachers were identified as key factors whose voices contributed to the improvement of language curriculum, time allocation for language teaching, as well as facilities (Nguyen, Fehring, & Warren, 2015). In Vietnam, the National Foreign Languages 2020 Project has been launched since 2008 to enhance graduates' foreign language competence so that they can be confident to compete in regional and international labor markets (Nguyen & Bui, 2016; Le, Nguyen, & Burns, 2017). To achieve the intended outcome of the policy, English teachers performed a crucial transformative role. They voiced their resistance to inequality of education policies, expressed their deep concerns about low-quality teacher education, and called for more attention to empowering teachers as active perceivers of policy change (Nguyen & Bui, 2016). Therefore, the educational policies of a monolingual society certainly have a significant influence on its foreign language learners. If policymakers consider English education as an essential factor for sustained social and economic growth, their policies may encourage learners' desire to invest in learning and mastering a foreign language. That is why transformative advocacy should be enacted to propose the students' attitudes and aspirations to shape macro level strategies and policies in language practice and assessment.

Why Advocacy Is Essential in Vietnam

Regarding learning and teaching English, various sociocultural factors challenge Vietnamese students. Firstly, the national school system is influenced by collectivism and Confucianism, which value top-down decision making (Nguyen, Terlouw, & Pilot, 2006; Tran, 2012). Although English teachers and ELs experience and understand most teaching and learning practices in this system, they have never been placed at the top level in the management of the Ministry of Education and Training and tertiary institutions.

In the context of Vietnamese education with prominent Confucian cultural features, students are always expected to be obedient, well-behaved, and good listeners. Sometimes there are unequal relationships between students and teachers, students and teaching staff, and even students and institution administrators because students are not encouraged to make their ideas known or to challenge teachers' and school administrators' conclusions (Bui, 2019). Consequently, their difficulties and aspirations in language learning may be abandoned. Teachers in this situation should be responsible for being their students' advocates, someone who can present problems to education authorities on behalf of their learners and offer solutions for students' academic and life matters.

Working in a Vietnamese educational context with high scores of collectivism and power distance index, teachers and other stakeholders, in general, would like to maintain harmony and avoid confrontations and conflicts in the education system (Bui, 2019; Hofstede & Hofstede, 2005). Teachers are considered core persons responsible for dealing with their students' issues within and beyond the classroom. However, they will hesitate to raise their voice for students if their actions may bring them into conflicts at the workplace (Truong, Hallinger, & Sanga, 2017). Firstly, maintaining harmony is of utmost importance; teachers and staff often avoid topics that may contribute to students' benefits but lead to shame and loss of face among colleagues. Secondly, most teachers consider this seriously before discussing learners' difficulties with their administrators due to the likely impacts of power distance. Because hierarchy is critical to preserve social stability, teachers are not expected to challenge their leaders' decisions. To be students' advocates, they may take the risk of being professionally marginalized (Linville, 2020).

According to the current situation, collectivism and power distance significantly impact Vietnam's higher education. Unequal power distribution was naturally accepted by teachers, who played a limited role in decision making and had to follow school committees' policies and directives. Management boards, whose members included principals, vice principals, and school party secretaries, enacted the decision-making function (Truong, Hallinger, & Sanga, 2017).

The inadequate learning conditions were also emphasized due to a lack of teaching facilities and study support materials (Dang, Le, & Ha, 2021; Trinh & Mai, 2019). Students had to study in hot, narrow classes without computers, speakers, or projectors. Moreover, some students and teachers worked with outdated or institutionally composed textbooks that only provided students with opportunities to develop their grammar rather than giving them interactive activities for the improvement of communicative competence. Therefore, transformative advocacy can be a feasible solution for an inequitable educational system where the voiceless continue to be powerless, whose rights go denied or unheard. What makes advocacy more critical in this focus is that all stakeholders, including teachers, staff, administrators and communities, are responsible for protecting ELs' holistic rights so that ELs are treated fairly and have unrestricted access to resources.

Students' English proficiency levels differ due to their varied learning conditions and backgrounds. The socioeconomic circumstances of an average Vietnamese household allow for the average quality of English education. While quality English language teaching (ELT) is only accessible to the affluent class, most of the population gets what they can afford. The foreign language policy in Vietnam states that English is officially taught as a compulsory subject since grade three in elementary and lower secondary public schools in the educational system. However, in reality, in mountainous villages or remote areas in the countryside, English education is subject to the availability of language teachers and the resources of those schools. As a result, pupils in these disadvantageous areas will not start learning English until they enter upper secondary schools, where they have only three years of learning English. They may not have enough conditions for private English classes, either. On the other hand, English education is easily accessible to pupils of all ages in urban areas or big cities. These pupils not only learn English officially in schools from grade three but also start learning it early in their kindergarten age with private English language tutors and schools. They may continue private English education until they complete upper secondary levels. When entering university levels, students from both disadvantageous and urban areas may be enrolled in the same class. In fact, the percentage of rural and inferior students accounts for a greater part in each class in comparison with urban students. Therefore, English teachers need to respond to the level of diversity in the classroom. They have to promote equity and help remove barriers for all students to succeed. They need to provide equal opportunities in regard to language and learning environments for all students. They also need to understand students' difficulties, needs and interests, from which they can support their students' learning and maximize the effectiveness of the English teaching and learning process (Cochran-Smith, 2020). When every student has the necessary resources, the entire classroom thrives.

Then there is the question of opportunity and accessibility. Teachers must ensure students are provided with equal participation in English learning, materials are provided in commonly used formats, the internet connection is stable, and the software is neither complicated nor expensive. However, although this equality may sound good in theory, it does not usually work in practice. This equality does not usually mean equitable learning. In fact, English teachers need to understand their students and provide them with targeted support. They also ensure students' language ability, language skills, and other needs will not negatively impact their ability to do well. English teachers need to understand that equity in the classroom is a process, not an immediate result, and promoting equity benefits all students in the class (Linville, 2020). And when English teachers promote equality and equity in the classroom, they practice advocacy for their students.

Overview of Vietnamese Tertiary Higher Education

Since Vietnam joined the World Trade Organization (WTO) in 1986 and the whole country moved to the market economy stage, Vietnam has seen a dramatic change in all aspects of society, such as economics, politics, culture, and especially education (Fry, 2009). The country's comprehensive integration into the world has brought about both positive improvement and controversial issues in education. Current Vietnamese higher education still has many unstable problems related to university autonomy; outdated teaching methods, curricula, and facilities; and students' unsatisfactory English proficiency (Tran & Do, 2022).

Thanks to the country's integration and internationalization, for ages, English has demonstrated itself as the most important foreign language in the teaching curriculum (Lam & Albright, 2019). Although English is a compulsory subject from primary to tertiary education, the number of students who meet the English output requirements is small, and many students do not qualify for graduation due to the failure to meet English requirements. Most of those who meet the English requirements belong to the English-major groups and come from big cities and towns with favorable conditions for learning English. The rest of the students' English proficiency levels are very worrying (Lam, 2019). Poor English ability also leads graduates to difficulties getting a good job. Many graduates are not qualified to apply for a job that requires skills and the ability to communicate in English. This is a waste to society, families, and the graduates themselves.

In such situations, English teachers and ELs in Vietnam are facing major advocacy challenges. The first advocacy challenge is the difference between students' learning needs and language levels. There will always be diverse language abilities in any language class that demand teachers' attention.

As a result, teachers need to think outside the box if they want to motivate their learners and satisfy them with different teaching strategies. They need to put extra hours and effort into their lesson plans while they are always short of time.

The second challenge is the number of students in each language class, which is closely related to the institutional lack of funding. To save resources, institutions tend to enroll many students into one language class. Consequently, teachers need to deal with a growing number of students in one class, which prevents them from providing careful attention to each student. Therefore, students may make lower achievements and have more dissatisfaction in their learning.

Another challenge goes with the ineffective communication between teachers and students. Communicating their needs to teachers is always a daunting task for most Vietnamese students due to the influence of Confucianism in the past. Vietnamese students are taught to respect and obey their teachers, so they find it difficult to communicate what they think or need to their teachers. Teachers need to build rapport with their students so that they have mutual understanding and trust, from which they can communicate effectively together inside or outside classrooms.

Finally, English teachers face the challenges coming from the conflict between the administrators and their students. Often English teachers serve as the bridge between students and institutions. As teachers understand students' difficulties, needs, and interests, they raise their voice on behalf of their students on some issues that may cause conflicts with their administrators. In those situations, teachers are easily marginalized in the workplace.

In short, the four issues above are the major advocacy challenges for English teachers in Vietnam. Dealing completely with those challenges is also the goal that "advocacy in Vietnam" would be trying to achieve.

Transformative TESOL Advocacy in Vietnamese Higher Education

A total of 19 EFL lecturers from three large, public, multidisciplinary universities in Vietnam were interviewed to share their viewpoints and experiences regarding advocacy, especially transformative advocacy practices. Those lecturers had a range of working experiences from 8 to 20 years. The majority (17) obtained a master's degree in TESOL, whereas the other two had Ph.D. degrees in education. The lecturers were participating in an advocacy-supporting workshop where the term "advocacy" was first introduced.

After that workshop, they were invited to be involved in the research. They were asked mainly about what advocacy, especially transformative advocacy, meant to them, what they did to support advocacy, and what they found difficult about fostering advocacy. The responses were meant to show an overview of transformative TESOL advocacy in Vietnamese tertiary language education so that the concept of advocacy would be more widely spread, and awareness would be better raised among educational stakeholders.

The interviews were audiotaped subject to the lecturers' consent, transcribed, and translated using the back-translation method before the data were analyzed thematically. The results indicated four critical themes of transformative advocacy described and discussed by the EFL lecturers: (1) manifestations of TESOL advocacy; (2) transformative advocacy in classrooms; (3) transformative advocacy beyond classrooms; (4) challenges to promote TESOL advocacy; and (5) lecturers' expectations toward enhancing advocacy.

Representations of TESOL Advocacy in Vietnam

EFL lecturers perceived TESOL advocacy mainly based on three dimensions: "classroom"-based advocacy, syllabus-based advocacy, and university-based advocacy. Specifically, classroom-based advocacy manifested in how lecturers supported their students inside classrooms and in unique virtual spaces so that the students could access language learning equally and equitably. The lecturers were expected to identify difficulties that ELs face in the classrooms. According to many lecturers, because language classes in Vietnam typically included varying levels of English, sometimes the advocacy could be the awareness of ELs' language proficiency to pay more attention to the weaker or more disadvantaged students. The lecturers gave those learners more encouragement and individualized exercises to boost their learning. Also, it could be simply asking ELs whether they understood the lessons well. Accordingly, the lecturers would either facilitate ELs' work or make proper changes in the lessons' speed. Notably, efforts were made by the EFL lecturers to motivate and engage their ELs in every lesson, using different strategies such as interactive games, technological applications, and online resources. Another vital aspect emphasized was that the lecturers encouraged and appreciated the ELs' feedback and questions raised inside classrooms to clarify unclear points and raise their concerns, as the lecturers believed that the ELs' voices should be listened to. Quotation marks are used above to highlight virtual classrooms such as Zalo groups—a unique social media of Vietnam—in addition to the traditional physical ones, in which both EFL lecturers and ELs share ideas, opinions, stories, and resources. They also talked comfortably there as friends to tighten the teacher-student relationship. Many lecturers valued those virtual classrooms, which worked as forums, because their ELs had private space to feel at home and tended to be more open-minded to share what they felt and needed than in traditional classrooms. Hence, virtual classrooms could be a new and promising way to promote TESOL advocacy.

Secondly, as defined by the participating lecturers, advocacy was represented in how the syllabus was designed, implemented, and evaluated. Although the syllabus is usually prescribed beforehand by the department or division, advocacy would appear if the curriculum could serve as an immediate response to the ELs' needs, ongoing feedback, and expectations. It means that although the lecturers had professional meetings to create the syllabus and select the textbook for the whole university, they should individually or collaboratively adapt the syllabus but still guarantee the core content required by the departments and universities. Such adaptation signified that ELs were being listened to and supported to equitably learn English even though it is more challenging to adapt the syllabus in mixed-level and/or large-sized classes and required the lecturers' harder work, including different types of exercises and assignments and more facilitative time. As one participant shared,

> Whenever I work with my students, especially weaker, I investigate the syllabus very carefully to make proper changes in activities and assignments so that they can learn more effectively and under less pressure because I find it nearly impossible for every student to follow just one syllabus.

Thirdly, advocacy in TESOL referred to how the EFL lecturers elevated their voices on behalf of the ELs to deliver the students' concerns, messages, and questions related to English language learning issues to the university authorities or leaderboards. This became more important in technical universities where English was a minor part of the curriculum. In the department of English, there were fewer teachers than in other departments. The students' concerns and inquiries could be about level of difficulty, workload, infrastructure, timetable, and even teachers' work. Accordingly, if the language lecturers became advocates at the university level, they would actively collect data from their students' opinions and feedback in different ways such as informal talks, class meetings, end-of-term feedback sessions, forums, and each lesson. Then, the data would be sent to the authorities, and the lecturers would wait for adequate answers before informing their students.

It can be concluded that the perceptions of the EFL lecturers well reflected the previous definitions and descriptions of TESOL advocacy. However, this term was initially coined in the United States due to the diverse backgrounds in TESOL among students in this nation (García & Kleifgen, 2010). Correspondingly, the term of advocacy applied to the Vietnamese context in two main points in the lecturers' perceived definitions of advocacy consistent with the previous ones, including "acting" and "access." The former refers to what the lecturers do and how they do it to make sure the students are supported equitably and have the latter—access to resources that facilitate their learning (Haneda & Alexander, 2015). However, there were some great points in the EFL lecturers' definitions of advocacy. Advocacy meant facilitation in English language learning so that the ELs did not feel disadvantaged in many aspects of their learning process at technical universities where English is taught and learnt in a short period of time. Moreover, unlike in the K-12 system, TESOL advocacy in tertiary education, according to the lecturers, did not involve parental roles since ELs were all adults with their decision-making rights. That is why advocacy was only relevant to educators and students.

Transformative Advocacy in Classrooms

At technical universities where English is regarded as a minor piece and the department of general English is small in scale, there are likely many inequities in teaching and learning English. As discussed above, the ELs experienced their language education in poor conditions, including large-sized classes; large classrooms with a small number of students; shortages of learning materials, resources, and equipment; and unstable or no internet connection (see more in Trinh & Mai, 2019). However, the authorities tended to pay little attention to English language teaching and learning practices, as reflected in marginal changes in the universities' policies regarding those practices.

To work as advocates, the EFL lecturers shared that they usually encouraged their students to share and raise their voices regarding what support they needed in the language classrooms, although Vietnamese students were generally reluctant to ask questions (Bui, 2019). One effective strategy reported by the lecturers to shorten the power distance between teachers and students was to sincerely talk to the ELs on a regular basis and regard them as friends.

As a result, the students had a feeling that they were warmly welcomed and listened to. The lecturers believed that the relationship between teachers and students should be more equal, although hierarchy was still maintained to a certain extent. Also, the students should not be afraid of conflicts or losing face. To illustrate, one lecturer contended,

> Beside teaching English, I always have an activity that allows students to share and reflect on what they want or need from me either anonymously or publicly. As a result, they share that I am a friendly and warm teacher that they can trust and tell their stories to. Also, I have known [sic] a lot in their thoughts and am motivated to help them more.

Moreover, the lecturers noted all the challenges above and made efforts to overcome them because the lecturers believed that their ELs should get equal and equitable access to better quality language education, as postulated by one interviewee: "My students come from different backgrounds and some of them are really disadvantaged in language learning. Therefore, one of my responsibilities is to help them to have better access and overcome difficulties in their own studies." Specifically, the lecturers "gave them more handouts and supplementary materials compiled by themselves and their colleagues" and "shared online open materials with students from American English, British Council Learning English, and live worksheets" to deal with the material deficiency. Also, they even equipped themselves with teaching-assistant machines and speakers without waiting for universities' financial support. Besides, the EFL lecturers self-funded packages of high-speed Wifi and 4G so their students could use the internet for their learning. Additionally, the lecturers kept asking those in charge to change their rooms into smaller-sized classes and smaller classrooms even though responses from the policymakers were being awaited.

It is apparent that despite difficulties and inequities, the EFL lecturers have made efforts to advocate for their students. Advocacy simply means being close to, sharing with, and supporting the students to learn English better in non-English-major contexts. Moreover, Vietnam is regarded as a collectivistic society with a high score on the power distance index (see more in Hofstede & Hofstede, 2005). As a result, the lecturers' perceptions revealed that reducing power distance and collectivism in classes was one way to represent TESOL transformative advocacy.

Transformative Advocacy Beyond Classrooms

While advocacy within the classrooms was reported frequently as what the lecturers themselves could do to tackle the challenges, the lecturers believed that advocacy beyond the classrooms was salient. To be more specific, they found that although language education had its own unique features regarding conditions (e.g., class sizes, classroom sizes, student placement of level, equipment, seat arrangements, decorations, and syllabus), it is obligated to share the same regulations and facilities with all other courses. The lecturers shared that their leaders who did not major in language teaching and linguistics did not understand much about those features. Therefore, EFL classes experienced inequity and inequality, and the policies lacked coherence and support to enhance the quality of and access to the language teaching and learning process.

The lecturers were aware of the importance of providing pedagogical suggestions and recommendations, because they acted as direct implementers of rules and policies and their students did not have as many chances to communicate with the policymakers as they did. They found it essential to help the institutional policy makers understand the curriculum and approaches that best satisfied the needs of their ELs, as the needs at their university differed from those at English-major ones or even non-English-major ones.

Moreover, they valued the ELs' feedback, noted all the difficulties they observed themselves and were reported by their students, and then publicly spoke about those challenges in further communications with the leaders, such as informal conversations, formal meetings, forums, and discussions. One lecturer, for example, stated that she usually mentioned the shortage of teaching equipment in every meeting with the faculty and university leaders, who kept promising to change the situation; however, she bought some necessary teaching tools on her own. Interestingly, the lecturers with higher qualifications (e.g., Ph.D. degrees) were more likely to express their opinions and ask for changes in the policies due to the influence of studying abroad, which enabled them to experience more advanced systems and feel free to raise their voices.

The lecturers took interpersonal actions to talk to their colleagues about equal access their ELs should have and to help their colleagues choose and adapt suitable teaching resources. These advocacy-fostering actions were popular among the participating lecturers and were taken regularly when they had professional development events. One participating lecturer postulated, "Our department has bi-weekly meetings to discuss how to make proper changes to language materials to improve the quality of teaching and learning. We are inspired to do so to support students' access." Also, the lecturers interviewed found the actions the most effective because they were immediately doing something good for their ELs without waiting for the policymakers' responses. The actions supported beyond-classroom transformative advocacy and also enhanced in-class transformative advocacy, as the lecturers, with the support of their colleagues, made changes in their classes to support the ELs' better language learning. Therefore, the interpersonal actions above symbolized the connection between advocacy in and beyond classrooms.

It can be inferred that two cultural dimensions of power distance and collectivism were related to TESOL transformative advocacy beyond classrooms. Despite philosophically predetermined social hierarchy, the EFL lecturers overcame power distance, raised their voices, and took action to ask for more equities in their TESOL contexts. Also, they were not afraid of institutional confrontations and conflicts when communicating directly with their colleagues, leaders, and management bodies regarding their students' issues. This can be explained by the fact that, more or less, in their previous preservice or in-service training, the EFL lecturers had time to approach Western cultures where voices are valued and raised if needed.

Challenges to Promote Advocacy

Some challenges affect TESOL advocacy in the context of Vietnamese tertiary education. The findings from the interviews and the information on the universities' websites pointed out two significant difficulties in fostering advocacy.

First, culturally, Vietnam is recognized as a collectivistic country with great power distance. Therefore, people, including students, are likely to appreciate harmony and avoid losing face as well as social conflicts when they say something different from the majority. Also, they highly respect their teachers and maintain a power hierarchy. As a result, the lecturers, despite endeavors for openness, sincerity, and encouragement, find it challenging to know their students' ideas, opinions, and voices, as there are too many students who are shy and passive (Bui, 2019; Nguyen & Habók, 2020; Trinh & Mai, 2019) and they tend to be silent. However, the lecturers postulated that students shared their viewpoints more in virtual groups such as Zalo or Facebook or in online classrooms such as Zoom or Microsoft Teams. Arguably, the students have their privacy in their own spaces, enabling them to feel free to talk and share.

Therefore, it is recommended that the spaces or environments where the students can raise their voices should be diversified so that the lecturers can listen to them and, on their behalf, deliver their messages to the policymakers regarding better access and quality of language learning.

Second, contextually, the disadvantage comes from the fact that their departments of English are merely minor in large universities whose main majors include engineering, economics, and technology. As a result, English language education is treated the same as majors without considering the unique characteristics of language education. If the EFL lecturers ask for policy changes, the leaders may promise to do something, but it takes a lot of time to realize their expectations. One of the interviewees shared that,

> My English department is the smallest unit at my university, and English is considered compulsory but not important, so if we ask for some considerations, for example, change in facilities, or syllabus, we have to wait long and sometimes the leaders' responses are not satisfactory. It seems they do not know much about language education. It is a pity for advocacy.

Thus, the leaders should pay special attention to English language education because it is different from other majors' training and plays a vital role in the students' future career path for integration and promotion.

EFL Lecturers' Expectations Toward Enhancing Advocacy

The EFL lecturers indicated their expectations based on three dimensions: student-based expectation, colleague-based expectation, and authority-based expectation. They insisted that the ELs should be aware of their rights and duties in and beyond classrooms; as a result, they can speak up for their rights if any inequities and inequalities are identified. The ELs are advised to cooperate reasonably with the lecturers in the language learning process by being more open-minded and comfortable in sharing concerns rather than considering them as models and sources of knowledge. If so, the lecturers can be better transformative advocates, at least in classrooms. One lecturer stated, "The students, no one else, really need to get on well with their teachers in language classrooms or even outside to say what they want confidently and comfortably so that we can be by their sides."

The interviewed lecturers contended that despite the recent progress in TESOL, professional development among EFL lecturers at non-English-major universities has still been limited, and their main activity is only teaching. To exemplify, "I have too many lessons in one week, week by week, month by month. Also, I am quite lazy after teaching lessons, so basically I do not attend professional development programs", one interviewed lecturer confessed. Therefore, the EFL lecturers expected their colleagues to participate in professional development events and improve their skills to work with the ELs. Such events also enable the lecturers to broaden their networking community of EFL lecturers and share more ideas to advocate for the ELs.

One notable fact at non-English-major institutions is that all the members of the leaderboards have majored in fields such as natural sciences and engineering, other than English. At one participating university, one lecturer felt unhappy because:

> All the leaders are majored in engineering, very different from our major. That is why they do not usually understand our concerns regarding language teaching and learning. For example, my leader told me not to arrange seats in class and not to make noise when having activities.

Hence, university leaderboards are expected to be more diverse in backgrounds. Accordingly, at least one member of the leaderboard should have majors in English language teaching and/or linguistics so that s/he can deeply understand the teaching and learning process and its uniqueness and help the department of English to raise voices if necessary.

Implications

Our discussion of TESOL advocacy in the context of Vietnamese tertiary education foregrounds issues, challenges, and expectations. To address these, some macro, meso, and micro level implications are proposed.

At the macro level, the policymakers are advised to have positive attitudes toward teachers' and students' opinions so that the policies can be informed, shaped, and implemented better in reality. As a result, students would be the center of the language learning process, and in particular, inequities and inequalities in English language education could be reduced. Accordingly, the policymakers should hold more public forums and discussions online and offline. In those places, the ELs should be encouraged to opine about the policies, rules, and regulations regarding what they are worried about, what they find challenging, and how these things influence their learning process. Those events should take place before any policies are enacted. Besides, the policymakers should be more open-minded and become good listeners to diminish power distance and collectivism in the community to enhance TESOL transformative advocacy. Also, among the influential leaders of the university, there should be one person whose specialization is language teaching and/or linguistics so that s/he can provide on-time helpful advice regarding language education.

At the meso level, the faculties or departments should encourage their staff to participate in regular professional development to enrich their knowledge and skills to work well with the ELs to contribute to equitable access to language education. The professional development events are also advised to aim at building up a stronger community of teachers who share opinions and raise voices together for better TESOL advocacy. They would be much better events with the participation of the university leaders, who should come and listen to know more about TESOL. Moreover, the faculty leaders should be the bridges to deliver the staff and students' concerns or feedback regarding policies and regulations to higher-level policymakers. Such delivery is one effective way to decrease power distance and collectivism.

At the micro level, the lecturers are recommended to always remember that they are the only direct agents who connect the students and the faculty or university leaders. Only if so can they work actively to help the students achieve better access to many aspects of the language learning process (e.g., facilities, learning resources, and networks). Therefore, it is advisable that they learn more about the advocacy activities to improve equity and equality in their students' language learning (see more in Haneda & Alexander, 2015; Linville, 2016; Linville, 2020). Also, in the context of Vietnam, the lecturers should limit the great power distance and collectivism in the traditional modes of teaching where teachers were centered and acted as models. Instead, they should value student-centeredness, encourage the students to speak up, listen to the students' concerns related to policies, and help the students as much as possible for better access and quality of the language learning process. Specifically, teachers can give students more autonomy (see more in Benson, 2011; Nguyen, 2022), create forums and platforms where the students can raise their voices up, and work collaboratively with other teachers and students in modifying teaching and learning resources suitably and acting as a bridge to deliver their concerns to the leaders.

Conclusion

Overall, the concept of advocacy and the related projects in the context of Vietnam are relatively new. The findings from the interviews with EFL lecturers and the websites represent some aspects of TESOL transformative advocacy in Vietnamese higher education in terms of equity, equality, policies, and regulations. Those aspects are associated with cultural dimensions popular in the nation's cultures, such as power distance and collectivism. According to the challenges and expectations shared by the lecturers, there are still many questions around TESOL advocacy, such as how it can be defined and how advocacy projects can be formulated and developed in the Vietnamese and other Asian contexts. The chapter is concluded by calling for further investigations into TESOL advocacy in different contexts in Vietnam and Asian countries for higher equitable access to language education.

Discussion Questions

1. How can TESOL advocacy be defined in your own context? What is consistent with the previous conceptualizations, and what is different?
2. What could you do as an advocate if your university rector consulted you in terms of policies in language learning courses?

References

Benson, P. (2011). *Teaching and researching autonomy in language learning* (2nd ed.). Pearson.
Bui, N. (2019). Learner autonomy in tertiary English classes in Vietnam. In J. Albright (Ed.), *English tertiary education in Vietnam* (pp. 158–171). Routledge.
Christison, M., & Lindahl, K. (2009). Leadership in public school environments. In M. Christison & D. E. Murray (Eds.), *Leadership in English language education: Theoretical foundations and practical skills for changing times*. Routledge.

Cochran-Smith, M. (2020). Teacher education for justice and equity: 40 years of advocacy. *Action in Teacher Education, 42*(1), 49–59. https://doi.org/10.1080/01626620.2019.1702120

Dang, T. B. D., & Ha, T. V. (2021). Factors affecting motivation of English-majored students towards learning English at a university in the Mekong Delta, Vietnam. *European Journal of English Language Teaching, 6*(6), 95–115. http://dx.doi.org/10.46827/ejel.v6i6.3952

Douglas Fir Group. (2016). A transdisciplinary framework for SLA in a multilingual world. *The Modern Language Journal, 100*(1), 19–47. https://doi.org/10.1111/modl.12301

Fry, G. W. (2009). Higher education in Vietnam. In *The Political Economy of Educational Reforms and Capacity Development in Southeast Asia* (pp. 237–261). Springer.

García, O., & Kleifgen, J. A. (2010). *Educating emergent bilinguals: Policies, programs, and practices for English language learners*. Teachers College Press.

Haneda, M., & Alexander, M. (2015). ESL teacher advocacy beyond the classroom. *Teaching and Teacher Education, 49*, 149–158. https://doi.org/10.1016/j.tate.2015.03.009

Haneda, M., & Sherman, B. (2018). ESL teachers' acting agentively through job crafting. *Journal of Language, Identity and Education, 17*(6), 402–415. https://doi.org/10.1080/15348458.2018.1498340

Harrison, J., & MacIlwain, M. J. (2019). ESOL teachers' experiences in their role as advocate: Making the case for transitive advocacy. *Tesol Journal, 11*(1), 1–18. https://doi.org/10.1002/tesj.464

Hofstede, G., & Hofstede, G. J. (2005). *Cultures and organisations: Software of the mind* (2nd ed.). McGraw-Hill.

Lam, H. T. L., & Albright, J. (2019). Vietnamese foreign language policy in higher education: A barometer to social changes. In J. Albright (Ed), *English Tertiary Education in Vietnam* (pp. 1–15). Routledge.

Lam, L. T. (2019). General English for non-majors in higher education. In J. Albright (Ed), *English Tertiary Education in Vietnam* (pp. 86–101). Routledge.

Le, D. M., Nguyen, H.T.M., & Burns, A. (2017). Language teacher proficiency and reform of English language education in Vietnam, 2008–2020. In D. Freeman & L. Le Dréan (Eds.), *Developing Classroom English Competence: Learning from the Vietnam Experience* (pp. 19–33). IDP Australia

Linville, H. A. (2015). ESOL teachers as advocates: An important role?. *TESOL Journal*, 7(1), 98–131. https://doi.org/10.1002/tesj.193

Linville, H. A. (2019). Advocacy skills for teachers: A real careful little dance. In H. A. Linville and J. Whiting (Eds.), *Advocacy in Language Teaching and Learning* (p. 15). Routledge.

Linville, H. A. (2020). A closer look at ESOL teacher advocacy: What we do and why. *TESOL Journal*, 11(3), e00508. https://doi.org/10.1002/tesj.508

Linville, H., & Whiting, J. (2019). Social justice through TESOL advocacy. *TESOL Journal*, 11(4), e553. https://doi.org/10.1002/tesj.553

Mai Ngoc, K. & Iwashita, N. (2012). A comparison of learners' and teachers' attitudes toward communicative language teaching at two universities in Vietnam. *University of Sydney Papers in TESOL*, 7, 25-49.

Nguyen, H. T. M., & Bui, T. (2016). Teachers' agency and the enactment of educational reform in Vietnam. *Current Issues in Language Planning*, 17(1), 88–105. https://doi.org/10.1080/14664208.2016.1125664

Nguyen, H. T., Fehring, H., & Warren, W. (2015). EFL teaching and learning at a Vietnamese university: What do teachers say?. *English Language Teaching*, 8(1), 31–43. https://doi.org/10.5539/elt.v8n1p31

Nguyen, M. P., Terlouw, C., & Pilot, A. (2006). Culturally appropriate pedagogy: The case of group learning in a Confucian heritage culture context. *Intercultural Education*, 17(1), 1–19. doi: 10.1080/14675980500502172

Nguyen, S. V. (2022). Learner autonomy in English language learning and factors influencing learner autonomy in the context of Vietnam: Non-English-major students' perceptions (Ph.D. thesis, University of Szeged), Szegedi Tudományegyetem Repository of Dissertations. https://doktori.bibl.u-szeged.hu/id/eprint/11238

Nguyen, S. V., & Habók, A. (2020). Non-English-major students' perceptions of learner autonomy and factors influencing learner autonomy in Vietnam. *Relay Journal*, 3(1), 122–131. https://kuis.kandagaigo.ac.jp/relayjournal/issues/jan20/nguyen_habok/

Norman, L., & Eslami, Z. (2022). English learner teacher advocates: A systematic literature review. *TESL-EJ*, 25(4), 1–28. https://tesl-ej.org/wordpress/issues/volume25/ej100/ej100a8/#back

Staehr-Fenner, D. (2014). *Advocating for English learners: A guide for educators*. Corwin.

Tran, J. (2012). Vietnamese higher education and the issue of enhancing graduate employability. *Journal of Teaching and Learning for Graduate Employability, 3*, 2–16.

Tran, L. T., & Do, T. T. Q. (2022). Higher education in Vietnam. In *International Handbook on Education in Southeast Asia* (pp. 1–25). Springer.

Trinh, H., & Mai, L. (2019). Current challenges in the teaching of tertiary English in Vietnam. In J. Albright (Ed.), *English Tertiary Education in Vietnam* (pp. 40–53). Routledge.

Truong, T. D., Hallinger, P., & Sanga, K. (2017). Confucian values and school leadership in Vietnam: Exploring the influence of culture on principal decision making. *Educational Management Administration & Leadership, 45*(1), 77–100. https://doi.org/10.1177/1741143215607877

Chapter 7
Using English Language Teaching as a Platform for Developing Self-Advocacy: English Is Our Future

Briana Rogers

Introduction

> *Lone Buffalo's passion to help young people is an inspiration for me to achieve more every day. It took a girl from the countryside and made her want to see the world and beyond.*
>
> —*Miss Bee Yangsaoye*

Have you ever been part of something greater? Over the last 12 years, I have worked on governmental English teaching reform programs in Malaysia, Tunisia, Uzbekistan, and Tajikistan. The goal was to change the face of how English was being taught across an entire country. It was a wave crashing down on teachers and schools, hoping for change. Unfortunately, waves often do not last long. They are swallowed back up in the ocean of educational reform. The initial approach was to write about one of these large-scale programs, but I wanted to write about a program that, rather than causing a huge wave, is creating ripples that expand and last for a long time. It is one small educational center in a rural area of Laos. Lone Buffalo is not trying to change the country. It is just trying to improve students' lives and provide opportunities. I was fortunate to be someone that helped create some of the ripples.

Overview

To understand the advocacy of an organization or person, you need to understand not only the message but also the culture and context (Mapes, 2019).

Therefore, I believe it is important to provide a background and context for the advocacy that was taking place in Lone Buffalo.

About Laos

Laos, officially the Lao People's Democratic Republic, borders Myanmar, China, Vietnam, Cambodia, and Thailand. It has a sizable ethnic population with 50 main ethnic groups and 200 sub-ethnic groups, with Lao being the predominant ethnic group and language in the country. (Open Development Laos, 2022). Additionally, Lao is the only official language accepted in the country and the only language of instruction in schools.

Education is compulsory for nine years. "While a Lao child goes to school for 10.8 years on average, she only receives the equivalent of 6.4 years of learning" (The World Bank in Lao People's Democratic Republic, 2022). All instruction in schools must be in Lao, and in this ethnically diverse country, many students enter school without knowing the language of instruction. Subsistence agriculture still accounts for more than half of the GDP. As of 2010, 10% of the population lived on less than $2 a day. In 2020, Laos was ranked 139th on the Human Development Index, putting it in the medium development range and making it one of the fastest-growing economies in the region (Open Development Laos, 2022). In 2019, the U.N. special rapporteur stated, "Despite important progress in reducing poverty, the government's economic growth strategies have too often destroyed livelihoods, entrenched vulnerability, and actually made some people poorer by taking away their access to land, livelihoods, and resources" (U.N. expert: Lao PDR's economic strategy entrenches poverty, 2022).

About Phonsavan

Phonsavan, or Xieng Khouang, is in the central highlands of Laos. It has a population of 70,000, with the largest ethnic group being the Hmong. It has become a popular tourist destination for two very different reasons. Firstly, it is home to the mysterious 2,000-year-old "Plains of Jars," which became a UNESCO world heritage site in 2019. These ancient burial jars are located throughout the province. Phonsavan is the hub for getting to the main archeological sites. Another unlikely tourist attraction is the remnants of the Vietnam war. The Mine Advisory Group (MAG) and UXO Lao are based in the town. They perform clearance work and mine risk education in schools and communities.

Figure 7.1 Lone Buffalo Students. Photo courtesy of Lone Buffalo Organization

About Lone Buffalo

The Lone Buffalo Organization is a grassroots organization named after a Lao man named Manophet, nicknamed, "Lone Buffalo." Manophet was self-taught in English and worked as a tour guide. Manophet decided he could help children, particularly those from the Hmong community, learn English and provide themselves with a brighter future. He started his school out of his house, charging only what a student could afford. Manophet would often bring tour groups he worked with to the school so that students would get the chance to practice their English. Tragically, Manophet died in 2012, and in his memory, Mark Steadman, a tour guide, and Nick Williamson, an English teacher, decided to build an English center and named it Lone Buffalo. Mark is still

Using English Language Teaching as a Platform 119

with the organization and is the school's chief officer. He oversees the logistics, finances, and fundraising in addition to developing a dynamic local team to take responsibility for teaching, administration, and youth development.

Lone Buffalo's mission has expanded to include not only English instruction but also the development of life skills that students will need for admission into tertiary schools and to lead successful careers. English provides the foundation from which they have been able to build other necessary programming, such as:

1. English Tuition: This is free English classes for students from 13-17.
2. Power Her Up: This is a female development program focusing on women's health and hygiene as well as life and leadership skills.
3. Develop Together: This is practical life skills workshops to help students become stronger contenders for tertiary education.
4. Sport and Fitness: This provides soccer and general health training for all students.
5. Creative Media: This is one of the first offshoots from English. Students learn about filmmaking to provide them with a stronger voice.
6. From Bombs to Beans: This is a student-run business. Students learn about business management and marketing by running a "company" that sells coffee to stores and retailers throughout Lao and even now globally. All the earnings go back into the company and the school.
7. Youth Aware: This is a safeguarding program for students to develop knowledge on online safety.

Lone Buffalo officially opened in 2011. It is in a rented three-room building where they hold classes and activities and that serves as a gathering spot for the students. It is the home and haven for 250 students between the ages of 11 and 18. A team of local managers and teachers runs Lone Buffalo. Its funding comes from private donations, embassy grants, and individual class sponsorships.

Lone Buffalo frequently brings in experts to assist with designing and planning the programs they want to run. I started consulting at Lone Buffalo while participating in the English Language Fellow Program. I was tasked with identifying non-profit, non-governmental English language programs in the country. In my research, I heard about a small school, Lone Buffalo, located in the northeastern part of Laos, providing free English classes to the region's poor and introducing a more inclusive environment that includes all ethnicities. I headed out to Phonsavan, in Xieng Khouang province, Laos, to learn more about the school and its activities. I was immediately taken in by the fantastic work at the school. Lone Buffalo was not just an English school, it was a place to build hopes and dreams and, as their logo suggests, to create futures.

Over the next two years, I tried to make it to the school as often as possible to provide teacher training for the Lao teachers they employed and workshops for students on presentation skills and intercultural communication. I also worked with the center school on choosing textbooks, creating connections with other organizations, and its alumni program. Each time I was there, it became more apparent what an amazing impact it had on its students and the community. I always felt welcome and quickly became like part of the Lone Buffalo family. However, this is not my story; this is the center school's, and it is a privilege to be a small part of it.

About Advocacy

In my mind, advocacy is supporting a person or cause. Advocacy does not have to be loud and showy. It can be the slow and steady helping of a person or a cause to build a solid foundation to grow from. As an advocate, you must be willing to listen as well as act. A true advocate does not take on "the cry" for that person but instead helps them build confidence to express themselves. It is giving a person the right to protect and promote their rights. To reach for goals that might go against what others think is right or appropriate. At the local level, advocacy is practiced by those who undertake a wide range of actions, from counseling or encouraging students to study languages to organizing college or school-wide programs (Chapelle & Ehlers-Zavala, 2013).

This approach to advocacy can be seen throughout the programs of Lone Buffalo. The center starts by providing free English language classes. Students sign up for English classes but end up getting much more, because English is the platform on which programs are built on. They are encouraged to take public speaking workshops. These workshops help students build confidence in themselves so that they then take on the main roles of presenters. Students at Lone Buffalo have presented in the capital of Vientiane on safeguarding and filmmaking. Additionally, the filmmaking has given the students another outlet to express themselves and share messages about the center, their lives, and their concerns. They have created videos about many of the lessons they learn and have shared them on various social media platforms. Their films have been showcased internationally and are usually in English and Lao.

Using English Language Teaching as a Platform

What struck me about Lone Buffalo was that it uses its success of providing free English classes as a platform to promote advocacy. It uses this base to address the needs of the whole student. The idea of focusing on the whole student made me a stronger advocate for the center and its students. As a supporter for Lone Buffalo and its students, I brought the United States regional English language officer to the center to share my enthusiasm for its work. As a result, the United States Embassy in Laos sponsored two of the English classes. Whenever the opportunity opened, I expounded on its fantastic work. Lone Buffalo is about giving strength and support to the individual. It understands that sustainable change in ethnic and gender rights must come from the people and not an imposition by outside entities. Lone Buffalo gives its students the confidence, skills, and knowledge they need to make themselves not just heard but also listened to! The students become advocates for themselves and their community. They have agency!

Neither Mark Steadman nor Chantal Vinthasai (student development manager) saw themselves as advocates or had a strong idea about advocacy. They were doing what they saw as right and needed to give the region's youth a chance at a better life. As an advocate, you are trying to provide information and bring support. You can give direction, but it is up to the person to decide what to do with the information and what approach to take (C. Vinthasai, personal communication, 2022). Mr. Steadman (personal communication, 2022) said, "We believe that all young people should have the right to education and the equal opportunity to develop themselves, irrespective of where they live in the world or their socioeconomic status."

When researching advocacy in Laos, it appears that the government is open to supporting its people. There are many international and domestic organizations doing advocacy work in Lao, ranging from autism awareness to unexploded ordnance (UXO) awareness. That said, according to the U.S. Embassy's 2019 Human Rights Report,

> Nongovernmental organizations (NGOs) generally exercised self-censorship, particularly after the 2012 disappearance of an internationally respected civil society advocate. NGOs said they also tried to avoid saying anything that might further delay government approval of a Memorandum of Understanding (MOU) needed to carry out their work. NGOs reported that citizens are taught at an early age not to criticize the government. (n.p.)

Working with the government at various levels is also one of the most difficult challenges of advocacy work in Laos. It is important to note here that when writing about government, we refer to local, regional, and national governments. To receive a Memorandum of Understanding, you must work with all three levels, all with different restrictions, rules, and desires. As mentioned above, going through governmental hurdles can prove challenging. Both Mr. Steadman and Ms. Vinthasai (personal communications, 2022) mentioned issues getting the government to understand the importance of what Lone Buffalo is doing and how it contributes to the region and country. The government would like things to remain as they are and to maintain the status quo. They are not very open to change. As a result, you must be cautious about how you phrase things so that they see you as staying within the lines they feel secure with. Mr. Steadman explained that while it is difficult to obtain the necessary approvals to run the school, after they are granted, there is very little governmental oversight, which allows them to mold projects to the needs of the students once they are up and running. For accountability, an effective advocate is a person that is versed in current research, especially on the local, state, national, and international issues affecting language education, policy, and practice (Chapelle & Ehlers-Zavala, 2013). While this statement makes sense in theory, Mr. Steadman stated that if he had known of the pitfalls in starting the center, he might never have moved forward. He was unaware of many of the constraints and hurdles that lay ahead.

When asked about the biggest constraint to their work, Mr. Steadman (personal communication, 2022) stated, "Financial is our biggest constraint. Finding people to fund what we do Full Stop." He went on to mention that he would like to be able to pay the teachers full-time wages so they could focus more on Lone Buffalo. Promoting one of them to full-time education manager would allow it to expand outside the town it is currently operating in and provide teacher training to teachers and English education throughout the province. Currently, Lone Buffalo relies on funding from private and corporate donors as well as grants from embassies.

Ms. Vinthasai discussed the challenge of working with parents: "Most of our students are minorities. Parents are not open-minded to what is happening, so we have meetings and engage with them. It takes time to change their minds." She continues, "Hmong students say because my brother is the asset, if I am the daughter, the son is given an opportunity. I will be an asset to my husband's family; therefore, my family won't invest in me" (personal communication, 2022). In rural areas, many families focus on current needs rather than long-term goals. Lone Buffalo has always done outreach in the town and with families to build awareness of the benefits of tertiary education. Families see alumni returning and being successful largely due to their child's experience at Lone Buffalo. This approach has led to an 85% rate of students completing the program and moving into tertiary education (Lone Buffalo, 2022).

By facing these challenges, Ms. Vinthasai commented that she has also developed herself. She has learned to advocate for herself! "I have become proactive, not reactive. I dare to make decisions! My voice is heard now."

What Are Lone Buffalo's Goals?

The overall goal of Lone Buffalo is to help the local youth develop the life skills needed to become successful, educated adults. "We are providing skills, both in the classroom and life skills, to ensure that as many of our young people can get a tertiary education as possible. We believe tertiary education is the way to change communities and societies" (M. Steadman, personal communication, 2022).

The standard of education in villages and towns is below that of the capital. There is a shortage of teachers and materials. When students receive an education, there is often a "brain-drain" to the city, where graduates feel they can get a higher salary and more support for their families. "Lone Buffalo's ethos of helping each other means former students play an important role in preparing current students for the future. Alumni return regularly from studies and work around the country to host senior student presentations, providing practical advice on final exams, studying at university, and life in the capital" (Lone Buffalo, 2022). "Young people are getting jobs in their community. They might go to university and get qualifications, but coming back to Xieng Khouang and using those skills to develop their province makes them feel good" (M. Steadman, personal communication, 2022).

While Lone Buffalo's priority is to provide better, free education for rural youth, it is constantly building and expanding on what it means to educate. During the time I was volunteering with the center, it implemented four new programs to assist its students. The center directors are always thinking of ways to expand and provide more opportunities for their students and improve the community. "Through a range of programs developing English proficiency, as well as creative and practical skills, we nurture leadership to increase confidence, knowledge, and ambition among students. Students complete high school as motivated, rounded individuals with a clear understanding of opportunities ahead of them—and the confidence to take them" (Lone Buffalo, 2022).

The expanding programming in the center shows that it is working toward whole-child development. "Students who walk out the door of Lone Buffalo feel confident in themselves. They are empowered. They don't feel lower than others" (C. Vinthasai, personal communication, 2022).

Advocacy Projects

Lone Buffalo Projects

Lone Buffalo is no longer an English center. It has developed into a youth center, developing self-confidence, leadership, and business skills in its students. Even more impressive is the connectedness among all the programs and projects it does. It is the truest definition of community and family. While at the school, it was clear that many of the programs started organically. The leadership staff is excellent at listening to the students' needs and dreams and, from there, developing programs that meet those needs and assist students in reaching their dreams. We will focus on the English language classes, as they were the platform for the school, and the other programs Lone Buffalo currently provides.

English Is Our Future

According to Low & Ao (2018), Laos is notable for its extensive diversity.

> Southeast Asia is a region characterized by historical, political, ethnic, cultural, and linguistic diversity, where English serves as a means for intra- and international communication. In other words, English does not only serve the purpose of communicating with people outside Southeast Asia but is also being used as a lingua franca among different ethnic groups within the region. (p. 131)

Laos relies heavily on outside support from other countries. In the Xieng Khouang province, where Lone Buffalo is located, there is now a UNESCO world heritage site and numerous international non-governmental organizations (INGO) running programs. These bring jobs into the area, and speaking English is a definite advantage.

Free English classes are the foundation of the Lone Buffalo project. "English opens doors, and it is still the common language in Asia. If you have a Burmese person talking to a Thai person, they will use English"

(Mr. Steadman, personal communication, 2022). The need for English shows in the number of students wanting to attend English classes at Lone Buffalo. Currently, there are 275 students attending classes and a waiting list of over 200 students hoping to get into the classes, mainly at the beginner level. They are required to attend three two-hour-long classes every week. The curriculum is based on the Common European Framework. Students come from a variety of backgrounds and ethnic groups. The student body is currently 54% female. "Lone Buffalo is important to a student who does not have money to pay for the English class. It's like LB [Lone Buffalo]; it's the best center that gives the opportunity to a student who doesn't have enough money to pay for the term" (anonymous, personal communication, 2022).

This dedication to providing free and high-quality English language classes drew me to Lone Buffalo in the first place. While working on a different project in Laos, I had the opportunity to visit many of the rural schools to do teacher training and learn about the Laos educational school system. One of the most significant problems in schools in rural areas is that the teachers themselves do not know English. In many schools I visited, the teachers were Russian teachers who were told they had to teach English even without knowing the language. English teachers at one school could not perform at an A1 level and could not answer basic questions, say the alphabet, or count. English is taught in public schools but is limited to two to three hours a week. Since English starts in the third grade, one may assume that students would acquire some proficiency, but students pass to the next level regardless of their proficiency level. Therefore, once they reach high school age, they often use textbooks that are above their level of English. Classes are very teacher centered, with teachers often writing on the chalkboard and students copying the text into their copybooks. Communicative skills are usually overlooked, usually due to the lack of the teachers' own ability to speak English. In addition, schools often lack basic materials like textbooks for students, pens, or paper. Souriyavongsa et al. (2013) found similar patterns in their research that explored why Laos students were weak in English. They said,

> First, most students stated that the English teachers are not well-trained; for instance, they use Lao language when teaching, so they cannot perform well to attract the interest of the student. Secondly, students lack an English foundation background. Third, students lack confidence to use English because they are afraid of making mistakes and feeling shy. Fourth, the curriculum is inappropriate for helping students to improve their English proficiency. (p. 180)

For these reasons, particularly shyness, fear of making mistakes, and inappropriate curriculum, during my two and a half years working with Lone Buffalo, I focused on three main projects: teacher training, public speaking, and intercultural communication.

Teacher Training

One of the first tasks I undertook while at Lone Buffalo was the professional development of the English teachers. The teachers varied in their experience levels, ranging from some who had never taught to those who worked as teachers at the nearby teacher training college. Lone Buffalo wanted to improve the quality of teaching and ensure teachers were using more communicative, student-centered approaches in the classrooms. Additionally, teachers were called on to use a holistic approach to language teaching due to the students' context of where they lived, economic situations, opportunities available, and cultural influences. Not all these concepts for teaching are the norm in Laos. Unfortunately, this means that not only are teachers uncomfortable facilitating student-centered classes but that students themselves need to adapt to a new role in the classroom. In Laotian culture, the teacher is often viewed as the knowledge provider, and mistakes are considered a weakness. According to Tan (2005, cited in Syarifuddin, 2017, p. 2), Asian students regard their teachers as the repositories of knowledge while the students are the recipients. In addition, they also tend to learn from their teachers without asking questions or challenging them.

Another hurdle faced when trying to introduce these Western-oriented methods into the classroom is that with a more holistic approach, teachers do not play the usual traditional role. They are expected to engage with their students at a much more personal level (Arnold, 1999 cited in Mousavi, 2007).

The communicative approach to language teaching focuses on interactions, whereas traditional language teaching in Laos concentrates on students' grammar competency. When working with the Lone Buffalo teachers, it was necessary to stress that while English grammar is important, the focus of their classes should be more on communicative skills, which the students would find more beneficial for their futures. Using a student-centered communicative teaching approach provides opportunities to develop additional skills valued in academia and business. Laos relies heavily on the NGO sector, and many students from Lone Buffalo have gone on to work for various NGO organizations. In fact, from my experience in Southeast Asia and working in

Using English Language Teaching as a Platform 127

various INGOs, independent thinking and being able to voice your opinions were often more important than the actual level of English proficiency.

Even though Lone Buffalo teachers were eager to incorporate new methodologies, they often reverted to their first language in their teaching. This could be due to their lack of confidence in their language abilities. Horwitz (1996) stated that teachers who suffer higher levels of foreign language anxiety tend not to use the target language in the classroom. They often did not feel confident enough in their own English to clarify and explain complex concepts in English. It was easier and safer to use L1. Horwitz (1996) also mentions that a non-native teacher's lack of confidence can inhibit a teacher's ability to effectively present the target language, interact with students, and serve as a positive role model as a language learner. Therefore, this lack of confidence could often leak into other areas of learning and affect the whole program. It could also translate into the activities and methods teachers use. Teachers who are not confident in their English language skills are less likely to utilize new, more communicative approaches (Horwitz, 1996). It was then necessary to address ways to build confidence in teachers' beliefs about their language abilities. At the center, I conducted several training sessions and attended classes to make sure I had a better understanding of the teaching context, students, learning environment, and current teaching strategies. Training sessions were kept small and personal so that teachers felt comfortable working on their skills. The sessions had many different focuses; we worked on using different interaction patterns in the classroom, including mingles, pair, and group work, and how to integrate these within the textbook they felt comfortable using. Since teachers designed lessons based on the textbook or followed it to the letter, we spent time on looking at ways to expand and adapt the book to make it more student centered and communicative. During the workshops a variety of games and activities were utilized and then discussed so teachers could analyze how to make them work within their teaching context.

Public Speaking and Intercultural Communication

While working with teachers was amazing, working directly with the students was even more rewarding. Mr. Steadman approached me to start teaching public speaking to the students so they could have the confidence and skills to advocate for themselves. Teaching public speaking in English provides opportunities for students to practice all four skills; they learn not just to speak but how to be influential speakers and share their message. Additionally, students practice reading and writing when they prepare a presentation and listen when doing peer observations (Iberri-Shea, 2009). Furthermore, I created an intercultural communication workshop, because given the closely intertwined nature of culture and language, Baker (2012) claims that it is difficult to teach language without an acknowledgement of the cultural context in which it is used. Since the students of Lone Buffalo would most likely be working with people from different cultures, it is necessary for them to have at least a small understanding that communication is different across cultures. I worked with Ms. Vinthasai so that she could continue the training after I left, and some of the first students I worked with are now assisting in presenting these workshops.

My goal was to help students to be able to self-advocate for themselves and to have the confidence to give agency to other students. "Agency refers to a person's ability to feel as though they can take action in the world that is meaningful. They see themselves as having the understanding, skills, and resources to make a positive difference" (Fassett & Nainby, 2021, p. 17). Facilitating the student's growth in their public speaking and intercultural skills was a way to give them agency. Public speaking has a long historical connection to advocacy. The ancient Athenian Greeks stressed the need for all citizens to become educated in rhetoric to be part of civil society (Mapes, 2019). When we advocate, we balance individual interests with those of a larger community or group (Mapes, 2019). Therefore, providing training on public speaking and cultural awareness to the students allowed them to build their confidence to advocate for themselves and the center. Many of the students and alumni now have the skills to advocate for the center when foreign nationals and embassies visit. They can express the importance the center plays in their lives, which ties back into my personal definition of advocacy: supporting people so that they have a voice to speak for themselves. It is giving them agency over their lives. Since the workshops were developed, Lone Buffalo students have participated in governmental study abroad programs, gone to medical school, won international filming competitions, started working at international non-profit organizations, and even become Miss Universe Laos!

Other Projects at Lone Buffalo

One of the reasons I am so passionate about my time at Lone Buffalo is their approach to English teaching. It is not about academia or passing exams. It is about creating opportunities. They used English as a building block, which enabled Lone Buffalo to expand its programs with a focus on the whole student. Without English at the core, the center would have had a harder time promoting other programs. Therefore, English remains the heart of the center and is used in all the other projects as well. Presentations for all the life skills courses are in English and in Laos, and most of the videos they produce include English subtitles. This strong foundation has led to the expansion of student engagement and growth in many areas.

Female Empowerment: Power Her Up

Laos has made many advances in women's rights, especially in the capital city. Women can be seen in leadership roles in business, educational institutes, and government. The national constitution advocates equal rights for women. However, in practice the idea of women's empowerment is still new, especially in rural areas. "In some regions, traditional attitudes about gender roles kept women and girls in subordinate positions and prevented them from equally accessing education, employment, and business opportunities. The law also prohibits discrimination in marriage and inheritance, although varying degrees of cultural-based discrimination against women persisted, with greater discrimination practiced by some ethnic minority groups in remote areas" (United States Embassy-Lao, 2019).

Having English as a foundation at the school is what led it to be able to support its students in so many more ways. Ms. Vinthasai recalls how the Power Her Up program started: "They [female students] start to put trust in me and talk to me about troubles they are facing at home with family and challenges they face building a living . . . Then this one student, she is the only daughter at home. She said, 'Sister, I don't know what happened to me. I was bleeding. There was blood coming out. I don't know what happened. I don't dare talk to my mom. What should I do?'" Ms. Vinthasai then realized there were other girls at the school that needed assistance and brought the matter up with Mr. Steadman. Together they worked toward creating a female development program. The program covers health and hygiene, financial literacy, IT literacy, leadership, and more! Additionally, they frequently held parent sessions, which provided parents the opportunity to develop their own beliefs on the role of women in their society. The students involved in this program are now leads in most of the other programs.

In southeast Asia and around the world, there has been a push for programs that concentrate on empowering women. There is a lot more on this, but sometimes supporting and educating girls is not enough. Lone Buffalo is a prime example of this. Power Her Up is a huge success, with most of the leadership programs being filled by the girls in the school, yet sometimes a girl slips back into more traditional ideas or beliefs because of family or because she is getting pressured by boys. I spent a lot of time discussing this with Mr. Steadman, particularly after one incident. He was very disappointed when one girl left to get married. She had been in Power Her Up. We talked about how she felt pressured by the boyfriend and that the boys need training on how to behave and change their own perceptions about how to treat women. This discussion, along with the request from male students to get some of the training the girls were getting, led to the creation of the Develop Together project. Lone Buffalo reached out to external partners, such as Laos Women's Union and BCEL International bank, to help with providing professional skills training for all students (Lone Buffalo, 2022).

Soccer and Fitness

Soccer is an integral part of Lone Buffalo. "Developing self-confidence, team building, and leadership skills are central to our project mission. Sport is a great medium for developing these skills as well as promoting friendship and understanding between different ethnicities" (Lone Buffalo, 2022). Soccer builds an even stronger community and provides work on both the students' physical and mental aptitude.

Safeguarding: Youth Aware

This program started as online safety training and now covers physical dangers. The Youth Aware project arose from shorter student workshops. The center now not only trains students on safeguarding but on becoming trainers themselves. Lone Buffalo has developed a contextual program that it has delivered both within the organization as well as to other youth organizations.

Creative Media

Lone Buffalo encourages its students to express themselves creatively and document their success. The students' short films have been featured in the Lao National Film Festival. They have also won awards at international student film festivals in South Korea and Taiwan! They also support the other programs by creating promotional materials and documenting the successes and achievements of the Lone Buffalo students. This program works closely with My Library, another free English center located in Luang Prabang, Laos, where the yearly Laos Film Festival is held. Students' work can be seen on Lone Buffalos Vimeo site: https://vimeo.com/channels/560896/155265472.

From Bombs to Beans

Bombs to Beans is a business program that allows students to develop their business prowess. The coffee cooperative is a fully functioning business with a business model and an active working environment. "Students manage recruitment, production, distribution, sales, and marketing as well as collecting sales revenue and preparing monthly accounts" (Lone Buffalo, 2022). Since most of the cafes and stores they sell to cater to expats, the need for English and presentation skills to promote the company is important. The program uses the funds it generates to help support other programs within Lone Buffalo.

Reflections and Future Directions

With all these programs, Lone Buffalo has worked with a variety of organizations to help assist with the training. It has had to overcome numerous funding issues and cut through the Lao government bureaucracy.

Lone Buffalo continues to strive to open the doors of future success to its students. It hopes to extend its reach within the community by offering teacher training. Additionally, in the next few years it hopes to expand its physical location to support more students. Mr. Steadman has a dream to open "Baby Buffalos" in even more rural areas. Their alumni support has widened, and alumni now can share the work they have been doing in Phonsavan with other youth organizations throughout Laos. It is amazing to see those that we once advocated for developing a sense of agency and becoming advocates for themselves and others!

Personally, even though I am no longer in the country, I still work with Lone Buffalo when possible. I have been working with Ms. Vinthasai on updating the intercultural communication workshop and developing workshops on soft skills and financial literacy. It has been an honor and privilege to be one of the small ripples within the organization.

To see how Lone Buffalo students are doing and their projects, visit https://www.lonebuffalo.org/.

Discussion Questions

1. There is some debate on communicative language teaching and culture. How would you propose to teach communicatively but also remain culturally aware?
2. This chapter focuses on giving a student agency. How can English language teaching allow for more student agency?
3. I came to this program as a foreigner and introduced Western concepts of teaching and communication. What are the pros and cons of having Western approaches employed in a school that has all local teachers? How can you assist them to advocate for themselves using their own voices?
4. This chapter discusses English as a foundation on which other programs can be developed. How does this idea differ from other chapters of the book?

References

Baker, W. (2012). From cultural awareness to intercultural awareness: Culture in ELT. *ELT Journal, 66*(1), 62–70.

Chapelle, C., & Ehlers-Zavala, F. (2013). Advocacy in language teaching. *The Encyclopedia of Applied Linguistics* (pp. 29–31). Wiley-Blackwell.

Fassett, D. L., & Nainby, K. (2021). *Empowering Public Speaking.* Cognella, Incorporated.

Horwitz, E. K. (1996). Even teachers get the blues: Recognizing and alleviating language teachers' feelings of foreign language anxiety. *Foreign Language Annals, 29*(3), 365–372.

Iberri-Shea, G. (2009) Using public speaking tasks in English language teaching. *English Teaching Forum, 47*(1), 18–36.

Low, E. L., & Ao, R. (2018). The spread of English in ASEAN: Policies and issues. *RELC Journal, 49*(2), 131–148.

Lone Buffalo. (2022). Retrieved from https://www.lonebuffalo.org

Mapes, M. (2019). *Speak out, Call in: Public Speaking as Advocacy.* University of Kansas Libraries.

Mousavi, E. S. (2007). Exploring "teacher stress" in non-native and native teachers of EFL. *English Language Teacher Education and Development, 10,* 33–41.

Open Development Laos. (2022, September 28). Sharing information about Laos and its development with the world. https://laos.opendevelopmentmekong.net/

Souriyavongsa, T., Rany, S., Abidin, M. J. Z., & Mei, L. L. (2013). Factors cause students low English language learning: A case study in the National University of Laos. *International Journal of English Language Education*, 1(1), 179–192.

Syarifuddin. (2017). Is communicative language reaching (CLT) appropriate to the Indonesian context. *Al-Makrifat: Journal Kajian Islam*, 2(1), 60–67. Retrieved from http://ejournal.koertais4.or.id/tapalkuda/index.php/makrifat/article/view/3024

The World Bank in Lao People's Democratic Republic (PDR). (2022). Retrieved from https://www.worldbank.org/en/country/lao/overview

UN expert: Lao PDR's economic strategy entrenches poverty. (2022). Retrieved July 23, 2022 from https://www.ohchr.org/en/press-releases/2019/03/un-expert-lao-pdrs-economic-strategy-entrenches-poverty

United States Embassy-Lao. (2019). *LAOS 2019 human rights report*. Retrieved from https://la.usembassy.gov/wp-content/uploads/sites/85/LAOS-2019-HUMAN-RIGHTS-REPORT.pdf

Chapter 8
Supporting Young Learners' English in Public Schools in Türkiye: Spoken Cafes Project

Sumru Akcan

Overview

English is the most common foreign language taught in Türkiye. If we consider the role of English as a lingua franca, the students should learn English as competently as possible, starting in the early years of schooling. This carries importance when they graduate and start their careers. This will be needed to advance in their careers. Since English is not used outside of the school context in Türkiye, it is highly important to create learning settings where students practice English as communicatively as possible. This project will increase the amount of exposure to learning English and also affect students' motivation to learn English positively. They will also develop a positive attitude toward learning English, which will help them practice English more often in order to develop their language competence over the schooling years.

The Spoken Cafes (Ders arası Dil Molası) project has been carried out jointly for a year by the Sarıyer District Directorate of National Education and the Foreign Language Education Department of Boğaziçi University, Istanbul, Türkiye. The main goal of the project is to support the English language proficiency of third- through fifth-grade students in seven public schools in Istanbul. The project was designed based on the need to improve primary students' spoken language. English language instruction in Türkiye's public schools is rather limited, so establishing learning environments to improve students' language skills was supported by the Spoken Cafes project. The students practiced English by using experiential, authentic tasks and hands-on activities, such as storytelling, games, and songs. We also aimed to help students increase their motivation toward learning English and their self-confidence in speaking it.

The English support program was designed by the university's Foreign Language Education Department based on the syllabi recommended by the Ministry of Education. Our senior-year teacher candidates taught regular supplementary English classes for two semesters to primary school students in classrooms specially designed and decorated for the project.

As the full-time faculty of my department, I served as the coordinator of the practicum program and one of the supervisors of our teacher education program; therefore, I was directly involved with the implementation of the project. In this chapter, I would like to share my experience and reflect on the process, implementation, and impact of this project from my point of view as the coordinator and one of the supervisors of the practicum program.

Advocacy: My Definition

My personal definition of advocacy is noticing the English learners' limited opportunities to learn English, which is the lingua franca, and taking action to improve and increase their learning experiences in order to help them advance in life. We care for our students, and offering them more hours of English instruction will bring them benefits in their process of learning English. I believe that advocacy brings the collaboration of the administrators, teachers, and parents. They need to work together voluntarily in order to support the initiative to create opportunities for the students. The schools and the parents believe that their children will improve their English language skills, and the teacher candidates know that having more opportunities to teach English will deepen their experience before starting their careers. As Linville and Whiting (2020) state, advocacy is a powerful tool to support educational, social, economic, and political equality within the field of TESOL.

I see advocacy efforts as identifying the challenges and constraints of learning English and offering opportunities for language learning to overcome these challenges. For this aim, the volunteer-based collaboration of the school (principal, teachers), university (university supervisors, teacher candidates), and communities (families) should be established in order to support students' English language learning process, because this widens the horizon of the students by teaching them English, which is the most commonly spoken language around the world.

With the collaboration of the Sarıyer District Directorate of National Education, the Department of Foreign Language Education of Boğaziçi

University started this advocacy project. Seven public schools in the District of Sarıyer and the teacher candidates at the Department of Foreign Language Education of Boğaziçi University were involved in the project. The school administration and the parents supported the project by ensuring the children would be in attendance during the scheduled hours. The teacher candidates also arranged their course schedules so that they could teach when they did not have their own classes at the university.

It was the voluntary effort of the District Directorate of Education, Boğaziçi University, public schools, parents, student teachers, and university supervisors that made this project come true and that positively continues to influence the language learning process of the students.

The Goals and Need for the Project

Learning English at a young age is essential for a child's early language development and brings many benefits to a child. Learning a foreign language at an early age has a high impact on problem solving, critical thinking, memory, concentration, and academic achievement (Butler, 2020; Cameron, 2001). Long (1983) states that participation in task-based learning environments in which communication is necessary facilitates the language learning process. In other words, language proficiency is promoted by interaction and communication in authentic learning contexts.

With the aim of enhancing students' opportunities to get exposed to English at public schools in which English language instruction is limited, the Sarıyer District Directorate of National Education, the Department of Foreign Language Education of Boğaziçi University, and seven public elementary schools collaborated and worked so this project could come true.

Senior-year teacher candidates at the Department of Foreign Language Education of Boğaziçi University took part in this project and taught English to students in these public elementary schools. Before asking for teacher candidates, we presented the project to the teacher candidates and explained how the project would proceed. They were informed about their responsibilities and how they would work together as a team with the schools. While designing the materials for the project, we followed the curriculum of the national Ministry of Education and generated the materials based on the level of the students with the aim of increasing their language proficiency. Since the hours of English instruction are limited in public schools (three hours per week), we aimed to increase the students' exposure to English and improve their language skills with the support of this project. We held a series of meetings with the schools and talked about the schedule and the design of the lessons. The learning materials and activities were prepared in line with the curriculum of the Ministry of Education. The focus of the activities was primarily on promoting the listening and speaking skills of students and engaging them with the learning experiences so they would use English in a more interactive and enjoyable way.

The project also had unintended, but positive, outcomes for the teacher candidates. This project provided additional teaching/learning opportunities for our teacher candidates; they improved their teaching skills and contributed to the community they live in. The teacher candidates were already doing their practicum at their assigned schools in our program, yet they had an additional teaching experience for their professional growth by participating in this project. The teacher candidates had already taken a course on teaching young learners; they had a solid theoretical and pedagogical background in teaching English to young learners. They knew that the aim of this project was to improve the students' speaking skills by exposing them to experiential learning activities where they could use language more meaningfully. English is the most commonly taught foreign language in Türkiye, yet the hours of classroom instruction are limited in public schools to improve students' English language proficiency. This project aimed to increase the exposure to the use of English more interactively.

The Freedoms and Constraints for Advocacy

In terms of the freedom of advocacy, designing the classroom environment and preparing the learning materials were the decisions of the teacher candidates. The teacher candidates worked with their supervisors and the classroom materials were produced based on the level of the students.

The parents were also involved in the project by decorating the classrooms, or Spoken Cafes. The project was the joint effort and collaboration of the Ministry, the university, schools, and the community. The Sarıyer District Directorate of National Education had already realized the need for improving students' language skills in primary schools, and our collaboration with them on practicum in our teacher education program gave momentum to start this project. We did not need to convince the parents and schools to support this project since they knew that the project was a unique opportunity for the students to get exposed to English more and improve their language proficiency.

The students were also highly motivated to practice English since they were told that they would practice English in Spoken Cafes and this would be a different experience for them compared to the classroom instruction. They were told that they would engage in activities using stories, games, songs, and puzzles, and they would have fun.

Sustainability has been a big challenge for this project. Due to the heavy coursework of our teacher education program, not every student teacher was involved in the project. Volunteer teacher candidates took part in the project. University supervisors also had limited time in monitoring the project regularly due to their time constraints. They were working hard to follow the coursework and administrative work of the department. These circumstances affected the sustainability of the project negatively.

In order to advocate for the continuation of this project so that it is sustainable, the university needs to improve the teacher candidates' advocacy skills by integrating projects, such as Spoken Cafes, into the teacher education programs and integrating them into the practicum course. This will be highly beneficial for the teacher candidates since they will be promoting their teaching skills, and the English learners will have a chance to develop their English language skills. When the advocacy course becomes a part of the practicum course, the material development for the project and the feedback process to the teacher candidate will be more systematic and continuous.

As Linville and Whiting (2020) indicate, when English language (EL) teachers learn and improve advocacy skills in their teacher education programs, they know how to support EL learners more effectively. In addition, integrating advocacy-focused projects/assignments into the curriculum of the teacher education programs makes the teacher candidates more confident in supporting EL learners.

Regular communication with the Ministry and the schools will strengthen the sustainability of the project and will allow us to monitor and revise the program regularly. The assessment component is highly crucial for sustainability efforts; with well-developed communication with the partners (Ministry, schools, teacher candidates, and parents), systematic and regular assessment will take place within the project. Both the program goals and student achievement will be monitored and evaluated constantly. Assessment tools and rubrics will be developed over time, and this will increase the quality of the program and lead the way to more student achievement. The advocacy projects, such as Spoken Cafes, need to be part of the curriculum of the Ministry of Education and the teacher education programs of the Faculties of Education. The gains are multidimensional: providing support for language instruction in public schools, expanding teacher candidates' opportunities for teaching, enriching the teaching experiences of the practicum courses at the Faculties of Education, and strengthening the connection among the Ministry, university, school and community to make a difference in young people's lives.

Advocacy Project

The project started in 2018 and took one year (two academic semesters: fall and spring). The volunteer senior-year teacher candidates were selected for the project on a voluntary basis and assigned their project schools. They were also doing their practicum work in their assigned schools. There were seven project schools, including a total of 400 students.

There were three main stages in the project. First, three to four teacher candidates were placed in each school and taught English four hours per week. Second, after the teacher candidates were placed, the classes took place in classroom settings specifically decorated for this project and called "Spoken Cafes." They taught in teams in an effort to give individual care and attention to each student. In each session, there were multiple teacher candidates, so the students were getting individual feedback frequently from the various teacher candidates.

The learning materials and activities were prepared based on the curriculum of the Turkish Ministry of National Education. The teacher candidates prepared hands-on activities for young learners who had limited opportunities to learn English and helped them practice English in meaningful contexts. They followed the curriculum, prepared by the Ministry of Education, but they supported the units with more experiential learning activities. In this way, the children were exposed to activities in which they practiced their speaking skills through stories, games, and songs. They solved a puzzle together, sang songs, and read stories.

The materials were circulated in the group and revisions were made. The learning materials were also checked and evaluated by the university supervisors. Lastly, the learning materials used in the Spoken Cafes were implemented in the project classes. The university supervisor visited each class and provided feedback to the teacher candidates in order to improve the level of instruction.

As this project became a reality, the students at the project schools were exposed to English more, and the teacher candidates benefited from this teaching experience and became more familiar with young learner contexts by improving their instruction.

Collaborations

The project was carried out jointly by the Sarıyer District Directorate of National Education and the Foreign Language Education Department of Boğaziçi University, Istanbul, Türkiye. The school administration and the parents supported the project a great deal by decorating the Spoken Cafes, finding equipment, providing classroom space, and getting spaces prepared for use. The Spoken Cafes were comfortably decorated so that the students were relaxed while they were practicing English with their peers.

The Sarıyer District Directorate of National Education and the Department of Foreign Language Education of Boğaziçi University have been working together on the practicum in terms of getting permission to access schools, entering schools, and assigning the student teachers to their schools for a long time.

The teacher candidates played a significant role in designing lesson plans, preparing materials, and actually teaching. The project provided our senior students with a valuable opportunity to actually teach and observe language teaching environments in different schools before they graduated.

The partners in this project were closely connected to each other; each partner's contribution to the project has been valuable. Since they have a common mission, they worked hard to organize the project and deliver the instruction.

The advocacy work was the effort of all the partners of the project. It would not have come about without the contribution of each partner. The project aimed to be a sustained effort, yet it took one year. There needs to be further preparation to integrate it into the practicum course and work on the assessment and advocacy issues with the teacher candidates.

Project Outcomes

At the end of the year, the teacher candidates reported that they benefited from this experience a great deal and were happy to contribute to the community. They added that they would continue to do voluntary work in different teaching contexts. I observed that the teacher candidates became more skilled advocates. They reported that they would continue their advocacy work after they graduated and make their own schools get involved with this kind of project.

Based on my observations at schools, the primary students had a positive experience in learning English. They became more eager and motivated to learn English since enjoyable, meaningful environments were provided to them by our teacher candidates. Improving students' English language proficiency and providing them with more opportunities to become exposed to English was the common goal of each partner. They were positively dependent on each other and worked to accomplish this goal.

The relationships among the project schools, the university, and the Ministry were improved. A trustworthy relationship has now been established among them, and they started to discuss further collaboration. The relationship between the university and the schools was developed in terms of having a connection to collaborate with professional development opportunities for the teachers in their schools. Identifying the need of the schools and communities, focusing on the need by making an action plan, planning the roles of the partners and their contribution, gathering regularly to evaluate the process, and offering systematic feedback to the process were essential components of this project. We trusted each other from the beginning, and the trust developed while working together because our mission was very valuable: supporting our students' language needs and well-being in the learning environment. We trusted each other because each partner would have a high potential and impact on the lives of the students. We believed in the goal and became more aware of the need for working together to achieve this goal. If one partner was missing, the project would not be able to work.

Challenges and Solutions

Since the practicum process was going on, the supervisors were busy with the departmental work, so they could not give enough time to visit the project schools, observe the classes, and give feedback to the teacher candidates regularly. As one of the supervisors in the project, I gave special attention to visiting the schools and talking to the candidates about their performance; yet, I could have visited the schools more often.

While planning for the sustainability of this project, this issue should be forefront, and the school visits and lesson observations should be organized in advance.

Preparing learning materials took extra time for the teacher candidates. Since the candidates mentioned that they were having difficulty preparing the materials, groups of teacher candidates were assigned for a particular week and they were responsible for preparing the materials and distributing them to other groups of teachers to use. Teamwork and collaboration were highly crucial in this project, and the teacher candidates worked together to prepare the materials.

Allocating time for the Spoken Cafes was a challenge for the teacher candidates. Since they were working hard to graduate and they had a heavy schedule for their coursework, we only had a few volunteer student teachers. Then we decided to give extra credit to our student teachers as part of the requirements of a practicum course, which worked well and increased the participation.

Project Completion

The project was completed in 2018 and took two academic semesters. Teaching experience in young learner classrooms has been an invaluable asset for the teacher candidates, and they are still talking highly about the importance of this project for their professional lives.

Due to the difficulties we experienced in the past couple of years, such as the pandemic, we could not continue this project. I strongly believe that we need to continue this project in the coming years and integrate the advocacy projects into the curriculum of the teacher education programs. The advocacy projects have a higher impact to strengthen the well-being of the communities. This project has also been presented at various local conferences in Türkiye, so disseminating the experience nationwide will affect and encourage other members of society to take initiative.

Another asset of this project has been the improved relationship between the university and the Ministry. Motivation for further projects had been increased. The success of the project has been shared with the media (https://www.aa.com.tr/tr/egitim/ders-arasi-dil-molasi/1118949).

The most significant benefit is the students' English language proficiency; it started to improve. However, regular and systematic assessments need to be conducted to assess how much the students' language proficiency improved.

I strongly believe that the sustainability of the project is highly important. Further work, such as planning, recruitment of the teacher candidates, material preparation, and assessment needs to be done to continue this effort.

Reflections and Future Directions

The research supports that strong communication and collaboration skills are essential to the advocacy efforts of English to speakers of other languages (ESOL) (Fiedler, 2000; Staehr-Fenner, 2014). Collaboration has been seen as a significant feature of effective advocacy (Linville, 2016). This project has been a successful example of how the strong collaboration with communication skills of each party makes the advocacy work advance by promoting learning contexts with limited opportunities.

The advocates first identified the need and then worked together to take action. They had a common goal, which was to improve the English language needs of the young English language learners. The advocates had varied responsibilities throughout the project. While they were gaining experience, they were also becoming aware of what would work better if they could do it next time. For instance, for the university supervisors, planning ahead carefully makes a difference in the efficiency of the project. All the contributors of the project realized the importance of working together and creating a strong impact on the community. The teacher candidates realized the value of working together both for the benefit of the community and the professional growth of their own. I have just received an email (September 19, 2022) from a teacher who participated in this project in 2018 asking whether the project is continuing and, if so, if her school could take part in it. In her email, she indicated that she benefited a lot from the experience she gained. I immediately forwarded her email to the head of the department to do further work on this project for continuation.

The university supervisors also found this experience invaluable and reflected on the need to integrate service learning/community service practices into the practice of teaching and community service practices courses. The volunteer teacher candidates realized that they needed to continue their effort to support their students' language learning process when they started their careers. Their awareness has increased toward advocacy work.

Dubetz and de Jong (2011), Linville (2016), and Pawan and Craig (2011) indicate that ESOL teachers maximize their advocacy efforts at the local level in their work with students, teachers, administrators, and parents, and this depends on rich interactions among all stakeholders in the context of each classroom, school, and community. Dove and Honigsfeld (2010) stress the importance of sufficient training for an effective relationship between teachers and other stakeholders.

The advocacy work needs to be a formal component of a practicum course in the teacher education program. The curriculum and the activities for the

Spoken Cafes should be organized in advance with the supervisors and the teacher candidates. Every step needs to be organized carefully, such as choosing classroom materials, monitoring and giving feedback to the teacher candidates, assessing the students' language proficiency, and evaluating the overall impact of the project.

Continuous assessment should be implemented in order to monitor how the students are doing. The challenges in the learning process should be noted and the research agenda should be kept during the process.

Staehr-Fanner (2014) states that advocates must know their students' family backgrounds well in order to advocate for students effectively and decide which action is appropriate. They need to have a clear goal in mind. In our advocacy project, there could have been a session(s) with the teacher candidates in which we talked about the background of the students and prepared materials more appropriate for them. Linguistic and content material could have been chosen accordingly.

I think that based on my experience with the advocacy project, the issues below need to be kept in mind in designing an advocacy work:

- Plan each step carefully to promote sustainability.
- Meet with the partners (ministry, university supervisors/teacher candidates, schools, and parents) of the project regularly to evaluate and revise each step.
- Integrate the advocacy efforts into the teacher education programs and the school experience/practicum courses systematically. Generate reading materials and assignments to be used in the course syllabus.
- Make a list of expected problems and have a B plan; get ready for the challenges.
- Integrate community service practices and advocacy work into the professional growth of teachers.
- Offer seminars in pre-service and in-service teacher education programs to provide information about service learning and advocacy to English language teaching (ELT) and make the teachers and teacher candidates informed about advocacy efforts.
- Disseminate your findings and share your experience with the university, school, and community.
- Explore the ways of using online technology to increase the impact of the advocacy work.

Discussion Questions

1. How can universities, ministries of education, and communities encourage teacher candidates' motivation to take part in community-based, advocacy projects?
2. How are the skills of the teacher candidates, such as establishing relationships; maintaining relationships; and developing interpersonal communication skills, empathy, emotional maturity, and understanding of the power dynamics, developed?

Inquiry Projects

Inquiry projects on key concepts in the following questions below would deepen the knowledge of advocacy and advocacy-based projects.

1. How do you identify a need for advocacy work?
2. What are the ways to encourage teachers' and teacher candidates' willingness to participate in the advocacy projects?
3. How do you increase awareness of the community to advocacy work via community-based projects?
4. How do you integrate advocacy work into a school experience/practicum course?
5. What are the pre- and in-service English teachers' beliefs about advocacy?
6. What are the professional factors that influence pre- and in-service English teachers' beliefs in their role as advocates?
7. What kind of school-based factors affect the English as a second or foreign language (ESL/EFL) teachers' practices in their roles as advocates?

References

Butler, Y. G. (2020). Cognition and young learners' language development. In Schwartz, M. (Ed.), *Handbook of Early Language Education* (pp. 1–29). Springer International Handbooks of Education. Springer.

Cameron, L. (2001). *Teaching Languages to Young Learners*. Cambridge University Press.

Dove, M., & Honigsfeld, A. (2010). ESL co-teaching and collaboration: Opportunities to develop teacher leadership and enhance student learning. *TESOL Journal, 1*, 3–22.

Dubetz, N. E., & de Jong, E. J. (2011). Teacher advocacy in bilingual programs. *Bilingual Research Journal, 34*(2), 248–262.

Fiedler, C. R. (2000). *Making a difference: Advocacy competencies for special education professionals*. Allyn and Bacon.

Linville, H. (2016). ESOL teachers as advocates: An important role? *TESOL Journal, 7*(1), 98–130.

Linville, H. & Whiting, J. (2020). Social justice through TESOL advocacy. *TESOL Journal, 11*(4), e553.

Long, M. H. (1983). Native speaker/non-native speaker conversation and the negotiation of comprehensible input. *Applied linguistics, 4*(2), 126–141.

Pawan, F., & Craig, D. (2011). ESL and content area teacher responses to discussions on English language learner instruction. *TESOL Journal, 2*(3), 293–311.

Staehr-Fenner, D. (2014). *Advocating for English Learners: A Guide for Educators*. Corwin Press.

Chapter 9
EFL Classrooms as Spaces for Advocacy Acts in Areas of Intractable Conflict

Julia Schlam Salman and Brigitta R. Schvarcz

Introduction

Efforts of advocacy enacted within English language classrooms can be important in deconstructing the legacies of linguistic colonialism. This may be particularly true in areas of intractable conflict, which can be defined as two "sides" experiencing irreconcilable moral and ethno-religious disagreements and where English usage continues to be tied to certain alliances and status markers. Additionally, at times it can be perceived as a drift away from local identities and toward an over-assimilation into tenets representing Western capitalism (Darvin & Norton, 2016; Schlam Salman et al., 2014).

The geopolitical region of the Middle East has been shaped by different colonizing forces. In addition to political, social, and cultural implications, this legacy can be seen in the languages that are present and used. English in the region, as an initially colonizing language, plays a complex role as both a language of past oppression and a language of potential emancipation. This emancipation is two-pronged and can be characterized by increased professional opportunities, access to higher education, and social mobility on the one hand, and colonialism, identity loss, and Westernized assimilation on the other hand (Amara, 2003; Le Ha, 2005).

One particularly unique context is the Israeli-Palestinian region, including the intractable conflict associated with it. The presence of English, amplified and made official during the British Palestine Mandate from the early 1920s to 1948, has paved the way for English to function as the language of wider communication (LWC). Additional contributing factors include the small size of the area; access to, use of, and development of technology; as well as the ongoing absence of normalized relations between Israel and most of its neighboring countries.

This chapter focuses on advocacy efforts we have undertaken as English language educators in teacher education institutions and institutions of higher education in Israel. We describe day-to-day practices that promote linguistic decolonization enacted within our classrooms. We elaborate on the following three measures, rooted in Freirean critical pedagogy and based on our experiences, for advancing advocacy-oriented pedagogies: (1) emphasizing appropriateness alongside correctness; (2) deconstructing binary thinking; (3) acknowledging societal inequities by building in pedagogical flexibility while simultaneously ensuring high educational outcomes and access to linguistic capital. Although these notions are embedded in the Israeli-Palestinian conflict, we will show how they may have relevance for English language teachers (ELTs) in other contexts, particularly those characterized by diversity, plurilingualism, and ongoing conflict.

Historical Overview of Language Policies in the Region

Local Languages: The Status of Hebrew and Arabic

During the Ottoman rule, and, prior to the British Mandate and the establishment of the State of Israel, the dominant language in the region was Arabic. Arabic was used as a vehicle for intergroup communication among distinct groups, including Ashkenazi Jews who spoke Yiddish, Sephardic Jews who spoke Ladino, and others who spoke a range of European languages. Turkish was also used and was the region's second official language (Deutch, 2005).

In 1922, Hebrew was recognized as an official language by the League of Nations.[1] The British Mandate of Palestine set forth an "official languages" act within the Constitution of Mandatory Palestine (article 82 of the Palestine Order in Council over the Land of Israel) (Deutch, 2005). English, Arabic, and Hebrew were designated as official languages. Government and official notices from local authorities and municipalities were to be published in English, Arabic, and Hebrew (Ginat, 2018).

Following the declaration of Israel's independence in 1948, the Law and Administration Ordinance provided that "any provision of the law requiring the use of the English language is repealed" (Deutch, 2005, p. 6). This legally ended the official status of English. After the establishment of the State of Israel, Arabic retained its status of an official language. However, de facto language practices favored Hebrew. Consequently, Hebrew was constructed as the main legitimate means for the production and reproduction of power.

The language continues to permeate day-to-day life in Israel and is a relevant and powerful linguistic tool for both first language (L1) and second/additional language (L2) users. In addition, as a language tied to the Jewish people, Hebrew also functions as an identity marker and a symbolic representation of Judaism and Jewish peoplehood (Nevo & Olshtain, 2007).

Until 2018, Arabic had the status as an official language in the State of Israel. Despite this classification, no bilingual arrangement was formulated, and political circumstances did not "grant Arabic the full and comprehensive status of an official language" (Saban & Amara, 2004, p. 20). In 2018, with the passage of the Nation-State Law Arabic was changed from an official language to having a "special status" (Basic-Law: Israel—The Nation State of the Jewish People, 5778–2018). Many language specialists and sociolinguists have viewed this policy change as unnecessarily inflammatory and a downgrading of the status of a language spoken by over 20% of the country's population (Green, 2018).

Within the Palestinian Territories, Modern Standard Arabic is the official national language. In addition, given the diglossic nature of Arabic, Palestinian colloquial Arabic is the spoken vernacular used in non-official settings. Although Hebrew has no official status, it is sometimes used in domains such as commerce, industry, welfare, and government to advance pragmatic and economic interests (Hawker, 2013; Khawaja et al., 2021; Suleiman, 2004). Hebrew is also sometimes represented in the linguistic landscape (Ujvari, 2019, 2021; Schvarcz & Khawaja, 2022).

The Status of English

Although English is not an official language, it has been awarded significant importance as an academic, global, and international language by both Israel and the Palestinian Authority (see Khawaja et al., 2021; Spolsky, 2004). It is often referred to as a first foreign language and can be categorized as a "quasi-official language" (Amara & Mar'i, 2002, p. 9). As Amara (2003) notes, "knowledge of English is a powerful status symbol and class marker" (p. 221).

English language instruction in both Israel and the Palestinian Territories is defined as EFL (English as a Foreign Language) and is regulated by the respective ministries of education. In Israel, Hebrew or Arabic are the mainstream languages, and English is added as a first foreign language. It is a compulsory subject, and instruction is funded from the third or fourth grade. However, many schools begin English instruction earlier and there is a new ministry of education initiative to introduce English at the preschool level (TOI staff, 2022). Students culminate their studies with a mandatory English Matriculation Exam (referred to in Hebrew as *English Bagrut*) that assesses their skills in reading comprehension, writing, listening, and speaking. Students can be assessed at one of three levels of proficiency, with the highest level approximately corresponding to the B1 level of the Common European Framework of Reference (CEFR) (Council of Europe, 2018).

For schools under the auspices of the Palestinian Ministry of Education, English is a compulsory subject, introduced from the first grade. Until 1994, Jordan regulated all schooling, including English instruction, in the Palestinian Territories (Alayan, 2018). Following the Oslo Accords,[2] the Palestinian Authority was awarded autonomy over their educational system (Dajani & McLaughlin, 2009) and subsequently, the *English for Palestine* English language curriculum was developed (Palestinian National Authority, 2015). Students culminate their studies with a matriculation exam called the *Tawjihi*, which includes an assessment component in English.

As evident from the above, English plays a critical role in the region and is an essential part of the linguistic capital needed to socially mobilize and gain access to higher education and the outside world. As an LWC, English also sometimes functions as an arbitrator between L1 Hebrew speakers and L1 Arabic speakers, advancing initiatives that promote shared society, shared education, and peace efforts (Khawaja et al., 2021; Yitzhaki et al., 2020). Alongside such initiatives remains the legacy of colonialism, imported nation-state ideology, and the constructions associated with a foreign language that represents Euro-American linguistic cultural expectations. As explored extensively by Pennycook and others (Pennycook, 2000; 2002) English is not solely a language of neutrality and wider communication but also a conduit for colonial discourses, meanings, and practices, which needs to be unpacked if we are to genuinely decolonize and use the language for emancipatory purposes.

Defining Advocacy-Oriented Pedagogies in Areas of Intractable Conflict

As stated previously, this chapter builds on research within Freirean critical pedagogy and on our experiences as English language educators in teacher education institutions and institutions of higher education in Israel. We define advocacy-oriented pedagogies as those that seek to dismantle hegemonic forces of oppression and colonization while promoting equity and social justice. We outline the following three advocacy-oriented pedagogies: (1) emphasizing appropriateness alongside correctness; (2) deconstructing binary thinking; (3) acknowledging societal inequities by building in pedagogical flexibility while simultaneously ensuring high educational outcomes and access to linguistic capital.

Efforts for Advancing Advocacy-Oriented Pedagogies

Emphasizing Appropriateness Alongside Correctness

Sociolinguists frequently make a distinction between "correctness" and "appropriateness" with respect to language usage (Stubbs, 2002). Thus, for example, "drive safe" would be considered a suitable and pleasant salutation in many parts of the United States even though it combines a verb with an adjective, which in standard English is a grammatical faux pas. Globalization and the spread of English as a LWC among speakers of other languages has resulted in numerous local varieties of English. Crystal has referred to this as a form of bilingualism wherein users of English speak one variety that allows them to communicate within their local context and a second variety that enables them to communicate within the wider world (Crystal, 2019).

Decolonizing EFL teaching and advocating for learners means introducing into classroom practices an awareness of the concept of "appropriateness" alongside "correctness." This includes the connection between "correctness" and symbolic power, grammatical form, and social conditions of acceptability (Bourdieu, 1991). Within their three-dimensional model for grammar teaching, Larsen-Freeman and Celce-Murcia (2016) highlight the importance of form, meaning, and use. As such, "correctness," described in a prescriptive sense, is but one component of language usage and no more important than exhibiting contextually and pragmatically appropriate usage. An additional dimension critical to an emphasis on appropriateness—a possible "fourth" dimension—is the intersection between language usage and markers of power. As Fairclough (2001) has written about extensively and Crovitz and Devereaux (2017) describe in their book on grammar instruction, language is tied to the production and reproduction of power relations and social inequities. From this perspective, "correctness" is understood as constructed within social communities of practice and cannot be separated from the contexts in which it is embedded.

Within language classrooms, a focus on appropriateness begins by clearly defining receptive and productive language learning outcomes and then aligning the linguistic expectations accordingly. For example, if the focus of the lesson or unit is on the use of the second conditional to write a respectful and polite funding request in formal English, then emphasis should be placed on the precise structure and usage of this form. However, if the learning outcome of the activity is, for example, "learners can informally talk about and discuss activities they like to do with their friends," then the utterance "my friends and me like to play basketball" sufficiently conveys communicative competence, meaning, and use. Although a prescriptive grammar approach would dictate the need to "correct" the speaker, the learning outcomes do not mandate such a need. Moreover, allowing the discussion to proceed authentically and without interruption can foster confidence, motivation, and communication skills.

The role of the language teacher is to clarify learning outcomes and to ensure that the vocabulary, structures, and expectations match what is "appropriate" for the task at hand. Care should be given to highlight the expected register and place emphasis on where there may be differences between the conventions used in the students' L1 and the conventions used in English. Explaining "appropriateness" is particularly valuable because of the connections between language use, power, and identity constructions. There are meaningful consequences related to power and social capital when users emulate "correct" usage and likewise when users are marked as "uneducated" or "improper" because of "incorrect" use.

In areas of intractable conflict where English frequently functions as a LWC, the need for an emphasis on appropriateness is even more paramount. "Inappropriate" usage can have widespread ramifications that can result in misunderstandings, mistrust, escalation, and even violence. All of these can sustain conflict.

An example of this from the local context can be exemplified by learners' regular use of imperative forms to address teachers, principals, and other authority figures. Thus, for example, blurting out "move" when a teacher is blocking the board or "give me my grade" when graded assignments are being returned are common utterances heard in EFL classrooms. As immigrants to Israel, when we initially encountered such discourse, we were appalled by the learners' "gall" and ostensibly disrespectful language. A few students were even reprimanded. Later, as we both acquired a better familiarity of the subtleties embedded in Hebrew and Arabic cultural linguistics, it became clear that such circumstances are sociocultural mistranslations, and they can

EFL Classrooms as Spaces for Advocacy Acts

provide opportunities for lessons in "correctness" and "appropriateness." The use of the imperative "move" is not "incorrect" but it potentially constructs a perception of rudeness that the learner may not be aware of and may not wish to convey. The EFL teacher can bridge nuances and pragmatic appropriacy embedded in such utterances.

A second example from the local context is reflected in the following anecdote shared by one of the author's language education students. Straddling the 1949 Armistice border, the city of Jerusalem and its surrounding areas remain disjointed, with West Jerusalem housing primarily Jewish-Israelis and East Jerusalem housing mainly Palestinians, many of whom are permanent residents of East Jerusalem but are not citizens of Israel. To pass from areas controlled by the Palestinian Authority into areas controlled by the Israeli government, there are checkpoints where Hebrew-speaking Israeli Defense Force (IDF) soldiers check people passing through. On one afternoon, a soldier was inquiring about where the student was from. Understanding his question quite literally, the student replied "Jerusalem." The soldier repeated the question, growing increasingly impatient. Veiled in the question was a request for the specific area of East Jerusalem from which the student came. Although the response was "correct", in this context it did not fulfill the social conditions of acceptability. Notably, in situations such as the one described above, where there is unequal power distribution, the one in power sets the conditions for acceptability. Failure to abide by these conditions of linguistic appropriateness can have dire consequences.

In the language classroom, we need not argue about the merit or the necessity of the checkpoint. The advocacy act is to equip those who must endure such circumstances with the linguistic capital needed to assert themselves in a manner that is "appropriate" and ideally empowering to the user. Based on his experiences, the language education student opted to develop a theme-based language learning unit around crossing checkpoints, aiming to ensure that his future pupils would be familiar with the forms and responses appropriate to this arduous situation. This can be seen as an act of advocacy whereby the student is linguistically empowering his future students.

Students may never choose to adapt or adopt such forms and expectations. However, we disempower them when we fail to highlight expected or appropriate discourse norms. At the same time, language educators perpetuate injustice when they pretend, sometimes quite indignantly, that there is a universal standard of politeness that governs all cultures, societies, and interactions into which students must assimilate to be "fluent" in English. One of the roles of ELTs is to acknowledge the constructed nature of appropriacy, to make explicit the discourse expectations, and to "translate" what is sociolinguistically acceptable. This gives learners the tools to shift between sociocultural contexts using "appropriate" language and to act as self-advocates in different situations.

Deconstructing Binary Thinking

People have multiple identities, and they construct them in relation to and in conjunction with the communities that shape their lives. Identity construction is not an autonomous process but is embedded in interactions transpiring within social settings.

When interacting with others, almost instantaneously, we construct conceptions of identity that may or may not be correct and may or may not be deemed salient by the interlocutor. These presuppositions tend to be conceptualized as binaries, such as educated-uneducated, rich-poor, or colonizer-colonized. These identity constructions can be difficult to undo. Thus, for example, the learner who is perceived as "unmotivated" or "bad at English" will have difficulty shedding this demarcation without substantial effort by the teacher and the pupil to reevaluate the identity construct. Such markers can contribute to learners' sense of marginalization and feelings of estrangement and impede their language learning potential (Darvin & Norton, 2016).

In societies characterized by religious, ethnic, and socioeconomic differences, binary thinking is pervasive and often governed by the underpinnings of the conflict. In intractable conflict, such as the Israeli-Palestinian conflict, where there may be irreconcilable moral differences; limited resources; and issues of power, control, and status, and the perceived "need" to delineate who belongs with whom is even more pronounced. The "us-versus-them" mindset is so reified that many times society members cannot see overlapping salient identities or even imagine alternative constructions. As such, concepts such as Jewish-Arab or non-Arab Christian are almost inconceivable. This occurs even though nearly half of Jewish Israelis identify as having roots in Arabic-speaking countries such as Iraq, Iran, and Syria (Lewin-Epstein & Cohen, 2019) and about one-third of the world population is non-Arab Christian.

A first step in implementing advocacy-oriented pedagogies that promote decolonization is to acknowledge the pervasiveness of binary thinking. Teachers can seek opportunities to "undo" such constructions by encouraging discourse that supports negotiating multiple identities. This requires recognizing the constructed nature of identities and viewing them as continually negotiated, changing, and, at times, intersecting. Such a perspective helps mitigate an either/or mindset and the tendency to reify learners into externally constructed identities. Language teachers who can engage with heterogeneity and difference, thereby beginning to dismantle binary thinking, can create classrooms where learners are more readily able to articulate multiple, salient identities. Such classrooms have been termed "pedagogical safe houses" for identity negotiation (Canagarajah, 2004), supporting learners who feel seen, validated, and represented.

Below we relay two general ELT practices that can encourage learners to recognize and reflect on their own multiple salient identities and the spaces in which these identifications intersect within diverse populations. The first example, "Find Four Things in Common: Where Do We Overlap?," is good for the beginning of the school year. The activity can both help teachers to become familiar with their learners and learners to become familiar with each other and their overlapping attributes and interests. Learners are given a list of questions, such as "What color are your eyes?," "Where were you born?," "What is your favorite food?," and "What do you like to do in your free time?" Learners are also encouraged to produce their own questions. Learners are then given a paper divided into four quadrants (one per group). Once they have identified four attributes or interests shared by all group members, they fill in the quadrants. The activity can be differentiated by providing a list of possible responses to the questions—attributes and interests from which to choose. More advanced learners can be given detailed instructions without the bank of questions. Although this is not an in-depth analysis of identity constructions, it is a suitable task for beginning to dismantle binaries and uncover similarities.

A second task that builds on the concepts presented in the previous activity is called "Me, Myself, and Others: The Identities We Share." Adapted from curricular materials developed by the United States Institute of Peace (n.d.), this activity asks learners to map out the groups they belong to using the following graphic organizer, adapted from Teaching Guide: Conflict Resolution in the EFL Classroom (p.27), by United States Institute of Peace (n.d.).

Students fill in each pie piece with an identity they feel is representative. Learners are instructed to avoid using adjectives such as "smart" or "beautiful" and instead to focus on categories such as "athletic" or "Christian." They are then asked to mark the identity they feel is most important and to reflect on whether that identity changes depending on who they are with and where they are. Learners are then asked to consider the following questions: (1) In what ways, if at all, do my identities change? (2) What role does

Me, Myself and Others: The Identities We Share

Directions: In each pie section, write a group that you are part of and identify with. These can include but are not restricted to: your position in your family, your religious identity, your ethnic identity, your gender identity, your professional identity, or any other activity you engage it that you feel defines you (for example, runner or singer).

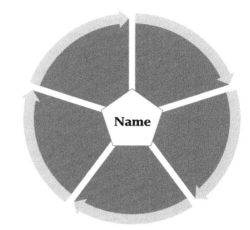

Figure 9.1 Identity Pie: Exploring Groups We Belong To

the surrounding community play in these changes in identity? (3) Now look at the responses from others in your group. Which identities did you have in common? Which identities surprised you? Mature English language learners can also be encouraged to think about whether there is any hierarchy among their identities and whether any of their identities are hybridized.

Both activities seek to dismantle binary thinking and an "us-versus-them" mindset by fostering an awareness of the context dependence of identity construction, the multiplicity of identities present in each person, and the circumstances in which identities may overlap. The subsequent two activities describe how we can begin to dismantle binary thinking, specifically within the Palestinian-Israeli conflict.

Shared Traditions

The first example was developed for a teacher education college in Jerusalem where there is a diverse student body including Jews, Muslims, and Christians. The reading comprehension and discussion was around the Muslim holiday of Eid al-Adha (i.e., the Festival of Sacrifice). This holiday references a passage in the Muslim holy book, the Quran, in which God commands the Prophet Abraham to sacrifice his only son, Ishmael. Crucially, this narrative is also chronicled in the Jewish holy book, the Torah, but with the sacrifice falling on Isaac instead of Ishmael. In both traditions, Abraham is commanded to sacrifice his only son to demonstrate his faith in God. Although the passage can be found in both traditions, Muslims and Jews may not be aware of the shared scripture. The aim of this activity is to recognize one another's religion and to raise learners' awareness of overlapping practices and religious commonalities, including dismantling the Arab-Jewish (Muslim-Jewish) binary.

The topic is also chosen to help learners see themselves and their cultures represented within the EFL classroom. Bringing in representative, authentic local content builds on the learners' prior knowledge, thereby denationalizing English and facilitating ownership of the language. In this activity, learners read about Eid al-Adha, and they are asked to think about how the holiday is similar or different from their traditions. In classrooms where Jews and Muslims are studying English together, they themselves offer recognition, saying, for example, "this sounds familiar" or "this is like the sacrifice of Isaac." This is an example of how the EFL classroom can become a space that promotes advocacy-oriented pedagogies, including intercultural dialogue and exchange, which help advocate for learners and promote peaceful relations among diverse populations.

Start-Up Nations

The second activity was implemented in an English for Academic Purposes (EAP) class at an engineering college in Tel Aviv. L1 Hebrew speakers, L1 Arabic speakers, as well as speakers of other languages (e.g., Russian or Amharic) were taking the class, which was conducted in English. The activity was part of a larger unit on start-ups.

The State of Israel has frequently been referred to as the "Start-Up Nation" (Senor & Singer, 2009) due to its exceedingly high number of successful start-ups as well as its economic prosperity, particularly within the high-tech sector. Less well-known is the creativity and drive for innovation taking place in the Palestinian Territories. Through the documentary entitled *Holy Land: Startup Nations* (note the plural "s"), learners are exposed to initiatives in both areas. In a pre-watching activity, learners are challenged to consider the plural reference, and they often express perplexity as to what it might be referring to. In post-reflection discussions, learners begin to dismantle the "us-versus-them" mindset and begin to see the inconceivable: that there are thriving start-ups in Ramallah as well as in Israel. In one discussion, an L1

Hebrew-speaking Jewish Israeli student described the transformation in his thinking from a soldier serving in Ramallah who witnessed the city as occupied and beset with danger and violence to a city characterized by innovation and day-to-day successes.

Without glossing over the intractable Palestinian-Israeli conflict and the real ramifications of ongoing occupation, activities that begin to dismantle binary thinking can be catalysts for seeing other and multiple perspectives. They can disrupt colonizing narratives that assume a binary of powerful and powerless, occupier and occupied. The English classroom itself becomes a space for advancing social justice where learners gain access to multiple viewpoints and perspectives.

Societal Inequities, Pedagogical Flexibility, and High Educational Outcomes

A critical component of advocacy within English language classrooms concerns acknowledging societal inequities with respect to privilege and power while simultaneously scaffolding and differentiating instruction to ensure achievement of success criteria and high educational outcomes. In her advocacy framework, Linville (2014, 2019) demonstrates the interconnectivity between English language learners, societal inequities, and the ultimate goal of improving learners' educational outcomes and life chances. Success requires recognizing societal inequities while still expecting high educational outcomes. Therefore, a first act of advocacy is acknowledging that there are standards and societal expectations. In fact, we perpetuate a form of colonization when we pretend that there are no "standards." Ignoring standards perpetuates the very inequalities we seek to dismantle by preventing learners from accessing the "required," albeit constructed, linguistic expectations (see, for example, Delpit, 1995). The fact that linguistic expectations tied to social capital are socially constructed does not make them any less real or consequential with respect to future opportunities and life chances.

Advocacy-oriented pedagogical practices in English language classrooms should require high expectations that facilitate access to linguistic capital while simultaneously bearing in mind ongoing injustices, which may marginalize students and play a role in the ways in which they are present (or not present) in the classroom. This includes honoring local differences, systematic marginalization, and disadvantages that may be a result of the ways in which the educational system is constructed (for example, only having monolingual instructions).

EFL Classrooms as Spaces for Advocacy Acts

There are physical, socioeconomic, political, and/or religious realities that might make it more difficult for specific populations to learn. A component of advocacy-oriented pedagogies is adopting flexible thinking and then introducing structural flexibility and pedagogical flexibility into the classroom. In the field of education, flexible thinking can be defined as a "competency necessary for adapting to new learning environments, for transferring knowledge to new situations, and for understanding and solving unfamiliar problems" (Barak & Levenberg, 2016, p. 40). Flexible thinking is a precursor to structural and pedagogical flexibility. Structural flexibility refers to an awareness of and willingness to modify the learning environment in order to optimize learning. Structural flexibility includes the lesson modality, the time and length of the lesson, and the lesson's unit and course outcomes, such as assignments and deadlines. Pedagogical flexibility refers to the ability and willingness to employ a wide range of techniques and methods for language teaching. Pedagogical flexibility is a proactive (rather than a reactive) pedagogy where teachers look at the cultural, linguistic, and socioeconomic makeup of their classrooms and then design and adjust their practices accordingly. Pedagogical flexibility depends on language teacher autonomy and localized, classroom-based practices.

Efforts to advance advocacy-oriented practices that acknowledge inequities while simultaneously ensuring high educational outcomes depend on context-specific structural and pedagogical flexibility. Inequities and legacies of colonization are embedded in specific historical-political milieux. Therefore, language teachers need to consider local circumstances and act accordingly when designing advocacy-oriented ELT materials and courses. Here we describe two examples from the local Palestinian and Israeli setting. Although context specific, the examples show how the described steps may advance equity and academic success.

In the Israeli context, there is a Jewish majority. Major Jewish holidays are vacation days, and educational institutions and schools are generally closed. In Arab majority settings, the Muslim or Christian holidays are marked, celebrated, and also constitute holidays. However, integrated Jewish-Muslim-Christian spaces tend to follow the Jewish calendar, and adjustments need to be introduced to ensure recognition and representation of all holidays. In educational settings, the need to safeguard minority rights, representation, and inclusion is particularly tangible. An apt example transpires in English classes in a teachers' college in Jerusalem each year during Ramadan, the Muslim month of fasting. During this month, adherers abstain from eating and drinking from sunrise to sunset. Despite this, classes and lessons proceed as usual. Clearly, when a percentage of the class members have not eaten or drunk all day and the lesson takes place at 5:00 in the afternoon, students' learning capacity and general well-being will be impacted. Instead of excusing these learners from their responsibilities and requirements, they can be given alternative timeframes and independent, asynchronous tasks that they can then complete at their convenience. Additional considerations for supporting students include having all the course materials clearly organized and accessible within a learning management system (LMS), such as Moodle, and indicating what is essential and what is optional within courses. Offering flexible pedagogical outcomes, for example, different formats for completing tasks, is also critical for success. A key component for ensuring educational outcomes is clarifying expectations from the outset and then allowing learners flexibility when choosing the path to achieving those outcomes.

Another example also connected to fasting relates to non-binding Jewish fast days, which, depending on the religious affiliation of the institution, are regular work and school days. In most educational institutions at the tertiary level, lecturers and students conduct their classes as usual. However, many institutions offer choice and flexibility. For example, in an EAP unit at an engineering college in Tel Aviv, the lecturer and the students can choose from one of the following options: (1) take part in the class as usual; (2) cancel the class and make up for it at later date; (3) offer an asynchronous class where the lesson materials are available online for a specific period of time and the students work at their own pace. Recognizing the unique challenges that fasting poses, irrespective of the religion, conveys empathy and recognition. Structural and pedagogical flexibility can ensure that all learners have equal opportunities to fulfill the course requirements and complete the expected educational outcomes. By recognizing the challenges, while simultaneously adapting our practices accordingly, we can create more just classrooms where advocacy acts transpire.

A final point regarding advocacy-oriented practices within English language classrooms is that they require innovation and a willingness to grapple with inequity, injustice, and conflict. Moreover, they necessitate institutional support and cooperation. English teachers need to be granted autonomy to structure and design their practices in ways that work best for their classrooms while bearing in mind the end goal of advancing equity, inclusion, and high educational outcomes.

Conclusion: English Language Classrooms as Spaces for Advancing Advocacy Acts

In this chapter, we have addressed three overarching means for introducing advocacy-oriented practices in English language classrooms. The first focused on emphasizing linguistic appropriateness alongside linguistic correctness. The second described steps for deconstructing binary thinking, and the third advocated for high educational outcomes and acknowledgement of societal inequities by building in pedagogical flexibility. An important premise of all these efforts is recognizing the subtle ways in which power is present in curricula and consequently within the pedagogies used to advance the curriculum. Ostensibly neutral pedagogies are never neutral but prioritize particular assumptions and worldviews. Part of decolonizing notions of advocacy is to first acknowledge that the need for advocacy emerges from legacies and expressions of colonialism where certain morals and values were imposed on other peoples, not necessarily with their consent or agreement. A critical step in advancing advocacy-oriented pedagogies concerns recognizing expressions of tangible and symbolic power and ensuring that we are guiding language learners toward accessing such expressions of power. Justice lies in empowerment, emancipation, and choice. Learners do not need to be beholden to arbitrary standards of correctness or externally imposed binaries. However, they must know how to navigate through such constructions and, should they choose, to exert the power located in them. English language teachers can further empower their learners by recognizing inequities and by prioritizing pedagogical flexibility alongside high expectations.

Within the Israeli-Palestinian conflict, there are layers of complexity, legacies of colonialism, and ongoing intragroup and intergroup injustices that cannot easily be categorized into a binary of right or wrong. As previously mentioned, particularly in higher educational settings, English language classrooms are spaces where these complexities come together when diverse backgrounds and populations interact. Depending on current events and the circumstances at hand, emotions can run high, and dealing with reality can be challenging. The easiest path is to "just teach English" and to pretend that language is a neutral vehicle for content carrying no political or ideological meaning. However, when we bring representation from the local context, including enduring conflicts and challenges, we create the possibility for deep learning where learners feel seen and also gain access to a language of power, which affords them the possibility of social mobility, self-advocacy, and choice.

For this chapter, we have provided examples that seek to advance advocacy-oriented practices at various levels in English language classrooms. We have brought in localized examples that attempt to shed light on the particular circumstances and challenges of our context. We acknowledge the specific lens and socialization processes influencing our understandings. They are solely representative of our own ideology and pedagogical priorities. At the same time, we hope our suggestions, although embedded in the Israeli-Palestinian context, may render insights pertinent to other educational settings dealing with ELT, in particular, those located in small, centralized countries grappling with hyper-diversity, plurilingualism, and ongoing intragroup and intergroup conflict.

Notes

1. The League of Nations was a conglomerate of countries formed to maintain world peace through treaties, agreements, and arbitration. This intergovernmental organization ceased to exist in 1946, but many of its components evolved into what is today known as the United Nations.
2. The Oslo Accords were a set of agreements signed in the 1990s between Israel and the Palestine Liberation Organization (PLO) that, among other things, transferred education regulatory responsibilities from the Kingdom of Jordan to the Palestinian Authority.

References

Alayan, S. (2018). *Education in East Jerusalem: Occupation, Political Power, and Struggle*. Routledge.

Amara, M. (2003). Recent foreign language education policies in Palestine. *Language Problems Language Planning, 27*(3), 217–231. https://doi.org/10.1075/lplp.27.3.02ama

Amara, M., & Mar'i, A. A.-L. (2002). *Language Education Policy: The Arab Minority in Israel*. Kluwer Academic Publishers.

Barak, M., & Levenberg, A. (2016). Flexible thinking in learning: An individual differences measure for learning in technology-enhanced environments. *Computers & Education, 99*, 39–52. https://doi.org/10.1016/j.compedu.2016.04.003

Basic-Law: Israel—The Nation State of the Jewish People, 5778-2018. SH No. 2743. https://fs.knesset.gov.il//20/law/20_lsr_504220.pdf

Bourdieu, P. (1991). *Language and Symbolic Power*. Harvard University Press.

Canagarajah, A. S. (2004). Subversive identities, pedagogical safe houses, and critical learning. In B. Norton & K. Toohey (Eds.), *Critical Pedagogies and Language Learning* (pp. 116–137). Cambridge University Press.

Council of Europe. (2018). *Common European Framework of Reference for Languages. Learning, Teaching, Assessment: Companion Volume with New Descriptors*. Council of Europe Publishing. https://rm.coe.int/cefr-companion-volume-with-new-descriptors2018/1680787989

Crovitz, D., & Devereaux, M. D. (2017). *Grammar to Get Things Done: A Practical Guide for Teachers Anchored in Real-World Usage*. Routledge.

Crystal, D. (2019). *The Cambridge Encyclopedia of the English Language* (3rd ed). Cambridge University Press.

Dajani, D., & McLaughlin, S. (2009). Implementing the first Palestinian English language curriculum: A need for teacher empowerment. *Mediterranean Journal of Educational Studies, 14*(2), 47–27. https://www.um.edu.mt/library/oar//handle/123456789/22501

Darvin, R., & Norton, B. (2016). Language, identity, and investment in the twenty-first century. In T. McCarty and S. May (Eds.), *Language Policy and Political Issues in Education*. Encyclopedia of Language and Education. Springer, Cham. https://doi.org/10.1007/978-3-319-02320-5_18-1

Delpit, L. (1995). *Other People's Children: Cultural Conflict in the Classroom*. The New Press.

Deutch, Y. (2005). Language law in Israel. *Language Policy, 4*(3), 261–285. https://doi.org/10.1007/s10993-005-7555-9

Fairclough, N. (2001). *Language and Power* (2nd ed.). Pearson Education Limited.

Ginat, A. (2018). British mandate for Palestine. In U. Daniel, P. Gatrell, O. Janz, H. Jones, J. Keene, A. Kramer, & B. Nasson (Eds.), *International Encyclopedia of the First World War: 1914-1918-Online*. Freie Universität Berlin. https://doi.org/10.15463/ie1418.11325

Green, E. (2018, July 21). Israel's new law inflames the core tension in its identity. *The Atlantic*. https://www.theatlantic.com/international/archive/2018/07/israel-nation-state-law/565712/

Hawker, N. (2013). *Palestinian-Israeli Contact and Linguistic Processes*. Routledge.

Khawaja A. J., Jakar, V. S., & Schvarcz, B. R. (2021). English as a mediator for communication and understanding: The case of Israel and Palestine. In K. Raza, C. Coombe, & D. Reynolds (Eds.), *Policy Development in TESOL* and *Multilingualism: Past, Present and the Way Forward* (pp. 217–230). Springer. https://doi.org/10.1007/978-981-16-3603-5_17

Larsen-Freeman, D., & Celce-Murcia, M. (2016). *The Grammar Book: Form, Meaning and Use for English Language Teachers*. National Geographic Learning.

Le Ha, P. (2005). Toward a critical notion of appropriation of English as an international language. In P. Robertson, P. Dash, & J. Jung (Eds.), *English Language Learning in the Asian Context* (2nd ed., pp. 202–211). The Asian EFL Journal Press. https://www.asian-efl-journal.com/main-editions-new/toward-a-critical-notion-of-appropriation-of-english-as-an-internatio nal-language/index.htm

Lewin-Epstein, N., & Cohen, Y. (2019). Ethnic origin and identity in the Jewish population of Israel. *Journal of Ethnic and Migration Studies, 45*(11), 2118–2137. https://doi.org/10.1080/1369183X.2018.1492370

Linville, H. (2014). *A mixed-methods investigation of ESOL teacher advocacy: "It's not going in and just teaching English."* (Publication No. 3624381). (Doctoral dissertation, University of Maryland, Baltimore County). ProQuest Dissertations & Theses Global.

Linville, H. (2019). Advocacy skills for teachers. In H. Linville & J. Whiting (Eds.), *Advocacy in English Language Teaching and Learning* (pp. 3–17). Routledge.

Nevo, N., & Olshtain, E. (2007). *The Hebrew Language in the Era of Globalization*. Magnes.

Palestinian National Authority, Ministry of Education, General Administration of Curricula (2015). *English Language Curriculum for Public Schools K-12* (New ed.). Retrieved from: http://www.englishforpalest ine.com/wp-content/uploads/2016/01/English-for-Palestine-Curriculum-Document-19.01.2016.pdf

Pennycook, A. (2000). The social politics and the cultural politics of language classrooms. In J. Hall & W. Eggington (Eds.), *The Sociopolitics of English Language Teaching* (pp. 89–103). Multilingual Matters.

Pennycook, A. (2002). *English and the Discourses of Colonialism*. Routledge

Saban, I., & Amara, M. (2004). The status of Arabic in Israel: Law, reality, and thoughts regarding the power of law to change reality. *Israel Law Review, 36*(2), 1–35.

Schlam Salman J., Olshtain, E., & Bekerman, Z. (2014). Examining markers of identity construction in English language learning. In B. Spolsky, O. Inbar-Lourie, and M. Tannenbaum (Eds.), *Challenges for Language Education and Policy: Making Space for People* (pp. 294–308). Routledge.

Schvarcz, B. R., & Khawaja, A. J. (2022). Linguistic landscape: The sign and the self in the Israel/Palestine region. In. B. Birch (Ed.), *Creating Classrooms of Peace in English Language Teaching* (pp. 117–134). Routledge. https://doi.org/10.4324/9781003147039-12

Senor, D., & Singer, S. (2009). *Start-Up Nation: The Story of Israel's Economic Miracle*. Twelve.

Spolsky, B. (2004). *Language Policy*. Cambridge University Press.

Stubbs, M. (2002). Some basic sociolinguistic concepts. In L. Delpit (Ed.), *The skin that we speak: Thoughts on language and culture in the classroom* (pp. 65–85). The New Press.

Suleiman, Y. (2004). *A War of Words: Language and Conflict in the Middle East*. Cambridge University Press.

Times of Israel staff (2022, February 11). Education minister said promoting a plan to start teaching English in preschool. *Times of Israel*. Retrieved from https://www.timesofisrael.com/education-minister-said-promoting-plan-to-start-teaching-english-in-preschool/

Ujvari, M. M. (2019). The effect of the linguistic landscape on Palestinian's language attitudes towards Hebrew in the West Bank. *International Journal of Linguistics, Literature, and Translation, 2*(4), 1–11.

Ujvari, M. M. (2021). The linguistic landscape of Palestinian C towns: The case of shop signs in Huwwara. *International Journal of Linguistics, Literature and Translation, 4*(4), 160–171. https://doi.org/10.32996/ijllt.2021.4.4.17

United States Institute of Peace (n.d.). *Teaching guide: Conflict Resolution in the EFL Classroom*. Retrieved from http://teachesl.pbworks.com/f/Confict+resolution+in+ESL+classroom+copy.pdf

Yitzhaki, D., Tannenbaum, M., & Shohamy, E. (2020). "Shared education" and translanguaging: Students at Jewish and Arab schools learning English together. *International Journal of Bilingual Education and Bilingualism, 25*(3), 1033–1048. https://doi.org/10.1080/13670050.2020.1740164

Chapter 10
Three Decades of Supporting English Teachers in Paraguay: PARATESOL's New Advocacy Response

Valentina Canese, Susan Spezzini, and Rocío Mazzoleni

Background

PARATESOL is a non-profit affiliate of TESOL International Association, an organization in Paraguay that aims to improve the delivery of English language teaching through the provision of professional development (PD) to teachers of English, among other activities. The organization has been operating in Paraguay for the last 30 years, and it has accomplished its mission through monthly workshops in different schools and language centers in Paraguay and in collaboration with publishers of teaching materials and private sector institutions. PARATESOL is a volunteer-based organization for English educators in Paraguay. It has been affiliated since 1989 with TESOL International Association, which was at the time called Teachers of English to Speakers of Other Languages (TESOL). During its first two decades, PARATESOL maintained an active presence and strong advocacy outreach. However, being operated solely by volunteer efforts, PARATESOL gradually lost momentum and entered a period of inactivity. Fortunately, the leaders of several local English-teaching entities (local language institutes and university departments) began reminiscing about PARATESOL's early years and joined forces to advocate for reviving this formerly thriving organization. Committed to serving the English language teaching profession, these educational leaders knew that a revitalized PARATESOL would be well positioned to promote widespread advocacy for the professionalization of English language teachers in Paraguay.

Led by an executive board and supported by committees, PARATESOL offers monthly (or semi-monthly) workshops and annual conferences.

English language educators serve as volunteers in leadership roles and on committees. According to Algren (2023), these educators understand that working together makes the work lighter and thus choose to dedicate their time and talent to support their associations and the English language teaching profession. As board members, these volunteers regularly collaborate with educators at local educational institutions, examine the field's evolving issues and challenges, build connections in a community of scholars, advocate for effectively preparing English language teachers, and initiate diverse pathways toward enhanced advocacy and professional engagement.

PARATESOL's Rebirth

In 2017 PARATESOL went through a rebirth, which was embraced by local English teaching entities (i.e., Centro Cultural Paraguayo Americano [CCPA], Stael Ruffinelli, Superior Institute of Languages [ISL]), major publishers of English teaching materials (i.e., Pearson, Richmond, Oxford), the U.S. Embassy, and the TESOL International Association. Thus empowered, PARATESOL's 2017 executive board quickly re-established monthly workshops and annual conferences, which had been hallmarks during PARATESOL's earlier years. The board was helped by volunteers who used different modes of digital communication and social media such as email, WhatsApp groups, Facebook, and Instagram pages, to promote and nurture PARATESOL's renewed advocacy efforts. These regularly scheduled events and virtual communication modalities propelled PARATESOL into its former role, that of being a major advocate for the preparedness of English language teachers. However, shortly after regaining its former strength, PARATESOL faced a new challenge—the COVID-19 pandemic. With a mission to provide quality PD, PARATESOL leaders immediately began converting their PD from on-ground to online. Within two years, PARATESOL was even stronger than before.

Since 2018, PARATESOL has been steadily increasing the number of professional development opportunities in the Paraguayan English language teaching community. Between the years 2018 and 2019, more than ten workshops and two international conferences were organized by the board, all of which were held face-to-face exclusively. Due to COVID-19 pandemic lockdowns in Paraguay during 2020, all forms of professional development activities organized by the association were put on hold. In May, the PARATESOL board decided to take the challenge of offering weekly free online workshops for teachers in Paraguay and Latin America through the Zoom platform, which would allow them to reach more people. Through a case study approach, this paper focuses on describing how this organization capitalized on the affordances of the virtual environment to offer an unprecedented number of professional development activities for their members as well as non-member English language teachers in Paraguay and around the world. The number of weekly workshops more than quintupled from previous years, reaching over 600 teachers in Paraguay and around the world. Likewise, the annual conference more than doubled the number of participants as well as countries represented, with presenters from 14 different countries sharing their expertise. Even though changing the way workshops were held was challenging and unknown, the association has grown in confidence with time and has transcended the frontiers. The board has also strengthened relationships with different TESOL associations in the region, which could be seen in the diverse attendance in the webinars.

In retrospect, PARATESOL's responses to a local challenge (inactivity) and a global challenge (pandemic) offer promising insights to how a volunteer-based association can respond to large challenges and continue building its advocacy role. By viewing challenges as opportunities, PARATESOL leaders strengthened their association's advocacy efforts for the preparedness of English language teachers and, in turn, enhanced the quality of English language teaching.

How PARATESOL's History Influences Current Achievements

As a TESOL affiliate, PARATESOL is charged with advocating for the preparedness of English language educators and the enhanced delivery of English teaching. To that end, PARATESOL provides PD workshops in schools and language centers across Paraguay and collaborates with publishers and distributors of teaching materials. PARATESOL serves educators from preschool through university who teach the English language, who use English to teach other subjects, who coordinate English language programs, and/or who direct educational institutions that provide English instruction. PARATESOL also serves pre-service teachers who are pursuing college degrees or teacher certificates. Through its website and social media presence, PARATESOL even serves educators across Paraguay and beyond. Its virtual venues (e.g., Facebook and Instagram) are of utmost importance for instructors who are the only English teachers in their respective region. This is especially important for teachers in remote schools who use their phones to access internet-based PD opportunities provided by PARATESOL.

Three Decades of Supporting English Teachers in Paraguay 169

PARATESOL was founded in 1989 as the culmination of two years of groundwork spearheaded by English language administrators at the Centro Cultural Paraguayo-Americano and supported by the U.S. Embassy in Asuncion. After having led this affiliation movement, Ms. Pacita Peña served as the association's inaugural president. In PARATESOL's first newsletter, Ms. Peña encouraged English teachers to participate: "From the first day of our acceptance as a TESOL affiliate, we have been dedicating our efforts to promoting our goals among all EFL teachers here in Paraguay . . . Increased contact among Paraguay TESOL members will make things happen" (Peña, 1989, p. 1). With 130 attendees at PARATESOL's first annual conference, the expectations of PARATESOL as a TESOL affiliate were met and surpassed.

Serving as PARATESOL's second president was Sonia Gallagher. Upon returning to Paraguay after several years abroad (which included an ESL master's degree), Sonia exclaimed: "I was surprised and pleased to discover many advancements and opportunities recently made available locally for enhancing our careers as English teachers" (Gallagher, 1991, p. 3). Two years later, when conference attendance dipped below 90, the board responded to this challenge by offering workshops in rural areas. Incoming president Mary Zorrilla identified a need at an even higher level of advocacy: "Our profession needs a voice at the policy making level. By mutually supporting one another, our organizations can work together to gain this voice" (Zorrilla, 1992, p. 1).

To better inform members of upcoming events, PARATESOL printed each year's PD schedule on its membership card. This led to increased participation at monthly workshops, resulting in 187 attendees at the 1993 conference. After several years as the inaugural newsletter editor, Susan Spezzini became PARATESOL's fourth president and described the growing participation as "contagious optimism": "Everyone wants to be a part of the action, and the wave of new PARATESOL members is cresting to an all-time high. This, in turn, creates a positive social atmosphere for learning and sharing" (Spezzini, 1994, p. 3). Two years later, PARATESOL welcomed 282 attendees to its 1995 conference. Mary Louise Baez, PARATESOL's fifth president, attributed this success to volunteerism: "It is a way to get involved in the community, serve others, and support a cause . . . PARATESOL Board of Directors are great examples of professionals committed to making a difference in ESL/EFL teaching" (Baez, 1995, p. 9).

PARATESOL was on the move! From its first seven years of operation, 17 newsletters describe a bustling world of advocacy-related actions. From the beginning, leaders knew how to advocate. Although the word "advocacy" rarely appeared in these newsletters, leaders were advocating for the professionalization of the English teaching profession, the optimal preparation of English teachers, and the effective instruction of English learners. For TESOL affiliates, TESOL serves to unify us and provides individual and collective strength (Algren, 2023); PARATESOL follows TESOL's advocacy focus and joins its collective voice.

Riding on this high wave of advocacy momentum, PARATESOL moved into the twenty-first century. However, as often occurs with volunteer organizations, we experienced an ebb and flow in activities and membership, which resulted in an extended period of inactivity. In 2017, PARATESOL started a revitalization process by several English language educators who focused their advocacy efforts on returning their professional association to its former strength. Armed with fresh ideas and digital skills, these new leaders forged a path for PARATESOL to meet the needs of today's educators. Mailings were replaced by social media, phone calls by WhatsApp, and physical classrooms by virtual venues. Yet, interestingly enough, some issues remained the same. For example, just like with PARATESOL's earlier leaders, its new leaders needed to find ways to motivate English teachers to want to belong and become active members. However, given today's technology era, solutions would be different from those used two or three decades ago.

Carolina Ortiz assumed the challenge of serving as PARATESOL president for the period corresponding to the years 2018–19. Carolina had been a preservice teacher in the 1990s and still remembered energetic PARATESOLers in packed rooms at yearly conferences. Determined to bring her professional association back to life, Carolina brought together a dynamic leadership team. With the scene now set for success, Harshini Lalwani presided over PARATESOL in 2020–21. She was followed by Rocio Mazzoleni, the 2022–2023 president, who together with the leadership team continued the organization's efforts to consolidate its advocacy efforts.

Advocacy Project

The energetic dynamic leadership team that assumed PARATESOL's helm in 2017 started by organizing and implementing monthly PD workshops and annual conferences. Just like in PARATESOL's initial years, frequent activities with quality PD again served as a catalyst for attracting attendees and increasing membership. Local, regional, and international professionals presented at these monthly workshops and at the annual conferences. The two-day conferences also provided attendees with an opportunity to see the latest language teaching materials offered by publishers and to exchange experiences with colleagues from across Paraguay and beyond.

For the first three years following PARATESOL's renewal, most of these activities were conducted in a face-to-face format. PARATESOL's renewed presence led to requests by members who lived in Paraguay's interior for workshops to be provided in their towns. Given travel complications, it was difficult for them to go to the capital city for a Saturday workshop, though they were often willing to do so for the two-day conference. Since 2018, PARATESOL has been steadily increasing the number of PD opportunities in the Paraguayan English teaching community. Between the years 2018 and 2019, over ten workshops and two international conferences were organized by the board, all of which were held face to face exclusively.

Due to lockdowns in Paraguay caused by COVID-19, during 2020 all forms of professional development activities organized by the association were put on hold—at first. In May, the Paratesol board decided to take the challenge; they leveraged their Zoom platform to increase their outreach to diverse educators in Paraguay by providing free weekly workshops to those who were often challenged by accessibility of professional development. The results of these activities were that over 600 Paraguayan and worldwide English language teachers participated in the weekly workshops, which is a fivefold increase more than previous years. Due to this shift to online modality, the annual conference expanded its global reach with presenters from 15 different countries and a twofold increase in the number of participants. Undertaking this new challenge of online professional development increased the association's confidence and allowed them to surpass their limits and professional development offerings. The board has also strengthened relationships with different TESOL associations in the region, which could be seen in the diverse attendance in the webinars.

During the past five years (2018–2023), PARATESOL has collaborated with both national and international organizations. These include, at the national level, schools, universities, and other educational institutions as well as publishers and other institutions serving the English language teaching community. Some of these institutions include the local universities, especially the National University of Asunción, with which the organization has a long-standing relationship, as many of its initial and current leaders have ties with the university.

The efforts made during the 2020 pandemic were extraordinary as they provided weekly support for English teachers, who encountered a very unusual situation having to migrate from in-person classes to virtual lessons from one day to another. PARATESOL provided not only professional support but a space that enabled teachers to be part of a community that gave them both professional and personal support. Through the weekly webinars, teachers had the opportunity to learn strategies and techniques as well as to share their experiences regarding how to handle the very challenging situation of having to teach their students remotely by whatever means necessary. These actions helped the organization with establishing and maintaining advocacy relationships with fellow teachers and teacher organizations in the Latin American region and further (Linville, 2019).

By the end of the first year of the pandemic, PARATESOL's leadership team realized that sustaining a weekly webinar was exceedingly difficult as the whole organization was done exclusively by a team of volunteers. Therefore, for the second year of the pandemic, a decision was made to cut back to a frequency of twice a month. This frequency has allowed the organization to accommodate workshops presented by volunteers from Paraguay and the region as well as presentations by publishers who, besides giving teachers strategies and ideas, promote assorted products aimed at English teachers. These commercial partners allow the organization to keep the membership fees to the minimum possible amount in order to attract not only established professionals but, most especially, students and new teachers.

As can be noted in Table 10.1, there was a significant growth from 2019 to 2020 due to the sudden change in modality and the number of workshops and activities organized to respond to the challenges presented by the pandemic. After the resounding success of the webinars and the online conference in 2020, the organization had to rethink the resources needed to continue with such a rhythm of activities. A decision was made to cut the webinars to twice a month for the next year. As can be noted in the table, the numbers decreased significantly, and this may have been due to a few distinct reasons. Regarding the webinars, many teachers started teaching in hybrid mode during 2021 and some even in person fully, so they did not have as much time to participate in weekly or even bi-weekly webinars. In terms of the international conference, the 2021 conference, unlike the previous year, had a cost, so that may have deterred many from attending.

As can also be noted in the table, getting paid membership for the organization has continued to be a challenge and a struggle. In the past three years, PARATESOL has offered combinations that included the membership fee in the conference registration to incentivize conference attendees to become members. Another challenge that has remained is to get new and existing members to get involved in volunteer activities, especially considering that

Table 10.1 PARATESOL Annual Conference and Workshop Five-Year Summary

	2018	2019	2020	2021	2022
Conference	International Conference: PARATESOL Face-to-Face Conference	International Conference: PARATESOL Face-to-Face Conference	International Conference: PARATESOL Virtual Conference	International Conference: PARATESOL Virtual Conference	International Conference: PARATESOL Hybrid Conference
Attendance	247	187	593	142	275
Attendees' Nationalities	Paraguay, Argentina, Peru, United States	Paraguay, Argentina	Paraguay, Argentina, Bolivia, Saudi Arabia, Venezuela, Uruguay, Great Britain, Canada, United States, Peru, Dominican Republic	Paraguay, Argentina, Venezuela, United States	Paraguay, Argentina, Uruguay, Venezuela, United States
Presenters	26	29	35	19	23
Presenters' Nationalities	Paraguay, United States, Peru, Argentina	Paraguay, United States, Uruguay, Peru, Argentina, Mexico	Great Britain, Canada, United States, Argentina, Peru, Venezuela, Bolivia, Uruguay, Honduras, Dominican Republic, Paraguay, Japan, Saudi Arabia Mexico	Canada, United States, Paraguay, Argentina, Great Britain	Paraguay, United States, Argentina, Spain, Uruguay, Peru, Russia, United Kingdom
Workshops given	7 (May to November)	5 (March to November)	26 (May to November)	15 (May to November)	10 (March to October)
Participants	200 attended in total	10 to 20 per workshop	15 to 45 per workshop 662 total	10 to 30 per workshop 200 total	10 to 152 per workshop 441 total
Feedback	Well organized 80% Go to the countryside 60% of attendees		Excellent to Outstanding organization 90%	Very Satisfied 90% Satisfied 10%	Very Satisfied 96% Satisfied 4%
Paid Members	98	45	40	0	59

many of them have schedules that do not allow for any activities besides those related to income-generating work. This is the case of schoolteachers, who during the weekend many times teach in language institutes. Therefore, finding teachers who are willing to spend their little and very precious free time in volunteer activities is exceedingly difficult, considering that many of them also have family to attend to during those times. In the last couple of years, the organization has offered free entrance to the conference to university student volunteers. After this experience, conversations have begun to start more aggressive campaigns to offer free and deeply discounted memberships to university students and public school teachers. This will allow the organization to reach out to publishers and other sponsors that would be more interested in sponsoring the organization considering its increased membership. This proposal is yet to be discussed at an assembly, which is the organization's maximum authority.

Meeting the Needs of Teacher Educators Through Open Access Materials

University students in resource-challenged contexts often experience limited access to affordable quality textbooks (Hilton, 2020; Trotter, 2018). Such was the case for students in Paraguay studying to become English as a foreign language (EFL) teachers. Their university library had an English collection, but it was small and outdated. To address student needs, administrators and faculty in the languages department conceptualized an online open-access textbook with chapters contributed by local and global English language teaching (ELT) professionals. The department director obtained university approval to publish this projected book as an Open Educational Resource (OER) via Creative Commons (https://www.oercommons.org/). She then sought collaboration from an ELT Fulbright scholar.

Energized and empowered from having revitalized PARATESOL, Universidad Nacional de Asuncion (UNA) faculty and administrators advocated for preparing their own textbook with chapters written by practitioners and researchers from Paraguay and other countries. Collaborating authors were contacted through the university and contacts from the book editors (Canese & Spezzini, 2023) as well as contacts made through PARATESOL sister organizations in Latin America and around the world. This year-long advocacy project resulted in a 55-chapter online textbook with 61 contributing authors in nine countries. This ELT book contains nine divisions: World of English Language Teaching, Language Learners, Language Learning and Use, Context for Teaching and Learning, Content and Language Integration, Methods and Approaches, Teaching Strategies, Assessment, and Career Development and Enhancement. Its 55 chapters are targeted toward teacher preparation courses at Paraguayan universities. Now approaching completion, the ensuing book is targeted for 2023 with a Creative Commons license. As an OER, this textbook can also be accessed for the preparation of pre-service EFL teachers worldwide (Hodgkinson-Williams & Arinto, 2017).

Lessons Learned and Future Directions

The organization learned that it is possible to reach both local and international teachers through digital means; however, in this era of fierce competition and information overload, it is challenging to convince some teachers to support the organization by paying for membership. The challenge remains to think of ways in which the organization can attract a substantial number of new members by offering special student memberships free of charge in exchange for volunteer work as well as partnering with educational institutions to provide bulk membership to their teachers.

Another outcome from PARATESOL's revitalization and its subsequent advocacy efforts is how many of the current PARATESOL leaders are also administrators and faculty in the English department at UNA. Through their self-advocacy experiences at bringing their professional organization back to life, these English language educators have built a self-awareness of also being able to meet the professional needs of their local work institutions (rather than waiting for outside support). The UNA English department identified a need for local-focused materials to better prepare pre-service teachers of English for working in the Paraguayan context.

Final Thoughts

Throughout this chapter, we have presented the advocacy efforts carried out by PARATESOL's recent leadership team. It is very noteworthy that the challenges presented by the pandemic also brought about opportunities granted by the affordances provided by the virtual boom experienced throughout the world. This pandemic created new opportunities and, even though it meant closing buildings, opened doors for PARATESOL to keep offering quality professional development to its members. It allowed the association to reach them more. We began this discussion with the challenges that transitioning to virtuality has represented for the educational community in general and English teachers in particular. PARATESOL has had an abrupt encounter with virtual environments, and it has learned to take advantage of this medium. It has facilitated its accomplishments of goals, and instead of distancing, it has cut distances and promoted better communication and collaboration. An unexpected outcome of this transition has been the opportunity it has created for members to exchange and share professional development opportunities with fellow local TESOL associations of the region. It has also allowed the internationalization of the organization, which in turn gives its members the opportunity to share glocally with colleagues. It can be fairly stated that the association has built a virtual professional community that is reaching its members and its local and regional community of teachers of English. A community of practice as defined by Lave and Wenger (1991) has been established with the common goal of professional development and a virtual community where opportunities for networking are possible. This community of practice now includes colleagues from around the world who collaborate with PARATESOL members in different endeavors to support and grow the teaching communities in their countries and regions. Through these efforts, the organization hopes to continue growing to better serve as an advocate for English teachers in Paraguay and throughout the region. In this way, the organization may serve both teachers and teacher candidates in developing their abilities to identify and work with co-advocates both locally and internationally (Whiting, 2016; Linville, 2019).

References

Algren, M. (2023). Building and engaging with your professional community. *Teaching English in Global Contexts: Language, Learners, and Learning* (chapter 55). Editorial de la Facultad de Filosofía de la Universidad Nacional de Asunción.

Baez, M. L. (1995). Words from our incoming president. *PARATESOL Newsletter, 4*(3), 9.

Canese, V., & Spezzini, S. (Eds.). (2023). *Teaching English in Global Contexts: Language, Learners, and Learning.* Editorial de la Facultad de Filosofía de la Universidad Nacional de Asunción. Creative Commons.

Gallagher, S. (1991). A message from our president. *PARATESOL Newsletter, 1*(4), 3.

Hilton, J. (2020). Open educational resources, student efficacy, and user perceptions: A synthesis of research published between 2015 and 2018. *Education Tech Research Development, 68*, 853–876. https://doi.org/10.1007/s11423-019-09700-4

Hodgkinson-Williams, C., & Arinto, P. B. (Eds.). (2017). *Adoption and Impact of OER in the Global South.* African Minds, University of Cape Town. DOI: 10.5281/zenodo.1005330

Lave, J., & Wenger, E. (1991) *Situated Learning. Legitimate Peripheral Participation.* University of Cambridge Press.

Linville, H. A. (2019). Advocacy skills for teachers: "A real careful little dance." In *Advocacy in English Language Teaching and Learning* (pp. 3–17). Routledge.

Peña, P. (1989). A note from our president. *PARATESOL Newsletter, 1*(1), 1.

Spezzini, S. (1994). Seize the opportunity. *PARATESOL Newsletter, 3*(1), 3.

Trotter, H. (2018, February 23). The challenge of open and accessible education. University World News: The Global Window on Higher Education. Retrieved from https://www.universityworldnews.com/post.php?story=20180223045659684

Whiting, J. (2016). Training ELL teacher advocates. *Fourth Estate, 32*(2), 9–10.

Zorrilla, M. (1992). Reaching out. *PARATESOL Newsletter, 1*(7), 3.

Chapter 11
Metagogy as Advocacy in Initial Teacher Education

Gabriel Díaz Maggioli

Overview

> Our advanced technological society is rapidly making objects of us and subtly programming us into conformity to the logic of its system to the degree that this happens, we are also becoming submerged in a new "Culture of Silence"
>
> —Freire (1970, 2002, p. 15)

How can a grassroots advocacy project have an enduring positive influence amid a nationwide neoliberal educational reform? What can an invested advocate specifically do when faced with the imposition of a version of the saber tooth curriculum (Peddiwell & Benjamin, 1939) that ignores the needs of educational institutions and favors outdated theories and praxes (Strohschen, 2009) intent on pauperizing the educational opportunities of those in public education under the guise of an educational transformation? I will attempt to answer these and similar questions by describing an emancipatory education advocacy project using the lens of Metagogy.

Context of the Project

The project was undertaken during a two-semester-long academic year at a branch of the National Teacher Education College in Uruguay within a course called Reflective Practice Workshop. This is a campus-based companion course to the early professional experiences that student teachers in a Bachelor of Arts (BA) in Teaching English to Speakers of Other Languages (TESOL) engage with as part of their final year in college. The purpose of the course is to provide student teachers with a safe and focused space to learn how to undertake classroom research as a way of promoting reflection *in*, *on*, and *through* action (Farrell, 2018). Authors such as Vaughan & Burnaford (2016) have suggested that classroom research provides "an integrative theoretical and practical" (p. 280) approach to inquiry, which can have three main purposes: to help student teachers reflect on teaching, to enable them to undertake participatory critical inquiry into their own reality, and to prepare them for teacher leadership in teaching and learning for social justice. I would add that the reification of classroom research as a form of professional development also acts as a sieve to perceive inequalities. These inequalities pertain not only to the student teachers but also to the students they serve, as the former engage in loops of practicing the theory learned in college while, at the same time, theorizing the praxes they enact in the actual school classrooms.

Educational Transformation or Saber Tooth Curriculum?

It was in this context that the need to develop an advocacy project emerged. Early in the academic year, national education authorities announced that they would be implementing a mandated nationwide reform of the whole educational system, including the teacher education sector. This would imply the adoption of a competency-based framework (Tobón, et al., 2006), the structure and contents of which would be decided by a group of consultants whose names, educational experiences, and institutional affiliations would remain unknown. In doing so, the authorities ignored the rich tradition of collaborative curriculum construction that had been the norm in the country since the year 1949. In previous scenarios, the needs for reform were diagnosed, and agreements made among the faculty and students of the various campuses of the National Teacher Education College. This new strategy aimed at silencing the voices of faculty and students was intended to minimize the alleged politicization of the national college. This perception results from the fact that, in a national teacher education system comprising 33 campuses, in a small country of only 3:500.000 inhabitants, the boundaries between the politicized demands from workers' unions and the political changes demanded by teaching collectives can be rather diffuse, at times. However, there are laws in place that strictly penalize proselytism in the classroom, and the code of ethics and conduct that instructors and students abide by clearly avoids such political biases.

As soon as documents from the team of consultants became known, there was a generalized sense of emergency as the proposals were drastically deficient in terms of academic rigor and suitability to the teaching profession. To start with, the core competencies of the model were the exact same ones as those specified for subject-specific contents as well as for general pedagogical courses. Also, the same core competencies appeared in all four years of the new BA curriculum (Consejo de Formación en Educación, 2022). This presented a very real impossibility of contextualizing the competencies to the learning needs of college students who undergo a very specific process of self-authorship (Baxter Magolda, 2014). Additionally, the few subject syllabi that composed the new curriculum framework presented severe epistemological inconsistencies. For instance, English Language Courses (a core component of the initial teacher education curriculum for future teachers who are still learning the language they will eventually teach) presented a strong structural approach characterized by a bottom-up conception of language as a system that is linear, and sequential. In this formulation, language is understood as the progressive combination of phonemes, morphemes, and, eventually, lexemes into sentences that, taken together, would constitute discourse (Administración Nacional de Educación Pública, 2022). The same kind of bottom-up approach is specified for the development of skills, with the most concerning being writing, where the voice of the author and the nature of the genre and the rhetorical organization of the texts are not mentioned. The recommendations in the aforementioned document are for learners to master phonics first, then individual words, and, finally, phrases, clauses, and sentences without regard to the systemic-functional nature of language (Administración Nacional de Educación Pública, 2022). Additionally, no reference is made to the many advances in the field of second language acquisition theories. In this way, teachers can supposedly learn (and teach!) how to read and how to write in a foreign language without discoveries in the field making any change to classroom procedures. The exact same orientation to language description was used in the new national curricula for primary and secondary education levels, which is where student teachers in this project currently do their practicum.

What is most worrisome in this scenario is the adoption of a perspective of the education of future teachers that sees them not as transformative professionals but as technicians who apply mandated, decontextualized teaching strategies. Additionally, the adoption of the particular epistemic perspective described above contradicts the very foundational assumptions of a principled communicative approach (Dörnyei, 2002), which is the one the National Educational System of Uruguay had been advocating for since the mid-1980s.

Metagogy as Advocacy in Initial Teacher Education

Seeing that there would be no possibility of reversing the decisions already made by the authorities. I chose to position myself as a broker between the academic and praxeological aspects of the discipline I teach. Because educators were unable to influence the decisions made by the authorities, as they ruled by decree, I found it necessary to intervene in the most hope-oriented way I could. I decided to engage in an advocacy project that would help raise awareness of what was being lost in this educational transformation both to future student teachers in the college and, also, to the students they will teach.

Understanding Advocacy

"Advocacy" is a very polysemic term that encompasses a wide gamut of meanings. Some interpretations of the term define it as acting on behalf of others to promote change. Other interpretations see it as collective activity oriented at influencing decisions and institutions. I have always been wary of definitions that position the advocate as a spokesperson for others. We cannot ignore the fact that advocacy is conceived of and enacted within contextual patterns that emerge from the identities, cultures, religions, politics, policies, histories, and economies of highly situated groups of individuals. Because of this, it cannot be denied that in this digital time and age, one key purpose of advocacy should be to haul inequalities into the open so as to provide alternative solutions to the problems these inequalities pose. Once these inequalities are open to public scrutiny, advocacy efforts and activities serve as catalysts to empower stakeholders with tools to propose the intended alternative solutions, while, at the same time influencing public opinion and building public consciousness. This endeavor is even more crucial in countries such as Uruguay, where mainstream media are controlled by a powerful few and society is constantly being exposed to half-truths or *alternate* truths.

Because of my critical epistemological positioning as an educator, I consider my advocacy role not as that of a helper but as that of a co-researcher and co-enactor of a reality that is co-constructed in highly situated historical moments. Hence, I take a decidedly Freirean (Freire, 1970/2002) stance to conscientization, defined as the process of becoming critically aware of our social reality through sustained engagement on reflection and action. In this context, action is crucial because it is through acting with and in the world that changes in reality begin to occur. Seen under this light, advocacy becomes an integral component of emancipatory educational practices. Furthermore, given my role as instructor in a higher education institution aimed at the education of future teachers, I see advocacy for concientization as an key professional commitment, as relevant to my role as teaching, research, service, and outreach. As Strothschen (2014) explains, "universities are defined as the places of knowledge production and dissemination, teaching and learning, and theory building that informs the practical in society" (p. 513) and advocacy should be an integral part of the university culture. Hence, it is one of the tasks of the teacher educator to constantly question the academic praxes they engage in, in light of the pressing needs of society.

Within this perspective, I see the role of the advocate as emergent and not as fixed or achieved at the culmination of a process. Taking an emergentist perspective to advocacy immediately makes it polyphonic. In this view, advocacy and advocates emerge from the interaction with stakeholders, with whom they are co-inquirers and co-enactors of praxes, which can be defined as principled and informed interventions *in* and *with* reality for the purpose of emancipation. As Freire (1970, 2002) aptly put it

> Humankind *emerge* from their *submersion* and acquire the ability to *intervene* in reality as it is unveiled. *Intervention* in reality—historical awareness itself—thus represents a step forward from *emergence*, and results from the *conscientização* of the situation. *Conscientização* is the deepening of the attitude of awareness characteristic of all emergence. (p. 109, italics in the original)

In light of the inability that teacher educators and student teachers would have to effect any change on the policies and procedures of the new curricula (both at the college level and at the secondary school level), the need was felt to explore ways in which the student teachers in the group could acquire the tools to advocate *for* and *with* the language learners they would eventually teach in the midst of an educational transformation that stands to negatively affect teaching and learning in public education, thus deepening the knowledge gap between the most and least privileged strata of society.

Goals of the Advocacy Project

One of the changes the new curriculum has put in place is the elimination of the particular subject I refer to in this chapter. The three weekly hours currently devoted to the Reflective Practice Workshop are to be substituted in the new curriculum by subjects such as Computational Thinking and the

Teaching of Phonetics and Phonology. Losing this curriculum space means that student teachers will have no equivalent space to engage in socializing their praxes so as to better align them to the needs of their learners in their four years of study.

Because of this, the goal of the advocacy project I refer to in this chapter was to model and co-construct principled interventions at the school level that would help compensate for the lack of pre-service exploratory experience, which constitutes an important form of professional development for future educators.

This goal sought to learn about, develop, implement, and reflect on—together with student teachers—a framework for their ongoing professional development. The intention behind this was that participating in the advocacy efforts of the course would help them advocate for their learners and build awareness within the individual schools in which they work. This awareness targets both potential obstacles and affordances to teacher and students learning.

The criteria by which we would gauge the impact of this project focused on the affordances of this particular intervention to build a network of advocates who, together, though acting from different milieux, would set in motion processes of inquiry aimed at enhancing the student experience of learning a foreign language in a principled way.

Because the targets of the project were groups of adults who are either studying to be teachers (the student teachers in the college) or working as teachers already (their colleagues in the schools where they currently work), a decision was made to frame it within the Metagogy theorem. Metagogy (Strohschen & Elizer, 2019) is defined by its creators as "an approach for facilitating learning within contextually developed, relevant education methods by, with, and for adults" (p. 3). To these authors, Metagogy "acknowledges the contextuality of geopolitical, national, psychological, or other boundaries, and with that, barriers to teaching and learning, that we have created and maintained within our sparring ways about whose ideology will prevail and grab all power" (p. 8).

What is more, the Metagogy theorem allows educators to design, develop, apply, and sustain the impact of learning activities that are grounded in very specific values. For example, it is grounded in the social value of interdependence, where respect for local knowledge is highlighted at all times. Also, this value blends the local knowledge with knowledge derived from global research and practices (if and when these are assessed by the local stakeholders as being of value to their community).

One key distinction between Metagogy and other approaches to adult learning is that the former incorporates cognitive, psycho-motor, and affective domains of human experience in the design, implementation, and sustainability of the practices oriented at engaging with and in their contextual reality. This integral view of the co-participants imbues interventions within this framework with the potential to promote the "emancipation of each Self" (students and teachers, author's phrase) in a liberatory context of freeing one's Self from assumptions and values that run counter to emancipation.

The current situation provided us with both affordances and limitations to reach our advocacy goal. In terms of the affordances, we counted on the generalized resistance among teachers to the new curriculum. Various college departments made their voices heard through social media, as well through non-mainstream media and press. Because of this, our project was readily identified as advocacy oriented. In this sense, the primary audience for the project was the staff of schools where student teachers taught, together with learners and their families, as well as other teacher educators in the department at the college. The secondary audience was the national authorities to whom the results of the project would be made evident through media campaigns reporting on the implementation of anti-hegemonic pedagogical projects. Hegemony, here, is understood as the specific mandates of the new curricula.

The limitations of the project involved mostly the unwillingness of the decision makers at the national level to engage in dialogue with local stakeholders, as well as the restrictions placed by participants' life situations, which, sometimes, left very little time for undertaking the collectively constructed activities. However, at all stages of the project, we made sure that both affordances and limitations were supported by relevant quantitative and qualitative data, as will later be explained.

The Advocacy Project

> Knowledge emerges only through invention and re-invention, through the restless, impatient, continuing, hopeful inquiry human beings pursue in the world, with the world, and with each other.
> —Freire, 1970, 2002, p. 72

The advocacy project started in our second month of classes. Ours is a yearlong course that starts in March and finishes at the end of November, with a two-week winter break in July and a one-week spring break in September.

Metagogy as Advocacy in Initial Teacher Education

Throughout this time, student teachers were in charge of their own group in a public secondary school where they undertook their practicum or early professional experience as these are called locally to avoid reinforcing the theory-practice dichotomy. During this last course, student teachers are supported by their English Language Teaching (ELT) methods instructor from college, who is also in charge of the Reflective Practice Workshop. As part of their teaching assignment, student teachers participate in a weekly faculty-wide coordination meeting in their schools where issues of teaching, learning, and institutional management are discussed and where professional development projects can be organized among faculty in all disciplines and grade levels. In turn, instructors in the college also have a two-hour weekly departmental meeting to the same avail.

During the second month of classes, and as soon as the first documents about the proposed reform began to surface and were made available, there was a generalized sense of urgency to engage in advocacy efforts as a form of resistance. These advocacy efforts were initially system wide, and they ranged from activism campaigns (e.g., student teachers sit-ins in the various campuses of the college, strikes, public demonstrations, appeals to the press for support, and similar activities), to lobbying at the congressional level by student, teacher, and professor unions, to more focused small-scale advocacy projects. Once it was made evident that the national authorities were completely reticent to engaging in dialogue, grassroots projects such as the one described here began to surface.

Starting Out

In our case, the genesis of our project can be traced to a very particular classroom discussion following a weekly coordination meeting that the student teachers had had in their schools. When they arrived in the college for our weekly class session, they were very concerned with the information about the new secondary curriculum they had received in the meeting and, being cognizant of the changes the teacher education curriculum would undergo as well, they wondered, "What can we do?"

Their main concern was that given the guidelines in the new secondary school curriculum, they anticipated learners would be unable to actually learn and use the foreign language they taught. If, they claimed, students in public schools already struggled to learn the language within a communicative paradigm, chances were that the turn toward a structuralist approach would render them even less able to learn the language. They reasoned that while a structuralist approach could perhaps yield better test results (since grammar and vocabulary drilling and the manipulation of syntax under very controlled conditions could easily be replicated in tests), the fact remained that students would be rendered functionally unable to use the language in real-life situations. In short, learners would be learning *about* the language, but they would not learn the language for actual use in social settings.

It should be noted at this point that throughout the first month of classes, the student teachers' main concern had been that their learners were reticent to communicate in English even though communicative-oriented teaching practices were in place. I, too, had noted that the student teachers were both tentative and reticent to actually engage in critical dialogue about teaching and learning in our weekly sessions and that they felt they were not authoritative enough to be able to make decisions about language teaching and learning that would prompt any sort of change. I made this point, noting it to them, and they reasoned that we needed to find a way in which we could all engage in activity oriented toward counteracting these perceived deficits. In doing so, they reasoned, they could collect highly situated data about their learners' language learning needs, while, at the same time, find ways to improve their own learning.

Getting On

At this stage we needed to find a framework that would allow us to undertake actions that would result in concrete data and praxes that would show to the wider educational audience the limitations of the current situation while highlighting the dangers of the proposed reform. I suggested we use Smith and Rebolledo's (2018) Exploratory Action Research (EAR) framework, as it complies with the main tenets of Metagogy, which is, in itself, a form of action research (AR). EAR is a form of AR that incorporates an additional step prior to the usual loop of planning—acting—observing—reflecting that is characteristic of AR. This prior loop is aimed at carefully exploring the current situation, highlighting local voices, and understanding affordances and limitations in the community to be able to take a principled approach to the design of an intervention. Hence, there is a cycle that starts with "reflect": reflect—plan—act—observe—reflect—plan, where the final "plan" is the actual intervention to be undertaken. Smith and Rebolledo (2018) point out that the need for this additional cycle lies in the fact that oftentimes, classroom researchers find out mid-way through the AR cycle that the intervention they have planned is not conducive to the change needed. Hence, by including an exploratory loop before deciding on a specific intervention, there is a deeper understanding of the local needs as well as the proposed intervention. One final difference between AR and EAR is the way in which EAR is intended to make research findings available to practitioners. It has long been discussed that there is a disconnect between classroom teachers and research in how research findings are obtained, communicated, and applied (for an interesting summary, see McLelland, 2016). EAR bridges this gap by promoting user-friendly ways in which results can be communicated to the wider school community.

The project started by developing our advocacy goal, identifying the primary target audience, and engaging in the EAR first loop. To this avail, we created surveys, performed one-to-one interviews, recruited the support of critical friends, and performed extensive literature reviews on the topic at hand. In the case of student teachers, the surveys were given in the learners' L1 for the sake of ease of response. The interviews were also undertaken in L1. Student teachers decided to request the support from a colleague teaching English as a Foreign Language (EFL) as their main critical friend but chose a college classmate as their second critical friend. In this way, they could feed back to our own community all their findings and reflections gathered along the way.

In my case, I undertook the same kind of exploratory activities to gather data. I then presented my exploratory findings to student teachers for their validation and discussion. I chose to have another instructor who teaches the same course as my only critical friend. The exploratory cycle lasted for two months, and our weekly class sessions were devoted to sharing and improving our understanding of the contexts we were researching.

Turning Points

Once the exploratory cycle was completed, we each engaged in designing interventions to answer our research questions. We counted on the support of our critical friends, who acted as sounding boards during the design and implementation stages of the intervention, as well as provided valuable feedback throughout the process. Not only did critical friends perform this function, but they also observed our lessons and audited our findings. The AR cycle lasted for two further months (from the end of the winter break to the spring break). Again, our weekly class sessions in the college were devoted to collectively analyzing data and reflecting on our findings. The findings were used as fodder to map out target audiences for advocacy as well as to craft advocacy messages and initiate advocacy activities at the school and college level.

Finally, after the spring break, the findings were communicated via social media to a wide range of audiences. We created short videos explaining our project, showing the data, and sharing our findings. We also built infographics for ease of reference. During every weekly class session, we reported on our project and sought to provide each other with further support to inform the wider education audience of our work.

Because this was a grassroots initiative, we did not seek to build a consortium. Instead, we aimed at developing networks of like-minded colleagues (both in the schools where the student teachers taught, as well as in the college). During weekly coordination meetings we provided information not only about our project but also about EAR as a tool to empower teachers. By the end of the academic year, each of us had developed a network of at least two other colleagues who were learning more about EAR to be able to implement their own projects during the 2023 academic year.

One of the areas we audited intensively during our weekly meetings in the exploratory cycle was how insider knowledge was gathered and used, and how this helped build personal connections among stakeholders. We understood insider knowledge as that "indigenous" knowledge derived from each co-participant's understanding of their reality. Having data about the co-participants' situated experience allowed us to keep our project honest and focused on the ultimate goal of raising awareness and prompting change.

While there were no major hurdles during the exploratory cycle from a methodological point of view, there were many learnable moments. In my personal case, I discovered that my teaching style and orientation toward a critical approach to joint knowledge construction sometimes prevented students from more fully participating in class. This was because they felt their voices were not qualified enough to give an opinion, suggest a course of action, or make a claim, even when data were readily available. Because of this they wanted to be taught explicitly and perceived any effort at co-construction on my part as a threat. This made me confront my own beliefs about teaching and learning and also my positioning as a co-advocate. Was I imposing my own views on them, or was I actually promoting a dialogic kind of interaction congruent with the Metagogy theorem? Was this advocacy effort worthy from both a social justice point of view and a pedagogic point of view or was I implementing a form of symbolic violence?

This led to many fruitful discussions with student teachers who contributed actively to the realization that for learning to be mediated and thus co-constructed, meaningfulness is paramount. When there is no meaning, joint activity is impossible. With that realization they turned to their own findings in terms of why their learners were reticent language users. They discovered that the faithful adherence to pedagogic paradigms characteristic of their survival stage as novice teachers (Díaz Maggioli, 2023) led them to act within a comfort zone that was difficult to leave.

Critical friends assisted us during this process. In my case, they observed my classes, audited my questions during class, and gave their own pedagogical interpretations of my praxis while helping me confront deeply held beliefs. In the case of the student teachers, critical friends also performed a more instrumental role by providing ideas and potential solutions to classroom problems that emerged during the exploratory phase.

Because of this, we arrived at the actual implementation of the intervention phase with sufficient data about and understanding of our realities so as to enact principled interventions. Throughout the implementation phase, we made sure to communicate relevant critical incidents emerging from our interventions. These were fed back to our critical friends and to our own college group for discussion, interpretation, and deliberation. From each of these encounters, a concise and concrete message was collectively crafted that would unambiguously convey to the general public our findings about the issue at stake. Our work was inspired by a set of questions proposed by Sharma (1997) as a guide to crafting advocacy messages. This author proposes reflecting on what we want to achieve by sending a particular message to a specific audience, envisioning the positive result of the message of the activity in question, and determining what specific actions we want the audience to engage in.

Opening Roads

Besides message crafting, we engaged in other advocacy activities, such as requesting a time slot within the weekly coordination meetings to address the issues in the messages. Additionally, we volunteered to demonstrate effective approaches to teaching and learning that had emerged from our collective engagement with EAR. These advocacy efforts were sustained over the course of the implementation of the interventions and until the end of the academic year.

Table 11.1 Policy Map for the Disadvantages of a Structural Approach to Language Teaching

\multicolumn{5}{l}{Policy map: Effects of a structural approach to language teaching on students' learning}
\multicolumn{5}{l}{Advocacy role: To raise awareness about the potential negative effects of an exclusive focus on form approach and to recruit advocates to spread the message.}
Audience	Audience knowledge about issue	Audience beliefs and attitudes about issue	Issues that the audience cares about (may be unrelated to the issue)	Sources of data
English language teachers	A focus on form exclusively is not conducive to communication	Resist the implementation of such an approach	Students' learning Teaching quality (professional pride)	Interviews Surveys Informal observations Anecdotal records collected
School administrators	They do not know how languages are learned	May feel that there is nothing wrong with this approach	Good learning results No complaints from parents	Interviews Minutes of coordination meetings Informal discussions on teaching and learning
College faculty	A focus on form exclusively is not conducive to communication	Resist the implementation of such an approach	Academic rigor Academic development	Professional theories Lived teaching experience
Parents	They do not know how languages are learned	May believe it is good because they may have experienced it themselves	Academic success of their children Differential advantage of knowing English	Surveys Interviews Records of parent-teacher conferences Anecdotal records
Students	They do not know how languages are learned	Tend to find grammar work boring and pointless, which may cause lack of motivation	Using the language to communicate Passing the course	Surveys Interviews Focused observations Analysis of students' work

Note: Inspired by and expanded from Sharma (1997, pp. 47–48).

Metagogy as Advocacy in Initial Teacher Education

Lastly, we undertook the establishment of a network of like-minded Exploratory Action Researchers whose understandings of their local reality we expected would cause the desired level of pressure in the educational system so as to make others realize that a change in policy was badly needed.

To this end, we used a tool called a "Policy Map" (Sharma, 1997, p. 47) that helped us plot our course and kept us on track. At this stage I should mention that because ours was a form of alternative advocacy, we centered on answering three key questions to help us construct our policy maps:

a. Who can implement changes to the enactment of the new curriculum without the need to involve government officials?
b. How can we reach these stakeholders and engage them in implementing the change?
c. Would these stakeholders help us in sustaining the advocacy efforts that would potentially help influence a change in policy?

In practice, a policy map helps us plot what our audience knows and thinks about a particular issue. In this sense, policy maps are ongoing constructions that, although future-oriented, are grounded in the present reality, thus helping advocates get a panorama of the current situation without losing sight of the end goal. Hence, policy maps are not static tools but devices that help advocates design multiple courses of action and messaging to clearly communicate intentions and information, raise awareness about the issue, and make calls to action in an ongoing manner. Such maps help to prompt reflection about what audiences know about the issue, what they believe, and what they care about. The following is one of our initial policy maps:

A Preliminary Assessment of the Project

One cannot give credit to the complexity of developing an advocacy project such as this by merely writing a narrative about it, even though that narrative may be supported with contributions from the literature on advocacy. In particular, academic writing requires us to be linear and sequential for the sake of clarity and rigor. In contrast, advocacy reality is both systemic and dynamic. It is systemic in that one single change has the potential to affect the whole system over time. It is chaotic because advocacy projects become self-adaptive to the many sociohistoric conditions, which are in perpetual flux as are the human actions at the center of advocacy activity. In this sense, claiming that the present project has already yielded results may prove to be a claim unsupported by enough quality data.

As this is an ongoing project, we can also account for what has been modestly accomplished in this first year. Firstly, the advocacy has acted as a catalyst for awareness-raising about the newly imposed curriculum and its limitations. This awareness has been expanding since the first advocacy messages were crafted and disseminated. Examples of these messages include some of the following, which were shared on social media.

Did you know that in the new teacher education curriculum:

- the voices of teacher educators and student teachers are completely silenced?
- future teachers of English will have significantly fewer courses than similar programs in the world and the region?
- future English teachers in Uruguay will know nothing about the culture of English-speaking countries because they won't have that course any longer?
- future English teachers will stop learning how to teach at the Primary level where English is compulsory? (Silva Quartiani, 2022)

Secondly, it has empowered student teachers to speak out. As one of the student teachers in the group expressed during an interview, "I believe I have developed a reflective stance that allows me, whenever there is a situation in which my students are put at risk, to not just notice what is going on, but act upon it" (student teacher #1). This simple testimony stands in contrast with the feeling of inadequacy for action felt by student teachers early in the project.

Thirdly, it has provided student teachers and the colleagues in their networks with a concrete tool for action that is ideally suited to the academic environment, while also innovating in terms of how teachers access knowledge and use it.

We can conclude that the outlook toward the future is at present a hopeful one. Co-participants show a commitment to enhancing their voices by engaging in collective inquiry and actions that directly target perceived and confirmed inequalities. They stand to be able to make a difference in the communities they participate in by actively voicing their concerns based on situated evidence. What is more, there is a general feeling of hope among co-participants that their EAR efforts may result in concrete, rigorous, and useful information that may help influence future and current policy development projects. As another student teacher reflected, "I want to be a teacher who acts morally whenever an issue arises because this is what my students deserve. I'll act because I know that change from the grassroots level is possible" (student teacher #3)

Reflections and Future Directions

> No pedagogy which is truly liberating can remain distant from the oppressed by treating them as unfortunates and by presenting for their emulation models from among the oppressors. The oppressed must be their own example in the struggle for their redemption.
> —Freire, 1970, p. 54

Even though the project described in this chapter is not finished, we can advance some relevant learning from the experience of engaging in it. To start with, we have learned to harness the power of Metagogy as an approach to teaching and learning that is inclusive and polyphonic and that allows co-participants to move from a dependent stance where they seek direction from authoritative figures to an interdependent stance where relationships, reflection, and action constitute the fabric for advocating for and with other co-participants.

This realization brought out into the open the fact that advocacy is not about speaking on behalf of others but about finding a footing for collective messages that incorporate all voices. These messages make evident realities that may be hidden to many and, in doing so, pave the way for collective action to have an effect on reality.

We also learned that advocacy is about community building and that communities do not have to be pre-existing. They can be born out of the common desire to change current conditions.

If given the chance to participate in a project such as the one described in this chapter, I would not hesitate to do so. Even though I may be a seasoned professional who has been in similar situations before, each iteration of an advocacy endeavor brings with it new learning and new ways of approaching issues. In doing so, we all grow as we act and live in multiple communities simultaneously. Even though these communities may not intersect, they do in fact constitute a network of advocacy efforts and activities that has the potential to effectively change conditions.

If we want to truly embody an advocacy stance we need to genuinely care about our students, their families, our colleagues, and their strife. We need to be willing to step out of our comfort zone and build new relationships. This may seem like a daunting task, but when understood as a community-building endeavor, it looks less daunting as we are no longer alone. Finally, we must be willing to learn about the cultures of other communities, which include those of the audiences we are trying to influence. In the process, we will necessarily have to examine our teaching practices to make learning relevant to all involved. This is the mettle of the true advocate, to promote equity, inclusion, and justice.

Discussion Questions

1. Can you establish a boundary between advocacy and learning efforts in this narrative?
2. How could you develop a similar advocacy project in your context?
3. What aspects of this project have left you wondering? Why?

References

Administración Nacional de Educación Pública. (2022). *Progresiones de aprendizaje [Learning Progressions]*. ANEP.

Baxter Magolda, M. B. (2014). Self-authorship. *New Directions for Higher Education, 2014*(166), 25–33. https://doi.org/10.1002/he.20092

Consejo de Formación en Educación. (2022). *Plan de formación de la cerrera de profesor de educación media [Curriculum Framework for the Education of Secondary School Educators]*. CFE.

Díaz Maggioli, G. (2023). *Initial Language Teacher Education*. Routledge.

Dörnyei, Z. (2002). Communicative language teaching in the 21st century: The "principled" communicative approach. *Perspectives, 26*(2), 33–43.

Farrell, T. S. C. (2018). Reflective practice for language teachers. In J. I. Liontas and M. DelliCarpini (Eds.), *The TESOL Encyclopedia of English Language Teaching*. Wiley. https://doi.org/10.1002/9781118784235.eelt0873

Freire, P. (1970, 2002). *Pedagogy of the Oppressed*. (30th Anniversary Edition). Continuum.

MacLelland, P. (2016, August 9). Why don't teachers use education research in teaching? *Education in Chemistry*. Retrieved from https://edu.rsc.org/analysis/why-dont-teachers-use-education-research-in-teaching/2010170.article

Peddiwell, J., & Benjamin, H. (1939). *The Saber-Tooth Curriculum*. McGraw Hill.

Sharma, R. (1997). *An introduction to Advocacy: A Training Guide*. Support for Analysis and Research in Africa (SARA).

Silva Quartiani, M. (2022, November 19). Did you know that they talk about educational reform and what is imposed is destroying teacher education? Facebook. https://www.facebook.com/MartinaSilvaQuartiani/posts/pfbid026vdxnNBTUynAYLfi7cZdzX3Kwp8aNwE6a0essDUYeASTh4yxio7AyUfDVXry0GZGl

Smith, R., & Rebolledo, P. (2018). *A Handbook for Exploratory Action Research*. British Council.

Strohschen, G. (2014). Education collaboration development: A blended shore education approach to sustainable development. In S. Mukerji and P. Tripathi (Eds.), *Handbook of Research in Transnational Higher Education*. IGI Global.

Strohschen, G. (Ed.). (2009). *The Handbook of Blended Shore Education: Adult Program Development and Delivery*. Springer Verlag International.

Strohschen, G., & Elizer, K. (2019). The metagogy theorem: A framework for teaching adults. *International Forum of Teaching and Studies, 15*(1), 3—15.

Tobón, S., Sánchez, A., Carretero, M., & García, J. (2006). *Competencias, calidad, y educación superior [Competences, quality, and higher education]*. Cooperativa Editorial Magisterio.

Vaughan, M., & Burnaford, G. (2016). Action research in graduate teacher education: A review of the literature 2000–2015. *Educational Action Research, 24*(2), 280–299.

Chapter 12
Global Efforts in Advocacy for English Language Teaching and Learning: Conclusions and Futures

Okon Effiong, Kate Mastruserio Reynolds, Debra Suarez, Georgios Kormpas, and Grazzia Maria Mendoza Chirinos

Patterns of Advocacy Identified in the Chapters

We began this project from the perspective that advocacy research and discussions often emerge from contexts where educators have some degree of enfranchisement to engage in advocacy activities. We aimed at having contributors from around the world share their work with us so the field could benefit from diverse global perspectives. Those educators who contributed to this volume exceeded our hopes and expectations. This conclusion chapter first draws together patterns gleaned across chapters prior to address takeaways from educators in other global contexts, principles, and skill sets for advocacy in sociopolitically and economically diverse, and possibly constrained, contexts, and future directions.

Pattern 1: Success and Sustainability Are Often Based on Access to Resources

The collective efforts that are portrayed aimed at providing access to opportunities, improving language learning, and creating more conducive environments for language learning to thrive. Contextual constraints, political support, availability of resources, and the willpower of advocates often determined the success of such endeavors. Advocacy efforts in more heavily resourced contexts are apparently more successful than in other contexts with fewer or less consistent resources, according to the authors' narratives.

Therefore, the examination of the patterns of resources reported in the volume, and the way that they highlighted the disparities, struggles, and successes of the contributing authors, showcased how in some cases, authors stepped up to find resources to support learning (e.g., Barrett, chapter 3 this volume). This is congruent with Linville & Staehr-Fenner's (2019) and Goode's (2019) discussions of teachers' classroom-based advocacy actions and the use of their personal funds to support learning. The role of individual motivation to serve as a change agent and take decisive action to obtain what learners need is echoed in the research of Garrone-Shufran (2022, 2023). Loder Buechel (2022) also notes that teacher dispositions are an indication of who is willing to effect change.

The diverse authors of this volume represent not only countries globally but also professionals who advocate at different levels of instruction and who work with varying academic backgrounds; the commonality here is the outcome of their efforts and the advocacy heart that guides their pathways. Overall, the authors have expertise and substantial knowledge of their learners or colleagues and leverage these to promote their work. There is no evidence here to suggest that greater professional experience and qualifications translated into greater success in a particular context. The majority of the advocacy actions did not appear to require a prohibitive amount of funding; although, substantial funds were needed by some, such as Oladejo, whose project involved the purchase of laptop computers, Paulino's need for a technical platform to implement her project, and Carranza Campos's need for funding from external government agencies to scale the project to the number of youth they had as a goal. These acts of advocacy required, mostly, the self-empowerment of the teachers and the support of others in power (Greenlee & Dedeugd, 2002; Norman & Eslami, 2022).

Some advocacy approaches are constrained by culture, politics, economics, and religion but can still be pursued by modifying the advocacy effort to suit the context (Haneda & Alexander, 2015). Absence of political will and finance are often major hurdles. Unless support comes from wealthier entities, those that are in economically challenged regions will continue to struggle. Perhaps, seeking support from the wealthier entities may go against the spirit of decolonization, which means to break free from the practices of former colonizers. If decentering means shifting from the practices of advocacy in the Western world, is it unacceptable to be self-directed in advocacy efforts and accept financial support for projects?

We need to clarify the term "Western," which often refers to nations such as the United States, Canada, Australia, New Zealand, and Europe. However,

Europe and the United States, for example, have locations that face similar economic realities to those in Southeast Asia, Africa, Latin America, and the Caribbean. Does "Western" suggest a developed economy, which includes Japan? In effect, "Western" perspectives portrayed in this volume should make space for other global approaches and the pursuit of diverse pathways to advocacy.

When we reflected on the idea of decentering advocacy, which we thought was an approach to shifting the lens to the ways advocacy was enacted in global contexts, we subsequently observed the entrenched nature of collective thinking. We recognize that the use of English as the lingua franca of international discourse, academic publications, and higher education is itself problematic and hegemonic. In the narratives, the use of English to discuss and enact advocacy may seem contradictory. English becomes the common link we see throughout the chapters, not as a tool for influencing culture and adapting to colonizing rules but as a tool language teachers leverage to promote change. English language teaching then becomes the available tool to drive change; meanwhile, the language itself can drive out local languages and promote unwanted colonizing influences. Furthermore, even our own reviews of the manuscripts struggled not to reinforce Western perspectives on advocacy as we looked for references to the relevant body of knowledge or existent research literature.

We noticed, too, that educators who live and work in formerly colonized contexts need to reclaim the power that was taken from them by colonization, or "decolonize themselves." In this way, decentering advocacy efforts are not something that comes from the outside, nor is it something that happens *to* non-Western contexts; rather, decentering advocacy is something that stems from within and is something that happens from, by, and inside the agents of advocacy within that context. Consequently, advocacy efforts in global contexts should be envisioned and shaped by the contextual nuances, constraints, and possibilities available in each geographic area, recognizing the complexities inherent around colonization and linguistic imperialism.

Pattern 2: Advocacy Efforts Are Based Directly on Students' Needs

The trends in the chapters suggest that the development of advocacy skills by the authors varies from context to context. Most of the authors view language teachers as those with the power to lead advocacy efforts through varied platforms, whether it be through English language teaching associations (ELTAs), within the classrooms, or outside of school projects (Canese, Spezzini, and Mazzoleni; Carranza Campos; Paulino; Nguyen, Lam, and Nguyen; Akcan). Many authors view advocacy as creating programs to meet the needs of their learners in their contexts (e.g., Barrett, Maggioli, and Schlam Salman and Schvarcz). The authors typically approached their projects to meet learners' needs while building on their assets.

Pattern 3: The Catalyst for Advocacy Efforts Can Be Intrinsic or Extrinsic

One can observe that some of the advocacy projects were situationally prompted, such as Oladejo's effort, and motivated by the educator's (or educators') drive to enact change within a given community. These educators saw the needs of learners, colleagues, school(s), or communities and empowered themselves to work toward equity.

It is seemingly easy for some authors to draw on their personal resources to advance their advocacy drive; others needed external agencies to augment their intellectual repertoire to succeed, especially where resources required for success had serious financial implications. Several chapters describe projects that focus on youth or vulnerable groups, such as imprisoned or out-of-school youth, who have historically been marginalized and who have had their needs and their rights overlooked (e.g., Carranza Campos, Paulino).

Some authors seem to suggest that ELTAs should be agents of advocacy. For example, Awanga claimed the local ELTA was not inclusive enough, especially for the female members, and opted to build "a ladder of the three collectives: collective awareness, collective development, and collective efficacy" (chapter 2). While others, such as Maggioli, were prompted by external changes in the educational system and his researched understandings of how language can and needs to be taught. This pattern again points to efforts to decenter advocacy, because there is no singular problem or challenge, nor solution or guidelines, of global advocacy.

Pattern 4: Educators Envision Many Approaches to Operationalizing Advocacy

We see the authors describing *practicing* advocacy or *operationalizing* advocacy in diverse ways, such as instructional advocacy, programmatic advocacy, and curricular advocacy. The power of the teacher/educator is in the operationalizing of classroom-based or schooling advocacy. According to Weng, McGuire, and Roose (2020), culturally responsive pedagogy emphasizes appreciating and sustaining learners' cultural differences and using cultural knowledge and prior experience of ethnically diverse students to make learning encounters more relevant and effective. As such, the practices of advocacy were socioculturally and contextually responsive.

Pattern 5: Context Dictates Efforts That Are Feasible

Not every advocacy effort involves the dual goal of improving educational access and promoting policy changes aimed at improving education for multilingual learners of English or working conditions of teachers. As noted in this volume, little has been reported on direct action for policy change; rather, most of the chapters focus on access to language education and creation of opportunities for language teachers to thrive. In terms of learning and teaching English, there are various sociocultural factors that could pose a challenge to learners. Nguyen, Lam, and Nguyen in Vietnam shared their approach to advocacy for opportunity and access, which connects schooling advocacy to larger advocacy realms, such as institutional advocacy and political advocacy. Maggioli's chapter described his approach to indirectly addressing a newly developed curriculum by the Ministry of Education that ran counter to research on ELT theory, principles, and instructional practices by engaging in-service educators with research on effective language teaching and learning, which was ultimately shared in a public manner to influence the implementation of the new curriculum policy.

It is important to have access to a wider range of intercultural practices (Perez et al., 2021), especially where English is viewed as a colonization tool that maintains unequal socioeconomic and power structures (Litzenberg, 2021). Therefore, the various perspectives presented in this volume in effect corroborate Litzenberg's suggestion of promoting intensive English programs as a means of positively influencing decolonization of the field if ELT educators strive to promote first language maintenance within their communities.

Authors in each of these book chapters have given a good account of their advocacy efforts, and having diverse voices from different corners of the globe suggests that more needs to be done toward decentering the advocacy construct from the ways advocacy has been treated within Western countries. This is just part of the initial efforts to decenter advocacy worldwide.

Lessons Learned from Educators' Advocacy Narratives

Having worked closely with the educators as they penned their advocacy narratives describing their efforts within their classrooms, schools, and communities, four main areas stand out for us. First, we found that individual educators' advocacy efforts required the sacrifices of time and energy, but the sacrifices yielded powerful outcomes for their learners and programs (Bradley-Levine, 2021). In Barrett's chapter, for instance, we see the degree of her personal and financial commitment to her advocacy work. Whereas in Oladejo's chapter, we can envision the transformation of learners' language abilities in the substantial improvement in students' listening skills as the result of her advocacy initiative. Since many of the narratives had similarities in contexts and needs that served as the impetus for advocacy actions, the initiatives are highly replicable.

Second, educators who engage in advocacy work take risks to challenge the status quo (Green, 2022; Linville, 2019, 2021). Although it may seem that some taboo topics are difficult to share with learners, especially in communities with strong cultural, political, or religious opposition, the eventual acceptance of differences by students in some contexts shows that advocacy strategies work to change minds and hearts. The Schlam Salman and Schvarcz chapter exemplifies how advocacy efforts can transform learners' thinking and mitigate conflict between Israelis and Palestinians by recognizing social inequities, deconstructing binary thinking, and promoting social and linguistic justice. Maggioli's chapter illustrates an informed resistance to a new ministry-sanctioned curriculum and how he and his collaborators prompted the participants' independent advocacy for and with each other.

The third area of learning for us was the lack of advocacy related to language policy in the narratives. The efforts were not driven by policy creation or change but instead by direct action focusing on implementing projects within the educators' locus of control. Dubetz & de Jong (2011) describe these areas as "within the classroom" advocacy (e.g., planning, instructional, and assessment choices related to social justice and equity topics) and "beyond the classroom" advocacy (e.g., ways in which educators strive to make schools and educational policy more equitable). It is myopic to claim that since there were no narratives submitted about ELT policy–related advocacy, it is not occurring in these locations. We wondered whether its absence in this volume is related to educators' self-perceived lack of agency and authority (Haneda & Sherman, 2015) or whether there are contextual constraints to engaging in direct-action, policy-driven advocacy in the countries they live and work in.

Varghese and Stritikus (2005) described the relationship among teachers' agency, policy-related advocacy, and context. They explained that teachers "are not seen as 'reproducers' of a particular policy but are viewed simultaneously as agents who make specific choices based on their own histories and their evolving professional lives as well as being 'constrained' or 'shaped' to a certain extent by the contexts in which they find themselves" (p. 75).

We remind ourselves that "advocacy" should not be treated in a vacuum. Teachers may have a harder time advocating for students in contexts where unequal power distribution is readily accepted. Therefore, advocacy agents must consider advocacy in larger schooling and community contexts. One thing is certain, however: it is a strong indicator that global advocacy is a field to be explored further, and it should not be viewed from the lens of advocacy in countries where actions might be more policy driven, have a broader impact, take longer, and might not necessarily reach those who need support. Nor should we view advocacy exclusively as actions taken to influence policy or bring about change; rather, advocacy seems to have various purposes depending on the situation, key players, and issues at hand. Clear examples are the types of advocacy that are evidenced in the literature, and these projects include:

- **Learner/learning-oriented advocacy** in which educators advocate for groups or individual learners and their instructional rights, or instructors advocate for what they need to be effective practitioners (Dubetz & de Jong, 2011; Linville, 2019, 2021).
- **Community-oriented advocacy** (Harrison & McIlwain, 2020) describes the advocacy efforts that educators enact to support the parents, families, and communities of multilingual learners of English (MLEs).
- **Materials-oriented advocacy** focuses on the tangible materials for learners' use (e.g., paper, pencils, books) or other physical materials, such as adequate desks, instructional space, and/or buildings (Harrison & McIlwain, 2020).
- **Social issues–oriented advocacy** emphasizes actions, such as peace, social justice, individual groups' rights, bilingualism/ multilingualism, and immigration/ migration.
- **Educator-oriented advocacy** encompasses employment and labor workforce concerns (e.g., visas, contracts, tenure, salaries) and professional recognition of the field of ELT.

- **Professional development–oriented advocacy** focuses on access to and funding for professional development and assistance for teachers to meet professional standards (Haneda & Sherman, 2018).
- **Policy-oriented advocacy** organizes to change instructional and programmatic standards, learners' rights, educational systems, teacher quality/preparation standards, and laws related to the instruction of multilingual learners of English.

Reconceptualizing Global Advocacy

Now that we have highlighted the patterns and learning, and as we explore the examples of the advocacy projects in this volume from contexts outside of Western countries, we ask the important question, "What can teachers/educators in Western contexts learn about advocacy from non-Western contexts?" As we discussed above, when we present examples of advocacy in global contexts, it is important to clarify how we use the term "Western." In this volume, we use "Western" to refer to Western Europe, the United States, Canada, Australia, and New Zealand.

As the volume editors, we suggest lessons learned from global contexts. We first harken back to one aim for this volume: to situate the decentering of advocacy within global efforts toward justice and equity. Notions such as "justice" and "equity" and even "advocacy" are not monolithic but are fluid and evolving. These are key reminders for Western educators not to be complacent in addressing their own challenges in educational advocacy. Global contexts, especially Western contexts, cannot be complacent because they have not yet "figured it out." Around the world, in every country, the "bend toward justice" continues to be but an arc on the long, moral universe. Educators' work toward justice, equality, and advocacy is ever continuing and relies on learning about successful efforts in multiple contexts.

When global educators read the contributions in this volume, we hope that they recognize the strength and courage of the contributors, as they claim their own contextual challenges, exercise their own agency, and assert their own power. The influential acts of advocacy described in these chapters may take diverse forms, such as instructional approaches as advocacy, program development as advocacy, or professional collaboration as advocacy. However, what many of these chapters have in common is how the writers had to first challenge some of the foundational notions of "advocacy" as the very starting point for their projects. Two examples: Awanga describes that in order to implement her daring project, creating a forum of women English language teaching professionals, she had to challenge existing notions of advocacy as oppositional, conducted by the "trouble fête" and a culture of "no," and Paulino dared support youth who are incarcerated to give them access to new opportunities. We encourage global educators to learn the lessons of strength, power, creativity, and resiliency demonstrated by this volume's contributors as they embark on, and succeed in, their advocacy projects. Those in power often meet educators' efforts to impact equity and justice with powerful and swift resistance, in contexts around the world, including all countries. Frederick Douglass's words are as true today as they were when he first uttered them in 1857 in his speech on West Indian Emancipation: "Power concedes nothing without demand. It never did, and it never will" (Douglass, 1857).

These narratives offer additional lessons learned that are useful and applicable to all global contexts. Another instructional point is to examine the impetus for many of these advocacy projects. For example, many of the projects in this volume have arisen in response to perceived inequity or injustice. Some projects arose in response to economic inequalities, where students' access to educational opportunities depended heavily on the students' wealth. Other projects arose in response to cultural differences and religious opinions, where the educators felt it necessary to advocate on behalf of minority students who may have been at risk. While these can be sensitive discussions, the writers in this volume did not shy away from addressing these perceived inequities and injustices through the respondent advocacy projects. We hope that all readers will explore the impetus for the advocacy projects offered by the contributors. Additionally, educators in global contexts would do well to follow the lesson of exploring the inequity and injustice in their own contexts, as an incentive for instructional, curricular, programmatic, school-wide, and community advocacy.

Furthermore, we encourage global educators to read this volume with an eye to view the world of educational advocacy with a broader lens. We encourage global educators to consider how diverse educational practices around the world are influenced by context, cultural values, desires, hopes, dreams, and visions of how the world (or at least one's corner of the world) can be a better place. And within the field of ELT itself, this volume highlights the necessity for global educators to view English, for advocacy purposes, within the teaching of other subcategories of English for specific purposes (ESP), such as business English, English for vocational purposes, English for academic purposes (EAP), English for air traffic controllers, English for science and technology, etc. (Mambu, 2011). To this end, as we have aimed to do in this volume, our final recommendation is to begin to move away from a "Western/non-Western approach" and instead move toward conversations in favor of true "global" advocacy. Throughout this volume, we have endeavored to communicate that advocacy is not one size fits all. Advocacy projects stem from specific, contextualized, and localized needs, challenges, inequities, and injustices, and are informed by emic insights and what is feasible in the local context. Thus rather than impose advocacy models, we can instead learn from each other's advocacy projects and apply what makes sense in our own contexts, what is possible, and what is most impactful. In this way, together, we can move toward more meaningful and more inclusive conversations of "global" advocacy.

Principles and Skill Sets for Advocacy in Constrained Contexts

In a world where education can be both a beacon of hope and a battleground over change, advocacy has emerged as a critical skill set practiced by teachers around the globe. However, this noble pursuit is not without its challenges and constraints (Staehr-Fenner, 2013). In the complex tapestry of education, there are cases that come to our attention, shining brightly under the spotlight of public awareness. Still, there are also countless others that remain hidden in the shadows, obscured by dangerous conditions or the absence of publicity. Advocacy is a global endeavor, and within its multifaceted realm, several principles and skill sets come to the fore.

Finance remains a significant handicap in advocacy. To address this challenge, advocates argue for various forms of support from wealthy donors and nations. This approach ensures that advocacy efforts remain focused on the needs and aspirations of the communities they serve.

Creative resourcing and fundraising become the cornerstone of advocacy in constrained contexts. Without adequate resources, even the most enthusiastic efforts may fail. For teachers advocating for their students and causes, knowing how to obtain resources effectively is an indispensable skill. It involves the ability to craft compelling narratives, connect with potential donors, and navigate the intricacies of grants and funding opportunities. In constrained contexts where financial support is scarce, the ability to secure resources can mean the difference between realizing a vision for change and leaving it unrealized. However, while some projects might require funds or fundraising, the main ingredient or component of advocacy is the will and drive, the commitment of those who advocate for the vulnerable populations who are facing varied challenges. Providing educators with knowledge and resources for raising funds will help them externally fund their advocacy projects.

Equally crucial is the principle of building capacity with like-minded individuals and organizations. Advocacy efforts must be sustainable over time to effect lasting change. This involves forming groups, collaborating with partners who share the same goals, and fostering a sense of collective responsibility. In countries where limited funding and access to opportunities are persistent challenges, the power of collaboration becomes evident. Together, advocates can pool their resources, expertise, and influence to amplify their impact and overcome constraints. When individuals stand together their voices are amplified.

In the chapters from Belize, El Salvador, and Vietnam we see an example of the importance of evidence-based advocacy. In constrained contexts, where resources are scarce, it becomes imperative to demonstrate the effectiveness of proposed changes. Without compelling evidence, advocacy efforts risk being dismissed or ignored. Therefore, the ability to gather and present persuasive evidence is a vital skill set for advocates, ensuring that their proposals are not cast aside in the face of skepticism.

Embracing diversity and responding to the evolving needs of society are essential components of effective advocacy. The projects in Malaysia, Tunisia, Uzbekistan, Tajikistan, Laos, Belize, and El Salvador provide examples of grassroots support that has managed to build a platform even in the most challenging circumstances, often through innovative language education programs that incorporate life skills and prepare students for successful careers in an ever-changing world.

However, some advocacy efforts are constrained by cultural, policy, or religious barriers, or a combination of these factors. In these situations, educators may place themselves or their jobs in jeopardy. In such cases, advocates may need to modify their approach to find a middle ground that respects these constraints while advancing their cause and protecting themselves.

One fundamental shift needed is to incorporate advocacy as a specific content area in teacher education programs and in professional organizations' offerings. Teachers play a vital role in advocacy efforts, and they should be equipped with the knowledge and skills to engage effectively in advocacy activities. This necessitates better treatment of advocacy in teacher education standards on a global scale.

Skills for enacting advocacy can be explicitly taught through instruction. These skills include collaboration, communication, negotiation, persuasion, planning, and more. By imparting these skills to teachers, we empower them to be effective advocates for change, even in the most constrained contexts.

In the intricate orbit of advocacy, these principles and skill sets serve as guiding stars, illuminating the path forward for teachers who seek to champion their students and causes in constrained contexts. With perseverance, collaboration, and a commitment to evidence-based change, advocates can overcome the myriad challenges they face and strive toward a brighter future for education worldwide.

Implications and Future Directions

As educators move toward the future, we must not forget these current global advocacy efforts, the nuances of the contexts, the different constraints and disparities, as well as the key advocacy players in the field. We must use the learning from this volume to guide our future directions in decentering advocacy practices based on what the local context is telling us now within the advocacy continuum: self-advocacy, advocacy for students and programs, advocacy for the profession, and public advocacy. Our efforts should be cognizant of the contextual sociopolitical trends and how these politics influence socioeconomic change and promote value to the work the authors are bringing to their communities.

Our future advocacy work must focus on the needs of each local community, but not in isolation. As a parallel to what Kumaravadivelu (2001) suggested in his post-method pedagogy, advocacy, like instruction, should consider what is particular to the local context, what is practical, and what is possible. When we gear our advocacy efforts toward understanding the sociopolitical and economic realities and the needs of the population in each geographic area, we can avoid promoting standardized advocacy approaches as we have done in the past. As we have succinctly summarized, what we have learned from the various chapters and experiences from our advocate-authors is that we cannot view advocacy from a standardized perspective, and it should not be approached as a one-time, short-duration project. Instead, we need to incorporate in future efforts all perspectives, focusing on what is operational, logical, and sensible to the population we are supporting. It means integrating projects and programs that have the potential to influence policy, based on the contextual needs, and systematizing the needed adaptations that will result in slackening the constraints and creating relevant breakthroughs.

We also want to view advocacy as a tool to build agency and empowerment for teachers, thus influencing learner agency and empowerment, which in turn will potentially trickle directly into the system and promote active, systemic change. It means implementing a learning-by-doing, trial-and-error approach where advocates pilot, follow up implementation, and make operational a variety of strategies through a collaborative learning approach until they identify the right pathway. This means a heavy lift on the side of advocates, but it also results in actionable change that is long-lasting rather than policies that could be reinforced or simply kept in a drawer with no real connection to the issues.

The educator-advocate authors have made us realize that as we move along the advocacy continuum, education is empowering and the key to understanding how our actions enact effective change. As we move into the future, the world will change and education will evolve. As new tools in technology, such as artificial intelligence (AI), virtual reality (VR), and expansion of interconnectivity, bring another layer of complexity, it is relevant to reflect how these trends will influence advocacy efforts both as tools to educate and as tools that raise up our learners, ourselves, and our profession. Hopefully they will erase disparities in access and equity and allow diverse perspectives and approaches, leading to agency, empowerment, and change while establishing diverse platforms where we hear all voices and support all initiatives.

We hope the ELT community and the local and global (glocal) communities involved in advocacy become stronger through all the grassroots movements. We hope that these direct driving forces toward change directly influence policymakers as educators and learners become more empowered, vocal, and active as change agents. The path, our journey, is still nascent, but through these narratives, stories, and projects we believe we are on track to challenge traditional status quo narratives, systemic injustice, and inequity, and to instead promote dynamic changes that build community, yield collaboration, and include everyone's voices at the discussion table. We believe this volume is just a first step toward creating awareness that advocacy is not and cannot be standardized, is not and cannot be a one size fits all, and that contexts speak to promote adaptation, evolution, and creation of the sustainable change we want to see globally.

Discussion Questions

1. What are the most influential patterns you see from the chapters and this discussion in global advocacy in ELT?
2. How do you think that teachers can advocate for students, programs, materials, policy, or the profession without jeopardizing themselves or their jobs?
3. What do you think is the role of advocacy in teachers' English language teaching?
4. How should teachers worldwide become prepared in advocacy work?
5. What are some examples that resonate and that you can relate to within your own context? How would you approach the challenges using similar strategies?

References

Bradley-Levine, J. (2021). *Promoting Teacher Advocacy as Critical Teacher Leadership*. Routledge.

Douglass, F. (1857). *West India Emancipation*. Reprinted 2001. Frederick Douglass Project, University of Rochester. Accessed August 20, 2023. https://rbscp.lib.rochester.edu/4398

Dubetz, N. E., & de Jong, E. J. (2011). Teacher advocacy in bilingual programs. *Bilingual Research Journal: The Journal of the National Association for Bilingual Education, 34*(3), 248–262.

Garrone-Shufran, S. (2022). "I think you have to be a fighter": Novice ESL teachers' descriptions of advocacy for emergent bilinguals. *Teacher Education Quarterly, 49*(3), 48–69.

Garrone-Shufran, S. (2023). Equity for emergent bilinguals: What every teacher needs to do. In J. Etim & A. Etim (Eds.), *Handbook of Research on Solutions for Equity and Social Justice in Education* (pp. 175–196). IGI Global. DOI: 10.4018/978-1-7998-9678-4.ch011

Goode, J. L. (2019). Leading for social justice: professional development experiences of K-8 urban principals (Doctoral dissertation, Rutgers The State University of New Jersey, School of Graduate Studies).

Green, V. (2022). "Use your teacher voice": How a podcast could support ESOL teachers' voices in advocacy. School of Education and Leadership Student Capstone Projects. 867. https://digitalcommons.hamline.edu/hse_cp/867

Greenlee, B. J., & Dedeugd, I. S. (2002). From hope to despair: the need for beginning teacher advocacy. *Teacher Development, 6*(1), 63–74. DOI: 10.1080/13664530200200157

Haneda, M., & Alexander, M. (2015). ESL teacher advocacy beyond the classroom. *Teaching and Teacher Education, 49*, 149–158. DOI: 10.1016/j.tate.2015.03.009

Haneda, M., & Sherman, B. (2018). ESL teachers' acting agentively through job crafting. *Journal of Language, Identity & Education, 17*(6), 402–415. https://doi.org/10.1080/15348458.2018.1498340

Harrison, J. & McIlwain, M. J. (2020). ESOL teachers' experiences in their role as advocate: Making the case for transitive advocacy. *TESOL Journal, 11*(1), e464. https://doi.org/10.1002/tesj.464

Kumaravadivelu, B. (2001). Toward a postmethod pedagogy. *TESOL Quarterly, 35*(4), 537–560. http://dx.doi.org/10.2307/3588427

Linville, H. A. (2019). Advocacy skills for teachers: "A real careful little dance." In H. A. Linville and J. Whiting (Eds.), *Advocacy in English Language Teaching and Learning* (pp. 3–17). Routledge.

Linville, H. A. (2021). Advocacy for student and teacher empowerment. In P. Vinogradova & J. K. Shin (Eds.), *Contemporary Foundations for Teaching English as an Additional Language: Pedagogical Approaches and Classroom Applications* (pp. 249–274). Routledge.

Linville, H. A., & Staehr-Fenner, D. (2019). Preparing teachers to be advocates for English learners. In L. C. de Oliveira (Ed.), *The Handbook of TESOL in K-12* (pp. 339–355). https://doi.org/10.1002/9781119421702.ch22

Litzenberg, J. (2021). Innovation, resiliency, and genius in intensive English programs: Decolonializing recruitment and contradictory advocacy. *Applied Linguistics, 42*(5), 905–923.

Loder Buechel, L. (2022). Teachers as agents of change: Unpacking EFL lessons through an anti-bias lens. In J. Crawford & R. Filback (Eds.), *TESOL Guide for Critical Praxis in Teaching, Inquiry, and Advocacy* (pp. 87–109). IGI Global. https://doi.org/10.4018/978-1-7998-8093-6.ch005

Mambu, J.E. (2011). English for advocacy purposes: Critical pedagogy's contribution to Indonesia. *Journal of Asia TEFL, 8*(4), 135–173.

Norman, L. N., & Eslami, Z. R. (2022). English learner teacher advocates: A systematic literature review. *TESL-EJ, 25*(4), 1–28.

Pérez Berbain, M., Banegas, D. L., & Beacon, G. (2021). Introduction: Diversity in ELT. In D. L. Banegas, G. Beacon, M. P. Berbain (Eds.), *International Perspectives on Diversity in ELT* (pp. 1–17). Palgrave Macmillan.

Staehr-Fenner, D. (2013). *Advocating for English Learners: A Guide for Educators*. Corwin.

Varghese, M., & Stritikus, T. (2005). "Nadie me dijó (Nobody told me)": Language policy negotiation and implications for teacher education. *Journal of Teacher Education, 56*(1), 7387. https://doi.org/10.1177/002248710 4272709

Weng, Z., McGuire, M., & Roose, T. M. (2020). Applying culturally responsive pedagogy to engage with cultural differences in an ESL composition course in the U.S. In P. Vinogradova & J. K. Shin (Eds.), *Contemporary Foundation for Teaching English as an Additional Language: Pedagogical Approaches and Classroom Applications* (pp. 113–117). Routledge. https://doi.org/10.4324/9780429398612

CONTRIBUTOR BIOGRAPHIES

Sumru Akcan

Sumru Akcan is a full-time professor in the Department of Foreign Language Education at Boğaziçi University, Istanbul, Türkiye. She received her master's degree in teaching English as a second language from the University of Cincinnati, Cincinnati, in 1997. In 2002, she received her doctorate degree on Second Language Acquisition and Teaching (SLAT) from the University of Arizona, Tucson. She has been teaching undergraduate and graduate courses in teacher education and foreign language teaching methodology at Boğaziçi University since 2002. Her research focuses on pre- and in-service language teacher education (specifically professional development of teachers and mentor training) and foreign language teaching methodology. She was a visiting scholar for her sabbatical at Hunter College, the City University of New York, in the academic year of 2022–2023. She can be contacted at sumru.akcan@boun.edu.tr.

Abigail Ekangouo Awanga

Abigail Ekangouo Awanga is an English language teacher in a state secondary school in Cameroon and has been in the field for 16 years. She is the current Cameroon English language teaching association (CAMELTA) Vice President for Outreach and founder of ELTWC SIG. For correspondence email: lahidechou@gmail.com.

Enita Elecia Barrett

Dr. Enita Elecia Barrett is a lecturer/special needs liaison in the Foundation Program Department of English at Qatar University in Doha, Qatar. She is a board-certified cognitive behavior specialist with a doctoral degree in education,

education leadership, and TESOL/special education. She also holds master's degrees in instructional leadership and in secondary education advanced studies in TESOL from the University of North Florida, Jacksonville, FL. Her bachelor's degree in secondary education English and literature was from the University of the West Indies, Mona Campus, Jamaica. Her current research interests include TESOL, special education in academic environments, neuro-education, and indigenous languages.

Miguel Ángel Carranza Campos

Miguel Ángel Carranza Campos has a M.Sc. in education from the University of Kansas. He is the coordinator of practicum programs at Universidad de El Salvador, where he is also professor at the Department of Foreign Languages. He is a Fulbright alum and was awarded "Teacher of the Year, 2022" by Teachers Up by the U.S. Department of State. For correspondence, email miguel.carranza@ues.edu.sv.

Valentina Canese

Valentina Canese is currently faculty and director at the Instituto Superior de Lenguas (ISL), Universidad Nacional de Asunción (UNA) in Paraguay. She holds a bachelor's in English (ISL, UNA), a master's in education (San Diego State University), and a doctorate in curriculum and instruction (Arizona State University). Her research interests include bilingualism, language education, information and communication technologies (ICT), and distance education. She is the editor in chief of the multilingual journal *Ñemityra: Revista Multilingüe de Lengua, Sociedad y Educación*. She is the founding president of the Paraguayan Association of Applied Linguistics and the current second vice president of PARATESOL, Paraguay's TESOL affiliate. Open researcher and contributor identification (ORCID): https://orcid.org/0000-0002-1584-7322.

Grazzia Maria Mendoza Chirinos

Grazzia María Mendoza Chirinos is a researcher at UW-Madison, School of Education, Wisconsin Center for Education Research-WIDA. She is a former education specialist at USAID Honduras, where she supported the Ministry of

Education through education development projects. She has been a language educator, teacher trainer, and consultant for 30 years. Recognized by the U.S. Department of State for professional development projects and by TESOL International Association for scholarship and service (Virginia French Allen Service Award 2018) and advocacy (Outstanding Advocate 2023). Grazzia has been a TESOL volunteer since 2007, a board member (2019–2022), and the finance committee chair (2021–2022), and is the founder/inaugural president of Honduras English Language Teacher Association (HELTA TESOL) and former president of the Latin America and the Caribbean TESOL (LAC TESOL).

Okon Effiong

Okon teaches English in Qatar University Foundation Program and holds a Ph.D. in applied linguistics. He is a member of the TESOL board of directors (2020–2023) and chair of the TESOL finance committee (2022–2023). Okon is the founder and past president of Africa ELTA. His research interests include foreign language anxiety and language teacher associations.

Georgios Kormpas

Georgios Kormpas has been an English language teacher for the last 20 years. He directs the Center for Executive Education and Teaching and Learning Development Center (TLDC) at Al Yamamah University in Saudi Arabia. He is currently the president of the International Association of Blended Learning (IABL) and TESOL Gulf. He is a doctoral researcher at Lancaster University in the United Kingdom.

Huong T. L. Lam

Dr. Huong T. L. Lam is currently an EFL lecturer at Thuyloi University, Vietnam. She earned her bachelor's and master's degrees in TESOL in the University of Languages and International Studies, and her Ph.D. in education at the University of Newcastle, Australia, in 2018. She has more than 20 years of experience in teaching and conducting research. Her research interests include (but are not limited to) TESOL methodologies, intercultural communication, language and culture, professional development, and educational management and internationalization of higher education. She worked as the project assistant for the book entitled *English Tertiary Education in Vietnam* in the series Routledge Critical Studies in Asia Education by Taylor and Francis group and published a chapter in this book. Her works have also been published in *Education Sciences Journal, Vietnam Journal of Educational Sciences,* and *VNU Journal of Foreign Studies.* She has presented her work at various national and international conferences, including VietTESOL International Convention and JALT International Conference. Her email is lamhuong@tlu.edu.vn.

Gabriel Díaz Maggioli

Gabriel Díaz Maggioli is a teacher who applies the lessons learned in the classroom to his roles as teacher educator, researcher, and author. He is currently academic advisor in the Center for the Advancement of Higher Education at Universidad ORT Uruguay, where he also coordinates the postgraduate diploma in English language teaching. He is also tenured professor of TESOL in the National Teacher Education College of Uruguay. He has been fortunate to be able to share his theory in praxis with colleagues in the Americas, Europe, the Middle East, and Asia. He was the first Latinx president (2020–2024) of the International Association of Teachers of English as a Foreign Language (IATEFL). Open researcher and contributor identification (ORCID): https://orcid.org/0000-0002-6686-2549. Correspondence about this chapter should be directed to: diaz_g@ort.edu.uy.

Rocío Mazzoleni

Rocío Mazzoleni holds a bachelor's degree in English from the Instituto Superior de Lenguas (ISL), Universidad Nacional de Asunción in Paraguay, a master's degree in applied linguistics from the Universidad Católica Nuestra Señora de la Asunción, and a master's in education and neuropsychology from the Universidad de la Rioja in Spain. Rocio teaches sociolinguistics and didactics and coordinates the ISL's English degree program. For several years, she taught English to K-12 students with special learning needs. Currently, Rocio serves as bilingual coordinator at an inclusive school for students with learning difficulties. Open researcher and contributor identification (ORCID): https://orcid.org/0009-0000-2429-5542. Emails for correspondence regarding this chapter: spezzini@uab.edu; vcanese@fil.una.py, rmazzol@gmail.com

Hong-Anh T. Nguyen

Hong-Anh T. Nguyen is currently a foreign language lecturer at Thuyloi University, Vietnam. She received her bachelor and master's degrees in foreign language teaching methodology at the University of Languages and International Studies. She has over 17 years of experience teaching English in high schools and universities in Vietnam. She has also served as a chairperson and reviewer of the English language studies session in annual conferences of Thuyloi University. Her proceedings have been presented in national conferences. Her works have been published in *Education Sciences Journal* and *VNU Journal of Foreign Studies*. Her research interests include language teaching, curriculum planning, and professional development. She can be contacted at anhnth@lu.edu.vn.

Son V. Nguyen

Dr. Son V. Nguyen is an EFL instructor at Thuyloi University, Vietnam. He obtained his bachelor's degree at the University of Languages and International Studies with distinction in 2015 and his master's degree at Victoria University, Australia, in 2017. He achieved his Ph.D. degree at University of Szeged, Hungary, in 2022. His research interests focus on learner autonomy, teacher autonomy, teacher beliefs, learner perception, and teacher professional development. He has published his work in *Heliyon, Electronic Journal of Foreign Language Teaching, Education Sciences, Language Learning in Higher Education, MEXTESOL, RELAY*, and *VNU Journal of Foreign Studies*. He also presented his research at many national and international conferences, such as the Hungarian National Conference on Education, the Training and Practice International Conference on Educational Science, and the VietTESOL International Convention. He can be reached at nvson@tlu.edu.vn.

Oluyemisi Oladejo

Oluyemisi Oladejo has an M.A. in English from the University of Ibadan. She was the winner of the 2020 African Writer's Prize for Creative Nonfiction. She was a co-winner of the Ogun State Academic Laurel in 2021. In 2022, she won the TOEFL English Researcher's/Practitioner's Prize. She taught English language across public secondary schools in Ogun State, Nigeria, before she won the Fulbright FLTA Fellowship and moved to the United

States, where she currently teaches Yoruba at the University of North Carolina in Chapel Hill. Oluyemisi has authored seven books, including a grammar textbook.

Ethnelda Paulino

Ethnelda Paulino is the founder/administrator/instructor of English and literature of Kaina Online High School, established 2014. She works with online students to increase the number of high school graduates. She teaches students of all ages, including incarcerated persons and those who cannot attend traditional schools for medical reasons. Email: ethneldabz@yahoo.com, ethneldap@gmail.com.

Kate Mastruserio Reynolds

Dr. Kate Mastruserio Reynolds is a professor of TESOL and literacy at Central Washington University. She has taught educators internationally at universities and public school districts and ESL/EFL in primary schools and universities in various contexts. Dr. Reynolds's publications include *Introduction to TESOL and Research Methods in Language Teaching and Learning* and *Approaches to Inclusive English Classrooms: A Teacher's Handbook for Content Based Instruction*. She has presented regularly at TESOL International Association, American Association of Applied Linguistics, National Association of Bilingual Education, and TESOL affiliates. She has attended the TESOL International Association Advocacy Summit three times since its inception and has taught undergraduate and graduate students the tools they need for teacher advocacy. In 2022, she was inducted onto the TESOL International Association's board of directors. Open researcher and contributor identification (ORCID): https://orcid.org/ 0000-0001-6528-2326. For correspondence, please email kate.reynolds@cwu.edu.

Briana Rogers

Briana Rogers is an English educational coach for the English-Speaking Nations program in Uzbekistan. She holds a master's in English language teaching from the University of East London and has certificates in Monitoring and Evaluation and Education in Emergencies. Ms. Rogers is an internationally experienced trainer of trainers, a teacher trainer, a curriculum designer, and a materials developer. She has over 25 years of experience in 15 countries. She has worked on teacher development programs advocating for teachers and students' rights in Uzbekistan, Malaysia, Laos, and Tunisia. For correspondence, please contact www.linkedin.com/in/brianalrogers.

Julia Schlam Salman

Julia Schlam Salman is a lecturer and teacher educator at the David Yellin Academic College of Education in Jerusalem. She also teaches in the MA TESOL program and in the division of languages at Tel Aviv University. For many years, Dr. Schlam Salman was an English as a foreign language teacher at the Max Rayne Hand in Hand School for Jewish-Arab Education. Her research interests include language education, language learning and teaching, and English language learning in areas of intractable conflict. Contact: schlam.salman@gmail.com.

Brigitta R. Schvarcz

Brigitta R. Schvarcz is the head of English as a Foreign Language at The Hebrew University of Jerusalem and a teacher educator for the Israeli Ministry of Education, Department of Professional Development of Teaching Staff. She is past chair of the English Teachers' Association of Israel (2020–23) and currently serves as vice-chair of the association. Starting from summer 2023, she also holds a position as lecturer in the M.A. TESOL program at Tel Aviv University. Her research interests include formal semantics, language awareness, linguistic landscape, and language in areas of intractable conflict. Contact: bridget.schvarcz@gmail.com,

Susan Spezzini

Susan Spezzini is professor and program director in ESL teacher education at the University of Alabama at Birmingham (UAB). Susan holds a bachelor's in linguistics (University of California, San Diego), a master's in language teaching (University of California, Berkeley), and a doctorate in ESL curriculum

(University of Alabama). Before coming to UAB, she worked 26 years in Paraguay, initially in the Peace Corps and then at the ISL/UNA and other ELT entities. A founding member of PARATESOL, she served in leadership roles during PARATESOL's early years. As a Fulbright Scholar, Susan returned to Paraguay to help create and edit this book. Open researcher and contributor identification (ORCID): https://orcid.org/0000-0002-6296-9365.

Debra Suarez

Dr. Debra Suarez is president of the TESOL International Association, serving in the presidential line and executive committee from 2023–2026. Dr. Suarez comes to this executive role after a lifetime of serving multilingual learners of English and the teachers, professionals, and organizations who serve them. Suarez has been a classroom teacher, university professor, international educator, and senior U.S. federal advisor. Dr. Suarez was senior advisor for the White House Initiative for Asian Americans. Prior to her work in the White House Initiative, she was a university professor and English language education specialist for the U.S. Department of Education, contributing to the national language advocacy efforts of multiple federal agencies and White House task forces. Further, as an English language specialist with the U.S. Department of State, Dr. Suarez served in Southeast Asia, the Middle East, South and Central America, and West Africa. Now, as a seasoned TESOL leader, Dr. Suarez focuses on coaching, mentoring, and developing the next generation of global ELT leaders. As such, Debra's current research, presentations, and upcoming books focus on leadership, advocacy, and mentoring of English language teachers worldwide.

INDEX

A
Abubakar, 45
Abubakar & Attanda, 42
academic achievement, 20, 23, 28, 69, 87, 136
academic backgrounds, 197
academics, 9, 11
access, 11–14, 24–25, 41, 48, 71–72, 79–80, 87–88, 95–97, 105–9, 111, 147–48, 150–51, 158, 196, 200, 203–4
action plan, 59, 141
action research, 186–89, 192, 195
actions
    advocacy-related, 19, 34, 95–96, 107, 169, 193, 197, 200–201
    interpersonal, 107–8, 191
activism campaigns, 185
Adams, 15, 90, 93
Adams & Newton, 2
adaptation, 21, 64, 104, 208
administrators, 62, 97, 99–100, 102, 135, 143, 174–75
advocacy
    agents of, 71, 197–99, 202
    beyond the classroom, 201
    classroom-based, 5, 96, 103, 197, 199, 201
    community, 204, 207
    curricular, 103, 199
    decenter, 4, 7–8, 199–200
    definitions of, 7, 33, 88, 96, 105, 128, 135, 199
    educational, 203–4
    effective, 33, 143, 206
    encourage, 4, 71, 103, 108–9, 167
    evidence-based, 206
    global, 15, 199, 202, 205, 209
    independent, 201
    institutional, 200
    policy-related, 202
    political, 96–97, 200
    programmatic, 199
    teacher, 16, 146, 209–10, 218
    teacher educator, 13
    teaching as, 5
    transitive, 12, 46, 96–97, 113, 210
advocacy actions, 3–4, 7, 16, 19, 101–2, 111, 114, 138, 188–89, 191, 196–98, 200–201, 206
advocacy acts, 13, 147–65, 197, 203
advocacy challenges, major, 101–2
advocacy change, 15
advocacy continuum, 207–8
advocacy efforts, 4, 7–12, 14–15, 121, 140, 143–45, 147–48, 167–68, 170, 175, 185, 188–89, 193, 196–202, 205–9
advocacy goals and frameworks, 11, 14, 96, 158, 184, 187, 204–5, 210

advocacy in English language teaching and learning, 1–2, 4, 6–8, 16, 28, 78, 150–51, 157, 159, 164, 177
advocacy initiatives, decenter ELT, 4, 6
advocacy messages, 188–89
advocacy narratives, 1–2, 15, 201
advocacy-oriented pedagogies, 148, 151, 154, 161
advocacy program, 19, 52
advocacy projects, 7–10, 13–15, 25, 27, 29, 60–61, 136, 138–39, 142, 144–45, 179, 181–85, 191, 194, 203–6
advocacy reality, 191
advocacy stance, 193
advocacy strategies, 48, 201
AERA, 84. *See also* American Educational Research Association
affordances, 168, 175, 183–84
agency, 2, 16, 87, 121, 128, 131, 199, 201–3, 208
agendas, 19, 24, 51, 58
ages, 11, 72, 74, 87, 100–101, 119, 121, 136, 181, 218
Akcan, Sumru, 13, 134, 199, 213
Akpoghome, 30
Akpoghome & Nwano, 21
Alam, 53, 63
Alas, 78
Alayan, 150, 162
Albright, 112–13, 115
Alexander, 16, 88, 113, 210
Algren, 167, 170, 176
alumni, 88–91, 122–23, 128, 131
Amara, 147, 149, 162, 164
Amara & Mar'i, 149

American Embassy, 90
Anderson, 63
anti-bullying, 5
anti-hegemonic, 184
Ao, 132
approach, 25, 27, 29, 116, 126, 185–86, 188, 195, 198, 203, 208
appropriateness, 14, 148, 151–53, 161
appropriation, 164
areas
    content, 71, 201, 206
    geographic, 21, 30, 66, 94, 100, 122, 125, 129, 131, 198, 207
Arinto, 177
Arno, 36, 45
Arnold, 126
Arshad, 21, 29, 31
artificial intelligence, 208
Ashikullah, 53, 63
assessment, 20, 48, 58, 60, 138, 140, 142, 144, 150, 191, 201
asset, 43, 122, 142, 199
association, 14, 33–34, 38–41, 167–68, 170–71, 176, 213, 215–16, 218–19
atmosphere, 33, 35, 51, 169
Attamimi, 28
Attanda, 45
attendance, 42, 65–66, 136, 168, 171, 173
attention, 3, 48, 50, 61, 71, 98, 101–3, 105, 139, 205
audiences, 8, 37, 184, 186–91, 193
authorities, 3, 7, 64, 66, 105, 109, 148, 152, 174, 179, 181, 184–85
autonomy, 2, 16, 83, 111–12, 150, 160, 217
Awanga, 11, 199, 204
Awanga, Abigail Ekangou, 1–2, 10, 32, 213

Index

awareness, 34, 36, 103, 121–22, 132, 143, 145, 156–57, 159, 181–83, 188, 190–92, 205, 208

B
Baez, 169, 176
Baez, Mary Louise, 169
Baker, 128, 132
balance, better work/life, 5, 35, 128
Ballantyne, 92–93
Banegas, 211
Barak, 162
Barak & Levenberg, 159
Barrera, 87–88, 93
Barrett, Enita Elecia, 11, 47, 197, 199, 201, 213
barriers, 61, 100, 183, 206
Barrow, 70, 84
Baxter Magolda, 180, 194
Beatty, 18, 27, 30
Bekerman, 164
beliefs, 35, 127, 129–30, 145, 188–89
Belmopan, 67
Benjamin, 194
Benson, 111–12
Berbain, 211
bilingual, 48, 64
Bilingual Education, 64, 165, 209, 218
Bilingual English Language Learning Association (BELLA), 5
bilingualism, 151, 165, 202, 214
binary thinking, 14, 148, 151, 154–56, 158, 161, 201
Birch, 165
Boatwright, 46
Boles, 50, 63
Bonner, 49, 58, 63
Bononno, 7, 16

boundaries, 179, 183, 194
Bourdieu, 151, 163
Bradley, 59–60
Bradley-Levine, 201, 209
Brigitta, 13, 147, 219
British Council, 106, 195
Brooks, 90, 93
Brulles, 5, 15
Buechel, Loder, 197, 210
Buhler, 69
Bui, 99, 105, 108, 112, 114
Burgess, 46
Burnaford, 195
Burns, 98, 113
Butler, 136, 145

C
Callejas, 87
Callejas Quijano, 93
Canadian Center, 30
Canagarajah, 6, 16, 155, 163
Canese, Valentina, 14, 166, 174, 176, 199, 214
Carranza Campos, 197, 199
Carretero, 195
Casey, 19, 30
catalysts, 14, 20, 48, 158, 170, 181, 192, 199
Cawich, 63
Cayetano, Isani, 80
Celce-Murcia, 151, 164
Centro Cultural Paraguayo-Americano, 167, 169
Challengers, 77
challenges, 7–8, 10–13, 23, 29–32, 34, 39–43, 52–54, 102–3, 106–8, 135, 144, 160–62, 167–68, 175–76, 203, 205–7
Chamba, 22, 30

change, 1–3, 6–7, 15, 19–20, 44–45, 48–49, 51, 56, 106–9, 116, 121–23, 155–56, 179–82, 185–88, 191–93, 197–203, 205–8
Chapelle, 132
Chapelle & Ehlers-Zavala, 120, 122
Chavez, Cesar, 3
Chen, 43, 45
children, 52, 55, 58, 66, 69, 71, 73, 76, 81, 83, 85–86, 135–36, 139
children's development, 53, 97
Chinpakdee, 2, 16
Cho, 34, 46
Christison, 112
Christison & Lindahl, 96
circumstances, contextual, 53, 100, 149, 159
Civil Disobedience, 3
Civil Rights, 3
civil society, 121, 128
civil unrest, 83
classes
   face-to-face, 57, 66, 105, 171
   groups of, 87, 92
   secondary, 18, 21
   virtual, 72, 74, 92, 103–4, 160
classroom discourse, 6–7, 10, 152, 154, 164, 180, 198
classroom materials, 137, 144
classroom problems, 189
classrooms, 4–5, 20–21, 24, 26, 28, 72, 79–80, 95–96, 99–103, 106–9, 126–27, 135, 155, 157–60, 165
   traditional, 72, 104
classroom settings, 21, 24, 58, 137, 139–40, 170
class sessions, 5, 125, 185, 187–88
class sizes, 21, 26, 104–7
Cochran-Smith, 100, 113

Cohen, 164
collaboration, 9, 11–12, 25, 27–29, 38–39, 79–80, 135, 137, 140–43, 174, 176, 181–82, 201, 203, 206–8
collectives, 34–35, 199
collectivism, 12, 98–99, 106, 108, 111–12
colonialism, 2, 6–7, 47–48, 50, 147, 150–51, 158–59, 161, 164, 197–98, 200
comfort zones, 189, 193
commitment, 24, 32, 37, 54–55, 87, 92, 182, 192, 201, 206–7
Common European Framework of Reference (CEFR), 91, 125, 150, 163, 194
communication, 17, 19, 48–49, 54, 67–69, 124, 126–28, 136, 138, 143, 145, 147–48, 150, 190, 214–15
communicative competence, 10, 12, 18, 21, 23, 26, 99, 152, 159, 180, 195
communicative language teaching approach (CLT), 34, 46, 91, 126–27, 133, 180, 185, 194
communities, 11–12, 50–51, 53–54, 61–62, 79–80, 97–98, 111, 120–21, 123–24, 130–31, 137, 139–45, 176, 186–87, 192–93, 199–202, 207–8
community activism, 54
community building, 193
community contexts, 202
community members, 59, 97
Community-oriented advocacy, 202
community stakeholders, 51
comparative analysis, 27
comparative study, 84
competence, 44, 46, 195
completion, 11, 18, 23, 49, 175

Index

computer-assisted language learning, 10, 18, 24–26, 28–30
Conflict Resolution, 56, 155, 165
conflicts, 99, 102, 106, 108, 147–48, 152, 154, 160–62, 165, 195, 201
confrontations, 99, 108
Consejo, 180, 194
constrained contexts, 2, 15, 205–7
constraints, 8, 15, 17, 22–24, 35–36, 98, 122, 135, 137–38, 196, 198, 201, 205–8
constructive role, 97
consultants, 179, 215
contacts, 20, 32, 174, 219
contagious optimism, 169
contemporary social movements/protests, 3
content material, 144
context dependence, 156
contexts, 1–4, 7–9, 12–15, 17–18, 22–23, 33–36, 95–97, 112, 116–17, 147–48, 151–54, 161–62, 178–79, 196–205, 207–9
contextuality, 183
contextualized practices, 17, 180
contextual patterns, 181
contextual sociopolitical trends, 207
continuous professional development (CPD), 3, 32, 45, 60
control, 30, 36, 43, 82, 154, 201
conversations, 6, 8–9, 21, 49, 60, 107, 174, 205
Coombe, 163
correctness, 14, 92, 148, 151–53, 161
cost, 42–43, 55, 59, 75, 89, 93, 172
countries, 38–39, 41, 49–50, 52, 70–71, 73–74, 76, 83–84, 86–93, 101, 116–17, 122–24, 168, 174, 201–4

collectivistic, 108
developing, 42
diverse, 117
neighboring, 147
small, 86, 179
country influence, 12
COVID-19, 14, 57, 76, 89, 167, 171
CPD. *See* continuous professional development
Craig, 69, 84, 143, 146
Crawford, 210
crime, 11, 48–49, 66, 75, 86
Crimmins, 46
critical epistemological positioning, 181
critical friends, 52, 187, 189
critical incidents, 189
Critical language, 64
Critical Pedagogies, 163, 210
critical social theory, 51, 64
Crovitz, 151, 163
Crystal, 151, 163
Cultural Conflict, 163
cultural diversity, 33, 64, 71
cultural entertainment, 51, 57
cultural exploitation, 48
cultural responsiveness, 58
culture of silence, 178
cultures, 47, 49, 51–52, 58, 63–64, 70–71, 99, 101, 112–13, 115–16, 128, 132, 192–93, 197–98, 204
curricula, 5–6, 14, 97–98, 104, 125–26, 136–39, 142–43, 161, 178–80, 182–85, 191–92, 194, 200–201, 217, 219

D

Dajani, 163
Dajani & McLaughlin, 150

Dang, 97, 99, 113
Daniel, 163
Darvin, 163
Darvin & Norton, 147, 154
Dash, 164
data collection, 53, 55, 60, 184, 186
Davis, Lawson, 15
Dawson, 80
decentering, 6–7, 10, 197, 200, 203
Decentering Advocacy, 1–2, 4, 6–8, 10–14, 16–17, 20, 22, 64–85, 148, 150–52, 154, 197–98, 200, 206–8, 210
decision makers, 19, 184
decisions, 41, 44, 48, 51, 53, 58–59, 61, 98–99, 172, 181, 183, 186
decolonization. *See* Decentering Advocacy
Decolonizing English language teaching, 6, 16
deconstructing, 14, 147–48, 151, 154, 161, 201
Dedeugd, 210
de Jong, 5, 16, 143, 146, 201–2, 209
DelliCarpini, 194
Delmarie Fuller, 81
Delpit, 158, 163, 165
de Oliveira, 210
Ders arasi Dil Molasi. *See* spoken cafes
destabilize, 33
Deutch, 148, 163
Developing Self-Advocacy, 13, 16, 116
development, 10, 12, 63, 69, 71, 119, 124, 132–33, 138, 190, 195, 198
  collective, 34, 199
  personal, 23, 32, 45, 175
  sustainable, 195
Devereaux, 151, 163

devices, 57, 60, 89, 191
dialogue, 157, 184–86
Díaz Maggioli, 14, 178, 189, 194–95, 216
difference, 36, 139, 143, 146, 152, 154–55, 158, 162, 187, 192, 200–201, 204–5, 211
difficulties, 11, 97, 99–103, 106–8, 142
diglossic nature, 149
dimensions, 48, 103, 108–9, 112, 151
direct-action, 201
discipline, 48, 83, 181, 185
discontent, 70
discoveries, 28, 180
discrimination, 129
dismantle, 150, 155–58
disparities, 48, 51, 88, 197, 207–8
disrupters, 1, 35, 45
dissatisfaction, 102
dissemination, 19, 142, 144, 182
distribution, 51, 99, 131, 153, 168, 202
diversity, 5, 48, 100, 124, 148, 206, 211
Dörnyei, 180, 194
Dove, 143, 146
Dréan, 113
Dubetz, 5, 16, 143, 146, 201–2, 209
duties, 10, 20–22, 24, 43, 66, 109
dynamics, 47–48, 50, 52
dysfunctions, five, 54, 63

E
EAP (English for Academic Purposes), 157, 160, 204
EAR (Exploratory Action Research), 186–89, 192, 195
Early Language Education, 145
Economic Development, 11, 47–63, 87, 89, 93, 117
economics, 75, 97, 101, 109, 197

Index

economic situations, 12, 126
economies, 87, 91, 117, 181, 198
Edmonds, 5, 16
education, 2, 11–14, 16–18, 20–22, 29–31, 46–63, 80, 101–2, 123, 136, 138–39, 145, 149–50, 162–63, 194, 205, 207–10, 213–17, 219–20
  accessing, 129
  basic, 65
  children's, 55
  distance, 214
  equitable, 12, 75
  formal, 65
  free, 66, 123
  high-quality, 79–80, 95–96
  improving, 200
  multilingual, 64
  post-secondary, 66, 72, 78
  public, 89, 150, 165, 178, 182
  risk, 117
  secondary, 11–12, 55, 66, 74, 214
  special, 214
  subtractive, 48
  transferred, 162
educational access, 5, 200
educational contexts, 1–2, 14, 49, 99, 176
educational experiences, 5, 88, 179
educational goals, 12
educational institutions, 48, 129, 159–60, 167–68, 171, 175, 178
educational opportunities, 178, 204
educational outcomes, 53, 96, 148, 151, 158–61
educational policy, 2, 4, 6, 65, 84, 97–98, 201
educational practices, 181, 204
Educational Reforms, 113–14, 116, 178, 195, 215

educational settings, 159, 161–62, 194
educational system, 21, 100, 150, 158, 179, 191, 199, 203
education initiative, 150
education leadership, 99, 122, 165, 179, 214
educators
  approaches, 14
  diverse, 5, 13, 41, 171, 201
  global, 203–4, 220
efficacy, collective, 34, 199
efforts, 2, 4–5, 9–11, 14–15, 29, 102–3, 106, 136–37, 139–40, 142–43, 169–71, 196–97, 199–201, 203–5, 207
EFL (English as a Foreign Language), 13, 22, 30, 38, 102–10, 112, 114, 132, 135–36, 147–65, 174, 187, 213, 215–17, 219
EFL teachers, 16, 95, 153, 169, 175
Eggington, 164
Ehlers-Zavala, 132
elders, 33, 58, 71
Elizer, 195
ELLs (English language learners) (*see also* Multilingual Learners and Multilingual Learners of English), 3, 5–6, 16–17, 19, 79–80, 92, 95–98, 100–101, 103–11, 113–14, 135, 138, 209–10
ELLs, advocating for, 3, 80
ELT. *See* English language teaching
ELT advocacy work, 8, 25
ELT book, 8, 174
ELT community, 208
ELT contexts, 3, 16, 52
ELT educators, 1–2, 4–10, 30, 33–34, 37, 40–41, 161, 164, 166–68, 174, 213, 215, 220

ELT inadequacy, 21
ELT policy, 201
ELT programs, 24
ELTWC (ELT Women of Cameroon), 10, 32–34, 37, 39, 43–44, 213
emancipation, 147, 150, 161, 178, 181–82, 184
embassies, 90, 121–22, 128–29, 167, 169
emergence, 182
emergent bilinguals, 113, 209
empathy, 19, 53, 145, 160
employment, 46, 65–67, 69, 87, 91, 129, 202
empowerment, 11, 47–48, 71, 129, 161, 208
enacting advocacy, 4, 78, 114, 191, 207
encourage, 9, 39–45, 90, 96, 111, 142, 204
encourage students, 10, 40, 74
English Access Microscholarship Program, 87, 93
English as a Foreign Language. *See* EFL
English as a Second Language, 18, 31, 91, 211
English Bagrut, 150
English classes, 10, 22, 88, 90–91, 100, 120–21, 125, 135, 159
English classes online, 25, 89
English classroom, 158
English communicative competence, 21, 23
English for Academic Purposes (EAP), 157, 204
English language, 18, 20–21, 23, 26, 33, 38, 63, 67, 69, 91, 94, 138, 143
English language advocacy, 19–20
English language and academic skills, 11

English language education, 4, 17, 95–97, 105, 107, 109–13, 122, 133, 200, 214, 219–20
English-language educators, 9, 37, 148, 150, 166–68, 170, 175
English language learning, 11, 23, 25, 31, 104–5, 114, 134–36, 146, 149, 164, 219
English language programs, 168, 180
English language teaching (ELT), 1–17, 19–20, 22–26, 28–30, 32–46, 48, 62–66, 88–90, 94–96, 100, 104–6, 112–14, 116–33, 144, 152–54, 164–68, 170–72, 174–77, 184–86, 197–211
English language teaching/learning, 19, 30, 65
English learner teacher, 94, 114, 210
English listening skills, 22
English-speaking countries, 68–69, 71, 192
English teachers, 21, 23–24, 39, 46, 97–98, 100–102, 118, 125–26, 145, 168–72, 176, 192
Enriquez, Alberita, 74
entities, 121, 166–67
environments, 20, 58, 96, 109, 141
  academic, 97, 192, 214
  authentic K-12 classroom, 13
  conducive, 196
  digital, 18, 23, 162, 168, 176
  inclusive, 119
  non-Western, 9
  physical, 72
  relaxed, 54
envision, 8, 51, 78, 189, 201
epistemological inconsistencies, 180
equality, 71, 96, 101, 111–12, 135, 203
equip, 34, 153
equipment, 24, 105, 107, 140

Index

equitable access, 106, 111–12
equity, 4–5, 46, 48, 51, 100–101, 108, 111–13, 159–60, 194, 199, 201, 203, 208–9
ESL. *See* English as a Second Language
Eslami, 94, 114, 210
ESL/EFL, 39, 145, 169, 218
ESL teachers, 46, 113–14, 143, 146, 210
Estados Unidos, 94
ethics, 48, 179
ethnic groups, 50–51, 69, 75, 117, 124–25
ethnicities, 51, 63, 68, 119, 129–30, 147, 164
Etim, 209
ETS (Education Testing Service), 10, 18, 22–23, 25, 29
European domination, resisted, 68
examinations, 22, 67, 77, 82, 123, 197
expectations, 59, 103–4, 109–10, 112, 152–53, 158, 160–61, 169, 196
exposure, 27, 54, 58, 134, 136–37

F

fabric, social, 71, 86, 193
facilitation, 25, 105
facilitators, 18, 59–60, 93
facilities, 66, 75, 78, 87, 98, 101, 107, 109, 111
faculty, 107, 111, 135, 138–39, 174–76, 179, 185, 214
failure, 43, 49–50, 101, 153
Fairclough, 151, 163
families, 10, 12, 19, 21, 53, 55, 62–63, 71–73, 79–80, 86–87, 90, 95, 97, 122–24, 129–30
Farrell, 179, 194
Fassett, 132
Fassett & Nainby, 128

Fedicheva, 26, 30
feedback, 25, 27, 41, 43, 58, 103–4, 107, 111, 138–39, 141, 144
fees, 56–57, 75, 80–82
Fehring, 97–98, 114
Fiedler, 143, 146
Figueroa, 63
Filback, 210
Filosofía, 176
Fleischman, 46
foreign language anxiety, 127, 132, 215
foreign language teaching methodology, 213, 217
Fragoulis, 27, 30
Fragoulis & Tsiplakides, 26
framework, 51, 62, 113, 179, 183–84, 186, 195
Franco, 63
Freire, Paulo, 2, 16, 51, 63, 148, 150, 178, 181–82, 184, 193–94
Fry, 101, 113
funding, 21–22, 40, 55, 61, 80–81, 83, 89, 93, 119, 122, 197, 203, 205–6
fundraising, 119, 205–6

G

Gallagher, 169, 177
Gandhi, 3
gang activity, increased, 66, 86
García, 64, 113, 195
García & Kleifgen, 105
Garrone-Shufran, 197, 209
Gatrell, 163
gender, 16, 36, 38, 71, 88, 129
gifted students, 15
Ginat, 148, 163
Giroux, 2, 16
global contexts, 2, 9, 14–15, 176, 196, 198, 203–4
Global Efforts, 2, 9, 14, 197–211

Globalization, 17, 101, 151, 164, 176, 216
global perspectives, 8, 196
Global Perspectives and Local Practices. *See* glocal
glocal, 1, 17, 208
goals, 44, 48, 54, 79–80, 88, 92, 134, 141, 143–44, 176
Goode, 197, 209
government, 13, 18, 20, 22, 24, 82, 86, 116–17, 121–22, 128–29, 148–49, 191, 197
grants, 10, 55, 61, 87, 119, 122, 149, 205
grassroots advocacy, 13, 118, 178, 185, 188, 206
Grassroots Development Theory, 62
Grazzia Maria Mendoza Chirinos, 1, 14, 196, 214–15
Greenlee, 210
Greenlee & Dedeugd, 197
Grijalva, 63
groups, 25, 33–34, 36, 39–45, 50–51, 56, 69, 71, 139, 142, 155–56, 179, 182–83, 185
growth, 42, 49, 52, 65, 87–88, 98, 128–29, 172
Guettler, 84

H

Habók, 114
Hadle, 69, 84
Hall, 164
Hallinger, 99, 115
Hamisu, 20–21, 30
Haneda, 16, 88, 113, 210
Haneda & Alexander, 6, 95, 105, 111, 197
Haneda & Sherman, 95–96, 201, 203
Harrison, 46, 97, 113, 210
Harrison & McIlwain, 12, 45, 97, 202
Hawker, 149, 163

Hebrew, 148–50, 152–53, 157–58, 164–65
Hegemony, 48, 151, 184
Heliyon, 16, 217
Herrera, Fernando, 88, 90
heterogeneity, 155
hierarchy, 99, 106, 108, 156
high school completion rate, 12, 49, 53, 66–67, 71–72, 74, 76, 78–79, 81, 88, 91
high school students, 11–12, 52, 55–56, 65–66, 71–74, 76, 83, 88–90, 92, 125, 217
high school teacher, 65
Hodgkinson-Williams, 177
Hodgkinson-Williams & Arinto, 175
Hofstede, 113
Hofstede & Hofstede, 99, 106
Holguin, 21–22, 30
home language, 6, 21–22, 48, 63, 146, 150, 157
Honigsfeld, 143, 146
hooks, bell, 7, 16
Hopkins, 70
Horwitz, 127, 132
humanitarian assistance, 83, 85
Humanity, 42, 44, 50–51, 82, 117, 182, 184
Human Rights Report, 121
Humes, 82, 84
hurdles, 122, 126, 188, 197

I

Ibadan, 217
Iberri-Shea, 128, 132
Ibrahim, 20–21, 30
identities, 13, 16, 47, 50–51, 54, 57–58, 63–64, 147, 149, 152, 154–56, 163–64

Index

ideologies, 20, 33–34, 36, 45, 97–98, 150, 161–62, 183
Ilaro, 10, 18, 20, 23
immigrants, 6, 68, 152
immigration, 6, 63, 84, 202
imperialism, 4, 6, 47–48, 198
implementation, 21, 28–29, 47, 107, 135, 184, 187, 189–90, 200, 208
Inbar-Lourie, 164
inclusion, 5, 16, 75, 159–60, 194, 218
indigenous, 6, 11, 50, 63, 68, 188
inequalities, 95, 98, 107, 109–10, 158, 179, 181, 192, 204
inequities, 48, 95, 97, 105–7, 109–10, 151, 159–61, 204–5, 208
INGOs (international non-governmental organizations), 124, 127
injustices, 2, 34, 153, 158, 160–61, 204–5, 208
innovation, 2, 17, 157–58, 160, 210
inquiry, 104, 145, 179, 183–84, 192, 210
Instituto Nacional General, 93
instruction, 4–5, 20–22, 67, 69, 92, 110–11, 117, 119, 135–40, 149–51, 155, 158–59, 180, 207, 210–11
instructors, 65, 71, 78, 81–83, 89, 96, 168, 174, 179, 181, 185, 187, 202
intentions, 11, 19, 61, 74, 86, 183, 191
interactional, 91, 96, 127, 154, 188
interconnectivity, 2, 158, 208
interests, 41, 43, 51, 74, 76, 100, 102, 125, 128, 149, 155
internet access, 24, 42, 57, 74, 78, 90–91, 100, 105–6
interpersonal skills, 12, 32
interruption, 76, 152
intersection, 47, 151, 155, 193
interventions, 50, 182–83, 186–87, 189
interviewees, 106, 109
interviews, 21, 51, 103, 108, 112, 187, 190, 192
intractable conflict, 13, 147, 150, 152, 154, 219
intragroup, ongoing, 161–62
isolation, 21, 207
issue, 6, 16, 36–37, 48–49, 115, 141, 189–92
Iwashita, 97, 114

J

Jakar, 163
Janz, 163
Jewers, 86, 94
job opportunities, 12, 87–88
jobs, 12, 37, 49, 87–88, 90–91, 93, 101, 113, 123–24, 206, 209–10
Joma, 92, 94
Jones, 163
Joseph, Angela, 81
Jung, 164
justice, 14, 16, 70, 113, 161, 194, 201, 203–4

K

K-12, 105, 210, 216
Keene, 163
Khawaja, 149–50, 163, 165
King, 20, 31
Kleifgen, 113
knowledge, 26–27, 34, 37, 109, 111, 119, 121, 123, 126, 145, 183–84, 197–98, 206
  cultural, 200
  insider, 183, 188
  professional, 3
Koenig, 49, 51, 63
Kormpas, Georgios, 1, 14, 196, 215
Kramer, 163

Kroshus, 49, 63
Kumaravadivelu, 207, 210

L
labor, 66, 87, 202
Ladino, 148
Lalwani, Harshini, 170
Lam, 101, 113, 199–200, 215
  Huong, 12, 95, 215
Lam & Albright, 101
Lambey, Pastor Agatha, 55
Landaverde, 93
language, official, 12, 20, 67, 69, 117, 148–49
language abilities, 26, 92, 98, 101, 127, 134, 201
language awareness, 219
language backgrounds, 68
language class, 101–3, 120, 125
language classrooms, 105, 109, 147, 152–53, 158, 160–62, 164
language curriculum, 98, 163
language education, better quality, 95, 106
language functions, 64, 91, 99, 147, 149–50, 152, 187
language learners, 20, 27, 97–98, 127, 143, 161, 175, 182
language learning, 13–14, 97, 99, 106, 108–9, 111–12, 133, 135–36, 145, 154, 196
language learning goals, 14
language learning process, 109–11, 136, 143
language policies, 12, 20, 47–48, 71, 97, 100, 113, 148, 162–65, 201, 211
language practice, 98, 133
language proficiency, 20, 24, 47–48, 97, 101, 103, 123, 125, 127, 134, 136–37, 141–42, 144

language programs, 22, 24, 112, 119
languages
  appropriate, 69, 154
  colonizing, 6, 147
  first, 47–48, 69, 127, 149
  global, 22, 149, 164
  indigenous, 20, 214
  instruction/official, 75, 124, 148–49
  local, 148, 198
  multiple, 12
  national, 149
  new, 27
  spoken, 134–35
  target, 75, 127
language teachers, 4–6, 33, 36, 39, 45, 47–48, 100, 102–12, 152–53, 155, 159–60, 171, 198, 200, 219
language teaching, 47–48, 69, 97–98, 107, 111, 114, 126, 128, 132, 190, 213, 215, 217–19
  communicative, 114, 132, 194
  traditional, 126
language use, 97, 151–52
Larsen-Freeman, 151, 164
Latin America, 167, 172, 174, 198, 215
Lave, 176–77
laws, 5, 43, 82, 129, 148, 164, 179, 203
leaders, 2–3, 41–42, 51–52, 61, 90, 99, 107–11, 166, 169–71
  educational, 90, 166
  global ELT, 220
leadership, 3, 34, 44, 112, 124, 129, 220
  instructional, 214
  nurture, 123
leadership programs, 130
leadership roles, 33, 129, 167, 220
leadership skills, 41, 83, 119, 130
leadership team, 170, 175
leadership training, 13
learner autonomy, 112, 114, 217

Index

learner-centered methodologies, 13
learners, 4–5, 10, 12–15, 18–23, 25–27, 38–39, 47–48, 97–99, 102–3, 151–55, 157, 160–61, 176, 183–87, 197, 199–203, 208
learning, 6, 10–14, 22–24, 26–28, 71–72, 94, 96–98, 100–103, 105–6, 113–15, 134–36, 161–64, 175–77, 179–80, 182–83, 185–86, 188–90, 193–94, 200–201, 203
  adult, 101, 163, 184
learning activities, 26, 93, 137, 139, 183, 208
learning environments, 13, 48, 100, 127, 134, 136, 141, 143, 159
learning experiences, 26, 44, 135, 137
learning inequalities, 14
learning outcomes, 152
learning process, 5, 26, 96, 98, 100, 105, 107, 110–11, 144, 194
learning resources, 23, 25, 95, 111
Lencioni, 54, 63
Leonardo, 51, 64
lesson plans, 29, 102, 127, 140, 159
lessons, 15, 23, 29, 36, 43, 103, 105, 110, 152–53, 159–60, 203–4
  virtual, 171
levels
  geographic, 4–5, 48, 79–80, 96–98, 110–11, 120, 143, 171, 184
  grade, 100, 150, 160, 180
  personal, 23, 126
  proficiency, 25–26, 51–52, 60, 62, 89, 91–93, 96, 98, 100, 103–4, 121–22, 125, 127, 136–37, 150
  second-highest, 73
Levenberg, 162
Lewin-Epstein, 164
Lewin-Epstein & Cohen, 154
Lewis, 65, 84

LGBTQ+ community, 6
Li, 2, 16
Liddicoat, 2, 17
life skills, 12–13, 90, 119, 123, 129, 206
limitations, 9–10, 21, 87, 184, 186, 192
limited opportunities, 135, 139, 143
limited resources, 12, 24, 59, 138, 154
Lin, 64
Lindahl, 112
lingua franca, 52, 69, 124, 134–35, 147, 150–52, 198
linguistic landscape, 47–48, 149, 165, 219
linguistics, 29, 107, 110–11, 165, 219
Linville, 16, 46, 48, 64, 78–80, 84, 96–97, 111, 114, 143, 146, 164, 176–77, 201–2, 210
Linville & Staehr-Fenner, 197
Linville & Vinogradova, 4–6
Linville & Whiting, 5, 36, 97
Liontas, 194
Liopoire, 9
listening comprehension, 10, 22
Litzenberg, 200, 210
livelihoods, 73, 117
local community, 22, 41, 52, 207
Local Practices, 1
Lone Buffalo, 13, 116–32
Loperena, 52, 64
Lopriore, 17
Low & Ao, 124
low-income communities, 18, 22, 29
Lugansk, 30
Lyon, 19, 31

M

MacLelland, 194
MacIlwain, 113
Maggioli, 199–201
Magnes, 164

Mahboob, 24, 30
Mahboob & Tilakaratna, 22
Mai, 63, 115
Al-Makrifat, 133
Mambu, 205, 210
management, educational, 96, 98–99, 108, 185, 215
Manophet, 13, 118
Mapes, 116, 128, 132
marginalization, 11, 47, 51, 58, 90, 154, 158
Mar'i, 162
materials, 5–6, 10, 13, 91, 98–100, 105–6, 123, 125, 136–37, 139, 142, 144, 159–60, 202
  preparing, 140, 144
Matthei, 64
Matthei & Smith, 58
Mazzoleni, 199
  Rocio, 14, 166, 170, 216
McCarty, 163
McGuire, 200, 211
McIlwain, 46, 97, 210
McLelland, 187
media, 142, 181, 184
Mei, 133
Mejia, Marsha, 56
Membreño, Danny, 90
Memmi, 7, 16
Mendez, 63
Menéndez, Francisco, 94
mentoring, 33, 39–40, 220
mentors, 11, 29, 37, 39, 54–55
Metagogy theorem of adult education, 14, 178–95
migration, 86, 94, 164
Miguel Ángel Carranza Campos, 12, 86, 214
mindset, 11, 40, 45, 154–57

Ministry of Education (MOE), 14, 71, 73–74, 82, 88–90, 93, 98, 135–39, 141–42, 144–45, 149–50
minorities, ethnic, 34, 48–49, 122, 162, 204
models, 5, 19, 29, 96, 109, 111, 180, 183
  positive role, 89, 127
Mohammed, 79
momentum, 137, 166
moral universe, 54, 203
Mosavian, 2, 17
motivation, 21, 27, 34, 39, 44, 58, 134, 142, 145, 152, 190, 197
Mousavi, 126, 132
movement, 2–3, 29, 69, 71, 169, 192, 208
Mukerji, 195
Mullens, 65
multiculturalism, 48, 69
multilingualism, 14, 20, 31, 64, 148, 162, 164, 202. *See also* bilingualism
multilingual learners, 4–6, 8, 14, 200, 202–3, 220
multilingual situation, 71, 113
Murillo, Virgilio, 80
Murnane, 65
Murray, 2, 17, 112
Muslims, 156–57, 159

N
Nainby, 132
narratives, 1–2, 7, 10, 15, 196, 198, 201, 204–5, 208
  colonizing, 158
Nasson, 163
national values, 28
nations, 20–21, 64, 69–70, 83, 86, 92–93, 105, 148, 162, 197, 205

Index

Navidad Morales, 93
negative effects, 47, 190
negotiation skills, 2, 27, 36, 61, 146, 207
Nelson Mandela Rules, 80
neoliberal, 14, 178
network, 11, 33, 41, 46, 111, 183, 188, 191–93
networking, 20, 61, 92, 110, 176
Nevo, 164
Nevo & Olshtain, 149
Newton, 15
Ngoc, Mai, 97, 114
NGOs (non-governmental organizations), 30, 38, 48, 52, 121, 124, 126, 128
Nguyen, 12, 95, 97–98, 111, 113–14, 199–200, 217
   Hong-Anh, 12, 95, 217
Nguyen & Bui, 98
Nguyen & Habók, 108
non-profit, 119, 166
norm, 33, 57, 126, 153, 179
Norman, 94, 114, 210
Norman & Eslami, 88, 95, 197
Norton, 163
Novelo, Hipolito, 79
nuances, 2, 4, 7, 15, 198, 207
Nunan, 26, 30
Nwano, 30

O

Obiegbu, 29–30
objectives, 33, 37, 44, 53, 57
observations, 21, 24, 48–49, 58, 72, 128, 141, 190
Okon Effiong, 1, 14, 196, 215
Oladejo, 10, 197, 199, 201
   Oluyemisi, 10, 18, 217–18
Olagbaju, 21, 31

Olshtain, 164
O'Neil, 19, 31
O'Niel, 53
online, 12, 14, 17, 41–43, 46, 65, 71, 74, 76, 167, 171, 174
online learning, 83, 89
online meetings, 11, 39, 90
online school, 65, 72–73, 108, 218
Open Educational Resource (OER), 174–75, 177
opinions, 3–4, 61, 104, 107–8, 110, 127, 188, 204
opposition, 61, 201, 204
oppression, 38, 51, 147, 151
organization, 9–10, 14, 18, 113, 116, 119–20, 130–31, 162, 166, 168–69, 171–76
   professional, 9, 166, 170, 175, 206
Orozco, 86, 94
Orozco & Jewers, 86
Ortiz, Carolina, 170
Oslo Accords, 150, 162
outcomes, 1, 5, 22, 27, 34, 137, 140, 159–60, 175–76, 197, 201
outreach, 122, 166, 171, 182, 213
ownership, 27, 52, 59, 62, 157

P

Palacio, 49, 58, 64
pandemic, coronavirus, 76, 78, 80, 89, 142, 168, 171–72, 175
Parada, 86, 94
parents, 20, 22–23, 54–55, 57–59, 62, 72–73, 77, 97, 122, 135–38, 140, 143–44, 190
participants, 18, 24–26, 28, 43, 53–54, 58, 87, 91, 168, 171, 173
participation, 9, 13, 18, 36–37, 89, 100, 111, 136, 142, 169, 179

partnerships, 14, 130, 138, 140–41, 144, 172, 206
passion, 10, 18–31, 45, 61
pathways, 7, 64, 167, 197–98, 208
Paulino, 12, 197, 199, 204
   Ethnelda, 11, 65, 218
Pawan, 143, 146
Peace Corps, 220
peace efforts, 150
pedagogy, 6, 13, 16, 63, 114, 159, 161, 193–94, 200, 207, 210–11
   critical, 6, 16, 148, 150
Peddiwell, 194
Peddiwell & Benjamin, 178
Peña, Joel, 91, 169, 177
Peña, Pacita, 169
Pennycook, 150, 164
Pentón Herrera, 9, 17
Peralta, 63
perceptions, 9, 36, 49, 56, 105–6, 114, 130, 153, 177
Perez, 200
Pérez Berbain, 211
personal characteristics, 44–46
perspectives, 7–8, 15–16, 49, 51, 151, 155, 158, 180, 182, 194, 196, 200, 207
   diverse, 158, 208
   emergentist, 182
   emic, 3
   epistemological, 49, 180
Pillai, 51, 63
Pilot, 98, 114, 208
plan, 1, 29, 58–62, 89, 91, 144, 165, 186, 194
planning, 19, 21, 59, 61, 91, 119, 141–43, 186, 201, 207
platform, 111, 117–33, 197, 206
Plewa, 86, 94
police officers, 48, 66–67, 78

policies, 3, 5, 7, 19–20, 30–31, 95, 98–99, 105, 107, 110–13, 181–82, 191–92, 200–202, 206, 208–9
policymakers, 48, 98, 106–11
Policy Map, 190–91
Policy-oriented advocacy, 203
political activism, 6
political biases, 179
political context, 6
Political Issues, 163
Political Power, 162
political tide, ever-changing, 51, 83
politics, 51, 101, 181, 197, 207
   cultural, 16, 164
   social, 164
population, 50–51, 58, 67–68, 72, 117, 149, 155, 157, 159, 161, 206–7
post-study test, 10, 27–29
Poteau, 16
Potts, 34, 46
poverty, 2, 49, 71, 117, 133
power, 1, 4, 48, 51, 129–30, 145, 148, 151–54, 158, 161, 163–64, 197–200, 203–4, 206
power distance, 99, 105–6, 108, 111–12, 151
practices
   advocacy-oriented, 36, 158–62
   community service, 143–44
   cultural, 58, 200
practicum, 89, 92, 135, 137–43, 145, 180, 185, 214
Prado, 5, 16
praxes, 16, 178–79, 181–83, 186, 189, 216
preservation, 11, 47, 71
pressure, 104, 191
pride, 20, 50, 53, 56, 190
Primary level, 66, 135, 192
prioritize, 20, 65–66, 161

Index

prison, 12, 49, 66, 78, 80
privilege, 120, 131, 158, 182
professional community, 176
professional development (PD), 3–4, 6, 13–14, 32–34, 36–39, 41–43, 60, 143–44, 166–68, 170–71, 176, 183, 203, 217, 219
professional development activities, 23, 32, 34, 38–39, 45, 167–68, 171
professional development events, 42, 107, 110–11, 127
professional development experiences, 178, 185, 197, 209
professional development opportunities, 5, 32, 141, 147, 167, 176
professional development programs, 37, 39, 110, 171
professionalism, 3
professionalization, 166, 170
professionals
    educational, 5, 8, 169, 172, 174, 197, 220
    female, 32, 34, 39–40
professional standards, 5, 203
proficiency, 22, 92, 125, 150
programming, 119, 124, 178, 204
programs, 13, 18, 39–40, 55, 59–62, 76, 78, 80–84, 87–93, 119–20, 123–24, 127–32, 137–38, 207, 209
    creating, 91, 124, 199
    scholarship, 89–90
progress, 22–23, 25, 29, 52, 54, 59, 61, 70, 76, 109, 117
project
    ambitious, 36, 90, 204
    collaborative, 12
    community-based, 145
project-based learning, 27, 30
project implementation, 61, 201
project mission, 130
promoting language learning, 4, 78–79
promoting social justice, 48
prosperity, 52, 157
protests, 3
public demonstrations, 185
public institutions, 30, 89–90
public opinion, 19, 181
public school environments, 112
public schools, 18, 21, 87, 100, 125, 134, 136–37, 139, 185
public school teachers, 174

Q

qualifications, 54, 107, 123, 197
quality education, 12, 48, 64, 86, 88, 94
quality textbooks, 174
Quintanilla Navidad, 87, 93

R

Rahman, 53, 63
ramifications, 152, 158
Rany, 133
Ravindranath, 58, 64
Raza, 163
reading program, 52, 59–62
reading skills, 28, 59–60
a real careful little dance, 16, 177
realities
    contextual, 2, 7, 184
    economic, 50, 198, 207
    local, 52, 56, 191
    political, 2
    religious, 159
    social, 181
    sociopolitical, 13
Rebar, 49, 64
Rebolledo, 186, 195

recognition, 2, 71, 157, 159–60
  negotiating, 13
  professional, 5, 202
recognizing social inequities, 201
Reconceptualizing Global Advocacy, 15, 203
Reflective practice, 178, 182, 185, 192, 194
reform, 113, 179, 185–86
  constitution, 71
  mandated nationwide, 179
  political, 70–71
  public service, 71
regulations, 107, 110–12
Reinoso, 22, 30
relationships, 3, 14, 26, 33, 51, 60, 106, 141, 193, 202
  close working, 62, 80
  effective, 143
  establishing, 145, 193
  good, 90, 142
  long-standing, 79, 171
  maintaining, 145, 172
  strengthened, 168, 171
  unequal power, 58, 99
Reliefweb, 83, 85
religion, 28, 157, 160, 181, 197
Rengifo, 22, 30
representation, 96, 149, 159, 161
Requena, 63
resilience, 19, 45, 53, 55, 58, 204, 210
resistance, 34, 64, 98, 184–85, 201, 204
resource-challenged contexts, 174
resources, educational, 79–80
responsibilities, 28, 43, 54, 96, 106, 119, 136, 143, 160
  collective, 206
  regulatory, 162
  social, 16

restrictions, 122, 184
revolutionaries, silent, 1, 35
Reynolds, Kate Mastruserio, 1, 9, 14, 17, 163, 196, 218
rhetoric, 52, 128
Rice, 6, 17
Ridley, 20, 31
rights, 3–4, 47–48, 96, 100, 109, 120, 199, 202–3, 219
  equal, 129
  gender, 121
  holistic, 100
  human, 3
  instructional, 202
  political, 2
  safeguard minority, 159
  territorial, 52
  women's, 129
rigor, academic, 180, 190–91
risks, 3, 73, 96, 99, 192, 201, 204
Robertson, 164
Rodriguez, 63
Rogers, Briana, 13, 116, 218–19
Roose, 200, 211
Rudolph, 17

S
Saban & Amara, 149
sacrifices, 156–57, 201
safety net, 11, 53
salaries, 75, 87, 123, 202
Salazar, 5, 17
Salleh, 21, 29, 31
Sánchez, 63, 195
Sanderman, 92–93
Sanga, 99, 115
Sari, 34, 46
scaffolding, 158
schedules, 11, 24, 40, 42, 136–37, 174

Index

heavy, 142
improved, 5
inclusive, 39
Schlam Salman, Julia, 13, 147, 164, 219
Schlam Salman and Schvarcz, 199, 201
scholarships, 33, 40, 43, 56, 80, 215
school actions, 5
school administration, 89–90, 99, 136, 140, 190
school-based activities, 10
school classrooms, 179
school committees, 99
school community, wider, 187
school days, 81, 160
school environment, 24, 75, 134
school equipment, 81
school experience, 145
school hours, 10, 19, 22, 24
schooling, 65–66, 134, 150, 202
schooling advocacy, 200
school leaders, 97
school leadership, 115
school levels, 20–21, 49, 52, 65, 95, 97, 100, 182–83, 185, 213, 217–18
school program, 12, 31, 81
schools
  inclusive, 216
  rural, 125, 168
school subjects, 20, 22–23, 28
school system, 49, 60, 74, 98, 125
school-to-prison pipeline, 11
school year, 92, 155
Schvarcz, Bridget, 9, 13, 17, 147, 163, 165, 199, 201, 219
Schvarcz & Khawaja, 149
Schwartz, 145
Second Language Acquisition (SLA), 27, 30, 93, 113, 213
sectors, 12, 25, 38–39, 65, 87, 91
security officers, 66, 79
self-advocacy, 15, 161, 207
self-advocacy experiences, 175
self-advocates, 5, 154
self-assessment, 3
self-authorship, 180, 194
self-awareness, 53, 175
self-confidence, 53, 78, 124, 130, 134
self-empowerment, 197
self-esteem, 11, 27, 33, 89
self-reliance, 58
Selvi, 17
semesters, 74, 78, 81–82, 135, 139, 142
Senor, 165
Senor & Singer, 157
sensitivity, 19
sensitization, 34
service
  community, 92
  public, 65
service learning, 144
Servio-Mariano, 50, 64
sessions
  face-to-face training, 59, 167, 171, 173
  parent, 129
setbacks, 11, 25, 37, 42–43, 75
shared experiences, 1
shared purpose, 54
Shared Traditions, 156
share responsibilities, 29, 97
Sharma, 189–91, 195
Sherman, 113, 210
Shin, 210–11
Shohamy, 48, 64, 165
shortages, 10, 69, 105, 107, 123
SIG (special interest group), 10–11, 32–33, 37–44

Silva Quartiani, 192, 195
situated experience, 188
Situated Learning, 177
skills
   communicative, 125–26
   competitive, 34
   digital, 43, 170
   endowed, 34
   indispensable, 205
   intercultural, 128
   listening, 28, 201
   presentation, 120, 131
   problem-solving, 27
   productive, 22
   soft, 11, 53, 131
   speaking, 137, 139
skill sets, 196, 205–7
Skutnabb-Kangas, 48, 64
SLAT (Second Language Acquisition and Teaching), 27, 93, 113, 213
Smith, 64, 186, 195
social acceptance, 69
social constructivist, 49
socialization, 27, 162
social justice, 5–6, 33–34, 36, 64, 71, 146, 151, 158, 179, 201–2, 209
social justice language teaching, 96
social media, 62, 103, 120, 167–68, 170, 184, 188, 192
social mobility, 147, 161
social movements, 3–5
social situations, 53, 71, 154, 186
societal inequities, 14, 148, 151, 158, 161
society, 36, 52, 63, 66–67, 75, 92, 101, 123, 129, 153–54, 181–82
   advanced technological, 178
   collectivistic, 106

fragile, 7
   monolingual, 12, 96, 98
   shared, 150
sociocultural, 2–3
sociocultural factors, 98, 200
sociocultural impact, 3
sociocultural mistranslations, 152
socioeconomics, 83–84
sociolinguistics, 149, 151, 216
Sociopolitics, 164
solutions, 8, 22, 31, 99–100, 141, 170, 181, 199, 209
   common, 40
   potential, 189
Souriyavongsa, 125, 133
spaces, virtual, 40, 103
Spaces for Advocacy Acts, 13, 147–65
speakers, 19–20, 25, 29, 52, 79, 99, 106, 143, 151–52, 157, 166
Spezzini, Susan, 14, 166, 169, 176–77, 199, 219
Spoken Cafes Project, 13, 134, 137–40, 142, 144
Spolsky, 149, 164–65
sponsors, 40, 43, 80, 174
sponsorship, 18, 22, 29
stability, 61, 99
Stachowiak, 62, 64
Staehr-Fenner, 4, 17, 19, 31, 95, 114, 143–44, 146, 205, 209–10
Stael Ruffinelli, 167
stakeholders, 4, 12, 28–29, 51–52, 97, 99–100, 103, 143, 181–82, 188, 191
   local, 183–84
standards, 5, 14, 46, 158, 161
   programmatic, 203
   teacher quality/preparation, 17, 203
start-ups, 55, 157, 165

Index

state legislators, 5
state level, 5
statistics, 28, 64, 85, 89
status, 49, 148–49, 154, 164
   official, 148–49
   socioeconomic, 121
   special, 149
status markers, 147
status quo, 7, 19, 122, 201
status symbol, 149
statutory obligations, 24
Steadman, 121–23, 125, 127, 129–31
Steadman, Mark, 118, 121
Stenner, 49, 64
stereotypes, 34, 44
stigma, societal, 10, 38
stories, 7, 27, 36, 104, 106, 120, 138–39, 165, 177, 208
storytelling, 25, 134
strategies
   effective, 105
   new, 179
strategizing, 19
strength, 10, 121, 167, 170, 203–4
   collective, 170
strengthen, 138, 142
stress, 37, 89, 126, 143
Stritikus, 202, 211
Strohschen, 178, 195
Strohschen & Elizer, 183
Strothschen, 182
Stubbs, 151, 165
student agency, 132
student body, diverse, 125, 156
student-centered approaches, 28, 126
student efficacy, 177
student engagement, 129
student enrollment, 82

student experience, 183
student participants, 26, 28
student placement, 107
students learning, 8, 146, 183
students work, 78, 160
Students' work, 131
student teachers, 136, 138, 140, 142, 178–89, 192
   empowered, 192
   volunteer, 92, 142
Suarez, Debra, 1, 14, 196, 220
subjects, 20–22, 79, 82, 84, 100–101, 149–50, 168, 182
subordinate positions, 129
success, 14, 19, 38–39, 89–91, 121, 129–31, 158, 160, 169–70, 196–97, 199
   academic, 5, 88, 96, 159, 190
   professional, 20–21, 54
   resounding, 59, 172
success criteria, 158
success rate, 59
Suleiman, 149, 165
Sun, 32, 46
superiority, perceived, 47
supervise, 57
supervisors, 135, 137, 141, 144
support
   financial, 87, 106, 197, 205
   institutional, 160
   interpersonal, 41, 172
support advocacy, 103
support educators, 14, 172, 210
support EL learners, 12, 108, 135, 138, 204
support employment, 12
support growth, 12
support learning, 197
support teaching, 22

sustainability, 7, 14, 88, 94, 138, 141–42, 144, 184, 196
Syarifuddin, 126, 133
syllabus, 22, 90–92, 104, 107, 109, 135, 144
system
  belief, 97
  colonial, 65
  learning management, 160
  oppressive, 47
  progress monitoring, 11
systemic disadvantages, 47–48
systemic-functional, 180

T

tactics, 3, 8–9
Tamaru, 19, 31
Tan, 126
Tannenbaum, 164–65
Task-based language teaching (TBLT), 15, 26
tasks, 21–22, 24, 26–28, 43, 45, 126, 132, 134, 152, 155, 160
teacher advocacy, 11, 32, 34, 36, 38, 40–41, 172, 198–99, 209, 213–16, 218–19
teacher beliefs, 217
teacher candidates, communities encourage, 138–39, 143, 145
teacher education, 3, 6, 13–14, 16–17, 113, 120, 122, 125–26, 145, 148, 150, 178–95, 210–11, 213
teacher education curriculum, 180, 185, 192, 206
teacher education programs, 8, 14, 47–48, 60, 126, 135–45, 176, 178–95, 206
teacher educators, 13, 174, 182, 184, 192, 199, 215–16, 219

teacher leadership, 96, 146, 179
teachers, 5–7, 19–21, 28–30, 32–33, 39–46, 59–60, 92–93, 96–102, 104–6, 108–11, 114, 122–23, 125–27, 141–45, 166–68, 172, 174–77, 182–85, 202–3, 205–10
Teachers' agency, 114
teacher stress, 132
teaching contexts, 127, 140
teaching equipment, 107
teaching experience, 137, 139–40, 142, 217
teaching facilities, lack of, 95, 99
teaching licenses, 60
teaching materials, 15, 21, 41, 107, 142, 166, 168, 174–75, 177
teaching methodology, 3, 11, 37, 186, 194
teaching practices, promoting ethical, 47–48
teaching profession, 166–67, 180
team, 9, 26–27, 54, 63, 119, 136, 139, 172, 179
team building, 54, 130
technology, 10, 22, 28, 38, 72, 109, 147, 170, 205, 208
Terlouw, 98, 114
tertiary education, 12, 95–115, 119, 122–23
TESL, 48
TESOL (Teaching English to Speakers of Other Languages), 16–17, 47, 81, 84, 95–96, 102, 104–6, 108–9, 111–12, 114, 163, 178, 210, 214–16, 218
TESOL advocacy
  better, 111
  perceived, 103
TESOL affiliates, 83, 168–71, 176, 218

Index

TESOL International Association, 17, 30, 166–67, 218, 220
TESOL International Association Advocacy Summit, 218
TESOL International Association's P-12 Professional Teaching Standards, 5
testimonials, 40–41, 80, 192
theme-based language learning unit, 153
themes, 15, 78
  critical, 103
theory-practice dichotomy, 185
thinking
  collective, 198
  critical, 136
  flexible, 159, 162
  independent, 127
  strategic, 58
Thoreau, Henry David, 3
threat, 52, 188
Tignor, 6, 17
Tilakaratna, 24, 30
Tobón, 179, 195
Toohey, 163
tools, 69, 135, 154, 181–82, 188, 191, 198, 208, 218
  academic, 53
  available, 198
  concrete, 192
  linguistic, 149
  new, 208
topics, 37, 39, 56, 89, 99, 157, 187
  taboo, 201
towns, 22, 37, 73, 101, 117, 122–23, 165, 171
traditions, cultural, 14, 36, 38, 72, 157, 179
Tran, 98, 101, 115

transformation, 158, 201
  educational, 178–79, 181–82
Transformative actions, 97
transformative advocacy, 6, 12, 95–98, 100, 102–3, 106–8, 111–12
transformative role, crucial, 98
transition, peaceful, 34
translanguaging, 165
translation, 7, 165
transportation, 93
treatment, equitable, 96–97, 206
Trinh, 115
Trinh & Mai, 98–99, 105, 108
Tripathi, 195
Trotter, 174, 177
Truong, 99, 115
trust, 102, 106, 129, 141
Tsiplakides, 27, 30
Tufail, 19, 31
tuition, 56, 66, 78
tutoring, 57
tutors, 78–79, 100

U

Ujvari, 149, 165
underachievement, 49
underrepresented gifted students. *See* gifted students
understanding, 3–4, 6, 8, 10–11, 128, 130, 153, 159, 162–63, 187, 189, 191, 207–8
  better, 53, 59, 127
  clear, 123
  mutual, 2, 102
  professional, 14
UNESCO, 50, 64, 117, 124
unexploded ordnance, 117, 121
UNICEF, 73, 83, 85
unions, 73, 85, 179, 185

United Nations, 64, 73, 88, 94, 162
university, 64–65, 87–93, 104–11, 113–14, 120, 123, 135–39, 141–42, 144–45, 168, 171, 178–79, 181–85, 187–88, 217–18
   technical, 104–5
university autonomy, 101
university culture, 182
university students, 92, 174
university supervisors, 135–36, 138–39, 143
urban areas, 75, 100
urban/rural, 73
USAID Honduras, 214
USDoS (U.S. Department of State), 87–90, 93, 214–15, 220
UXO. *See* unexploded ordinance

V

Varghese, 202, 211
varieties, 68, 151
Vaughan, 195
Vaughan & Burnaford, 179
vernacular, spoken, 149
viewpoints, 49, 102, 108, 158
village, 48–49, 51–55, 57–58, 123
   mountainous, 100
   neighboring, 58
   small, 49
villagers, 55, 58
village school, 54
village's size, 51
Villiers Scheepers, 46
Vinogradova, 16, 210–11
Vinthasai, 121–24, 128–29, 131
   Chantal, 121
violence, 21, 152, 158, 188
   domestic, 38, 73
   increased gang-related, 83

vision, 13–14, 34, 52, 75, 204–5
vocabulary, 25–26, 28–29, 91, 152, 186, 204
voices, 1–3, 7, 19–20, 78–79, 94–96, 98–99, 102–5, 107–11, 127–28, 169, 179–80, 192–93, 206, 208, 210
   collective, 1, 7, 170
   diverse, 2, 200
   local, 186
volunteerism, 32, 46, 123, 169
volunteers, 13, 37, 43, 57, 62, 73–74, 88–92, 139, 167, 172
vulnerability, 47, 117

W

war, 86, 165
Warren, 97–98, 114
waste time, 3, 24
webinars, 11, 40, 168, 171–72
Weiner, Markus, 17
Weng, 200, 211
Wenger, 176–77
Western contexts, 4, 200, 203
Western-oriented methods, 126, 132, 205
Western perspectives, 4, 7, 198
WhatsApp, 40, 43–44, 54, 56, 167, 170
Whiting, 16, 31, 46, 78, 94, 114, 135, 138, 146, 164, 176–77
Willett, 65
Williamson, Nick, 118
Windodo, 44, 46
Winkle, 16
Wisconsin Center for Education Research-WIDA, 214
Wodwall, 91
women, 32–34, 37–40, 42–44, 66, 71–72, 82–83, 129–30, 204

Index

women ELT professionals, 36, 42
work
  income-generating, 174
  volunteer, 140, 175
workers, voluntary, 78
workforce, 12, 52, 74, 87
workload, 5, 24, 104
workplaces, 97, 99, 102
workshops, 11, 39, 42, 55, 59–60, 103, 120, 127–28, 166–68, 171–73
  advocacy-supporting, 102
  developing, 13, 131
  face-to-face, 93
  free online, 167
  intercultural communication, 128, 131
  life skills, 119
  public speaking, 120
  self-development, 54
  soft skills, 53
workshop sessions, 43, 169
World Bank, 117, 133
world peace, 162
World Trade Organization (WTO), 101
worldviews, 14, 161

X
Xu, 46

Y
Yafaei, 28
Yangsaoye, Bee, 116
Yaro, 21, 29, 31
Yazan, 2, 17
Yi, 20, 31
Yitzhaki, 150, 165
Yoon, 20, 31
young learner classrooms, 142
young learner contexts, 140
young learners, 13, 76, 135–45
young people, 66, 83, 87, 94, 116, 121, 123, 139
youths
  at-risk, 11–12, 66, 78, 86
  local, 13, 123

Z
Zalo, 103, 108
Zhen, 2, 17
Zoom, 37, 59, 108, 167, 171
Zoot Suit Protest, 3
Zorrilla, Mary, 169, 177

Printed and bound by CPI Group (UK) Ltd, Croydon, CR0 4YY
31/07/2025

14712026-0002